From Martyrdom to Power

RECENT TITLES FROM THE HELEN KELLOGG INSTITUTE
FOR INTERNATIONAL STUDIES

Scott Mainwaring, *general editor*

The University of Notre Dame Press gratefully thanks the Hellen Kellogg Institute
for International Studies for its support in the publication of titles in this series.

Víctor E. Tokman and Guillermo O'Donnell, eds.
Poverty and Inequality in Latin America: Issues and New Challenges (1998)

Tristan Anne Borer
Challenging the State: Churches as Political Actors in South Africa, 1980–1994 (1998)

Juan E. Méndez, Guillermo O'Donnell, and Paulo Sérgio Pinheiro, eds.
The (Un)Rule of Law and the Underprivileged in Latin America (1999)

Guillermo O'Donnell
Counterpoints: Selected Essays on Authoritarianism and Democratization (1999)

Howard Handelman and Mark Tessler, eds.
Democracy and Its Limits: Lessons from Asia, Latin America, and the Middle East (1999)

Larissa Adler Lomnitz and Ana Melnick
Chile's Political Culture and Parties: An Anthropological Explanation (2000)

Kevin Healy
*Llamas, Weavings, and Organic Chocolate: Multicultural Grassroots Development
in the Andes and Amazon of Bolivia* (2000)

Ernest J. Bartell, C. S. C., and Alejandro O'Donnell
The Child in Latin America: Health, Development, and Rights (2000)

Vikram K. Chand
Mexico's Political Awakening (2001)

Ruth Berrins Collier and David Collier
Shaping the Political Arena (2002)

Glen Biglaiser
Guardians of the Nation? (2002)

Alberto Spektorowski
The Origins of Argentina's Revolution of the Right (2003)

Caroline C. Beer
Electoral Competition and Institutional Change in Mexico (2003)

For a complete list of titles from the Helen Kellogg Institute for International Studies,
see http://www.undpress.nd.edu

FROM
MARTYRDOM
TO
POWER

The Partido Acción Nacional
in Mexico

YEMILE MIZRAHI

University of Notre Dame Press
Notre Dame, Indiana

Library of Congress Cataloging-in-Publication Data
Mizrahi, Yemile.
From martyrdom to power : the Partido Acción Nacional in Mexico /
Yemile Mizrahi.
p. cm.
"From the Helen Kellogg Institute for International Studies"
Includes bibliographical references and index.
ISBN 0-268-02867-2 (cloth : alk. paper)
ISBN 0-268-02870-2 (pbk. : alk. paper)
1. Partido Acción Nacional (Mexico) I. Title.
JL1298.A3M59 2003
324.272'04—dc21
2003009030

∞ *This book is printed on acid-free paper.*

CONTENTS

FIGURES, TABLES, AND CHARTS

ACKNOWLEDGMENTS

In 1989, when Ernesto Ruffo won the governorship of the northern state of Baja California, I became convinced that a great political transformation was under way in Mexico. This was the first opposition victory at the state level since the PRI was created in 1929. Although the PAN had scored important victories at the municipal level since 1983 in various other states, the victory at the state level was an important qualitative step forward in the path toward democracy. I knew that the transition to democracy in Mexico, unlike most transitions in other Latin American countries, would take a "federalist" path, moving from the local to the state level and then, eventually, to the presidential level. I also understood that political parties would play a major part in this transition.

In 1991 and 1992, as the PAN won the states of Guanajuato and Chihuahua, my conviction increased. Many of my colleagues and friends at the time thought that I was too optimistic, that these were isolated political events and that the PRI still had a secure hold on power. After the presidential elections of 1994, when the PRI won the elections by a comfortable margin, it seemed as if my colleagues' predictions were true. However, soon after these elections, more and more states fell into the hands of the opposition, both the PAN and the PRD. When Vicente Fox announced his intention to seek the PAN's nomination for the 2000 presidential elections, I began to imagine a possible PAN victory at the presidential level. After doing research in the state of Guanajuato, where Vicente Fox was governor, and witnessing the dynamism and commitment of his cabinet, I thought that he was perhaps the only candidate capable of provoking a critical electoral realignment and defeating the PRI. I was proven right.

My interest in the PAN was sparked in the early 1990s. At that time, with few notable exceptions, the PAN did not attract many scholars. Most studies about the PAN had been conducted during the 1960s, and they were historical in nature. Although the absence of scholarly work on the PAN seemed a great disadvantage at first, for I had to generate my own data, in the end this intellectual void proved extremely beneficial for my research. PAN officials, militants, and candidates were eager to talk and share their stories with me. They found it quite exciting to find a U.S.-trained scholar interested in their party and writing a serious academic study about it. Moreover, having no partisan connection to them whatsoever and coming from a Jewish Mexican background, a background totally unfamiliar to them (starting with my uncommon name), they felt free to express themselves openly and were wonderful interview subjects.

Over the years, I interviewed hundreds of panistas, and it is impossible to thank them all individually. However, I want to express my special gratitude to some individuals who made this book possible: Ernesto Ruffo (Baja California); Francisco Barrio, Luis H. Alvarez, Salvador Beltrán del Río, Héctor Chávez Barrón, Arturo Chávez Chávez, and Francisco Villarreal (Chihuahua); Vicente Fox, Martha Sahagún, Eduardo Sojo, Carlos Arce, and Carlos Gadsden (Guanajuato); Carlos Castillo Peraza, Felipe Calderón Hinojosa, Luis Felipe Bravo Mena, Rosendo Villarreal, José Luis García Valero, Juan Antonio García Villa, Arturo García Portillo, and Concha Lupe Garza (Mexico City). My special thanks also go to Eugenio and Janine Villarreal from Chihuahua. Although they are not panista officials or militants, they played a very important role in putting me in touch with numerous people in the state. They not only gave me valuable information, they also opened their hearts to me and adopted me as their child when I conducted research in Chihuahua. I have remained their "adopted daughter" since.

I also wish to express my deep gratitude to two institutions that generously funded different stages of my research for this book. From the Consejo Nacional de Ciencia y Tecnología (CONACYT), I received a grant to analyze and develop a set of indicators of government performance in four states controlled by different political parties. The Ford Foundation funded the design and conduct of opinion polls in the states of Puebla and Chihuahua, which enabled me to analyze and compare people's opinions about their governments and attitudes about political parties in states controlled by the PRI and the PAN. Together, these two research grants allowed me to conduct the most important part of the research for this book. I want to especially thank Kimberly Brown of the Ford Foundation for her support and enthusiasm throughout this project.

In 1999 I received a fellowship from the Woodrow Wilson Center for International Scholars in Washington, D.C., where I wrote most of the manuscript. I want to thank the Wilson Center and, in particular, Joe Tulchin, Latin American Director, and Andrew Selee, Mexico Project Coordinator, for their candid support and intellectual contribution during my writing. They both read and commented on substantial portions of the manuscript. I also want to thank my colleagues at the Wilson Center who also read and commented on parts of the manuscript, in particular, Kurt Weyland, Stephen Clarkson, Richard Mitten, and Paul Gootemberg.

In Mexico, I worked at the Centro de Investigación y Docencia Económicas (CIDE) from 1991 to 2001. These ten years were extremely rich and formative, and I cannot emphasize enough my gratitude to this institution for allowing me to develop and grow as an academic. I want to express special thanks to CIDE's president, Carlos Elizondo, for his consistent support and my colleagues who shared with me the "pains" of giving birth to a book. In particular, I want to thank Joy Langston, Benito Nacif, Enrique Cabrero, Jose Antonio Crespo, Guadalupe González, Leticia Santín, Ignacio Marván, Fausto Hernández, Alfonso Hernández, Alfredo Ramírez, Enrique Borja, Jorge Shabat, Teresa Bracho, Judith Mariscal, and Jorge Schiavon. I also want to thank several colleagues from other academic institutions in Mexico. Soledad Loaeza, of the Colegio de México, shared her ideas and knowledge with me. She is one of the few scholars who has written an excellent study about the PAN in recent years. Gina Zabludowsky, of the National Autonomous University, also read parts of the manuscript and offered insightful comments. Alejandro Moreno, of ITAM and *Reforma*, gave me valuable advice on conducting and interpreting surveys in the states of Chihuahua and Puebla, and he also gave me access to the survey data *Reforma* had obtained in the state of Guanajuato.

Like most research projects, this one would not have been possible without the valuable contribution of my research assistants, who worked on various stages of the book. My special gratitude goes to Luisa Ortíz, Javier Díaz, Erika Contreras, Dora Guernika, Rubén Munoz, Juan Cristián Iturriaga, Juan Espíndola, Griselda Melo, Gabriella Duvignau, and Claudio López-Guerra.

Many friends and colleagues in the United States also read and commented on earlier drafts of this book. My gratitude in particular goes to Kevin Middlebrook, Roderic A. Camp, Scott Morgernstern, Steven Wuhs, Ben Schneider, Sylvia Maxfield, Victoria Rodríguez, Peter Ward, Scott Mainwaring, Kenneth Greene, Pamela Starr, Edward Gibson, Timothy Kessler, and Richard Snyder. I also want to thank the anonymous reviewers for their insightful comments and suggestions and the editors at the University of Notre Dame Press, particularly Jeffrey Gainey for his enthusiastic endorsement of this book.

My family has been a source of unconditional support and love. I could not have written this book without them, and I dedicate it to them. My children, Eliana, Gabriel, and Andrea, are my source of inspiration and happiness. Although they still prefer to become astronauts, engineers, architects, lawyers, or Broadway actresses, I am sure one day, as they grow older, they will become interested in politics, and I hope they will read this book to gain an understanding of the political evolution of their own country. My husband, David, has been supportive and loving throughout this long journey and has allowed me to enjoy life even when the research and writing were difficult. I thank him for teaching me to keep things in their proper perspective. Finally, I am grateful to my parents, Moisés and Mery, for their support and trust in my academic endeavor. I would not be who I am without them.

I N T R O D U C T I O N

Vicente Fox Quesada once said that kicking the official Partido Revolu-cionario Institucional (PRI) out of office would be the equivalent of putting a man on the moon. On July 2, 2000, Fox did just that. For the first time in seventy-one years, the PRI lost the presidential election in Mexico—and by a substantial margin.

The victory of the Partido Acción Nacional (PAN), the oldest and most consistent opposition party in Mexico, represents a watershed in the country's political life. The PRI was not just a political party; it was part and parcel of Mexico's political regime.

From its founding in 1929 in the aftermath of the Mexican Revolu-tion, the PRI had been the most important vehicle for gaining and main-taining power. Until the mid-1980s the PRI held a virtual monopoly on Mexico's political life. It not only controlled the presidency uninter-rupted since 1929; it also controlled all state governments, the over-whelming majority of municipalities, and an uncontested majority in both chambers of Congress. While opposition parties were tolerated, they were marginalized and ineffective in exerting any significant po-litical influence, other than testifying to the "undemocratic" nature of Mexico's political regime.

The victory of the PAN is even more impressive if we consider that only fifteen years ago it was still an insignificant electoral force. In 1985 the PAN controlled only three municipalities, representing less than one million people.[1] It did not control any state government and had never won a seat in the Senate. Until 1988 the party had not been able to win

1

more than 17 percent of the total vote in presidential elections and more than 18 percent in congressional elections.[2] Moreover, in the 1988 presidential elections, the PAN was relegated to third place by the left-wing coalition organized by Cuauhtémoc Cárdenas, a PRI dissident and future leader of the center-left Partido de la Revolución Democrática (PRD).

This book analyzes the evolution of the PAN over the past twenty years, during which the party's electoral fortunes have changed. It examines why this small and virtually insignificant political party was able eventually to defeat the PRI at the national level. More important, it explores the consequences of electoral success on the party's internal life and organization, as well as the implications of the party's internal organization for the future of democracy in Mexico.

In the age of mass media and candidate-centered elections, political parties seem to have faded to the background. Mexico is no exception. Vicente Fox and his campaign organization received greater attention from the media and political analysts than his own party did. Yet I make the central claim here that political parties play a crucial role in the stability and consolidation of democratic regimes. Although political parties are not exclusive channels of political participation, in democracies they are the most important actors for political representation, interest aggregation, and the formation and functioning of government (Diamond and Gunther, 2001). Democracies require political competition, and competition in turn requires that citizens know something about the political choices available to them. Political parties play a central role in structuring these choices: they define certain ideological and policy principles that distinguish them from other parties in the electoral market. Further, strong parties, not only clean elections and high levels of political participation, are necessary for the stability of democratic regimes. Parties reduce the costs of information for the average citizen, they reduce the level of uncertainty when voters choose new leaders, they provide a degree of continuity and consistency in their policy and ideological positions, and they become crucial mechanisms for making public officials accountable to the electorate.

The centrality of political parties is even more evident in emerging democracies, where the fluidity, weakness, and instability of parties become a major threat. If Mexico's "old regime" suffered an unequivocal blow as a result of the defeat of the PRI at the presidential level, the "new" and, one hopes, more democratic political regime that is emerging depends on the fate of its most important players: political parties (Aldrich, 1995; Mainwaring and Scully, 1995; Klingemann and Fuchs, 1998; Middlebrook, 2000).

Political Parties and Democracy

There is little doubt that the PAN victory in the 2000 presidential elections owes a great deal to the charismatic Vicente Fox. In fact, no other candidate could have pushed the PRI out of office. Fox was able to attract the votes of a diverse electorate whose main concern was defeating the PRI once and for all. Indeed, in the eyes of many panista activists, Fox's personal and aggressive style, his unwillingness to submit to the party line on highly controversial issues such as the role of the church in politics, Mexico's relations with Cuba, and the privatization of the oil industry, and his campaign's relative independence from the party apparatus all became matters of concern. Fox was perceived as an unorthodox panista with great personal—rather than partisan—appeal. However, even to the most skeptical panista activists, it became clear that Fox was the only candidate capable of winning.

The weight of candidates in elections is not a novel or unexpected phenomenon. All over the world, the personal attributes of candidates and in particular their attractiveness in the media are decisive elements in people's voting decisions. The central question, then, is why we should concern ourselves with the future of political parties if candidates seem so decisive and often give the impression of winning elections in spite of their own parties? If Fox was more important than his party in the elections, why should we care about what happens to the PAN?

Since the 1970s many academics and journalists, particularly in the United States, have been discussing the decline or weakening of political parties. This is evident, it is claimed, in the growing number of independent voters, the decline in party membership, the higher levels of electoral volatility, and the multiplication of social movements (Crotty, 1984; Dalton, Flanagan, and Beck, 1984; Crewe and Denver, 1985; Kitschelt, 1993; Katz and Kolodny, 1994; Katz and Mair, 1994; Ignazi, 1996). Yet, as Schlesinger (1994) and Aldrich (1995) persuasively argue, there is also evidence that political parties are stronger than ever. Indeed, as *political organizations*, political parties have become stronger over the years. In the United States, for example, both the Democratic and the Republican Parties are better financed; they have larger and more professional staffs that operate on a continuous basis (Schlesinger, 1994, 2). Like no other organizations, political parties provide candidates with valuable support—money, workers, and resources of all kinds (Aldrich, 1995, 15).

According to Aldrich, Schlesinger noted the irony that in the age of party decline and candidate-centered elections, politicians' affiliation with major political parties has increased. And he asked, "Why are then politicians' affiliations with a major political party more today if they need them less?" (Aldrich, 1995, 52). The answer, according to Aldrich, is that politicians do not need parties less, regardless of the seeming decline in parties' significance. Affiliation with a party gives candidates a reputation; parties provide a "brand name," which helps to reduce uncertainty and convey information to the public in a more expedient way. In the United States, nomination by a major party still remains a necessary condition for anyone with serious hopes of being elected to a major office (Aldrich, 1995, 273).

In addition to recruiting elites and mobilizing the electorate, parties order the legislative process, reduce the number of proposals to manageable proportions, and discipline politicians both in Congress and in the executive branch. Strong parties can have a stabilizing effect in the political arena and promote beliefs about legitimacy and trust in the political order (Schmitt and Holmberg, 1998). Moreover, as intermediaries between citizens and the government, parties represent, aggregate, and articulate diverse interests, form cohesive policy, and provide the only means for holding elected officials accountable for their collective actions. As Fiorina (1980, 26) argues, "The only way collective responsibility has ever existed, and can exist . . . is through the agency of the political party; in American politics, responsibility requires cohesive parties."

Political parties thus remain critical actors in maintaining the stability of democratic regimes. Parties, however, are no absolute guarantee of either stability or predictability. As Stokes (1998, 28) notes, elected officials can still say one thing during the campaign and act differently once in power. But where parties are strong, this behavior should have electoral consequences. If what public officials do significantly violates their party's basic commitments and produces negative results, people will not continue to vote for that party. As long as officials do not go against their party's central principles, they might undertake innovative actions, even when the latter differ from what they promised during their campaigns. If these actions yield positive results, they can even help to redefine or enrich the party's political platform. The central question, then, is what makes political parties strong?

Strong political parties are those that in addition to acquiring the necessary organizational resources to operate in democratic environments—financial resources, professional staff, and activists—are able to generate more permanent bases of support among the electorate and greater partisan identity among its constituencies. This electoral entrenchment gives parties a cushion of support that *stabilizes* them in the electoral arena and grants their elected officials some *flexibility* to adapt and innovate in the policy domain. In the end, parties gain a reputation for what their elected officials are able to accomplish in office and for the ways in which they respond to their constituencies.

Political parties are not static. They evolve and adapt to changing environments. Elected officials play a crucial role in this process, for when new challenges and issues emerge, they are responsible for translating the party's core principles into government policies. Party officials also play an important role in adjusting to new situations, for they are responsible for maintaining the party's links with the electorate, representing and answering to the shifting demands of its constituents, and fostering greater partisan identity. In many cases, this adaptation involves a fundamental change in the party's internal rules and organizational strategies. The electorate becomes the final judge. To the extent that voters are satisfied with government performance, they might be willing to continue to give their support to the incumbent party and eventually identify with it.

Stokes (1998) notes that parties can have a negative impact on democracy when they become factional, that is, when they cease to concern themselves with the public interest and become too entrenched in defending their own interests. Parties that are too ideological or that are sectarian, for example, can be pressed by their own members to remain committed to their particular interests even if they lose elections. In Chile, the military coup of 1973 was a product of deep political polarization that resulted from the failure of parties to see beyond their own interests (Valenzuela, 1978; Stokes, 1998, 16). Similarly, according to Coppedge (1994), party factionalism and the penetration of parties (through clientelism, patronage, and corruption) into all areas of society were responsible for discrediting democratic institutions in Venezuela.

Public opinion surveys have demonstrated that people in most Latin American countries, including Mexico, distrust and dislike political parties.[3] This can be explained by the way in which parties in these countries, including the PRI in Mexico, have behaved. The alternative, however, is not to eliminate parties altogether but to reform them. Getting rid of parties threatens the very stability and viability of democracy. The central issue is thus to recognize what types of political parties are most suitable for stable democratic regimes.

Parties that are concerned with appealing to the larger electorate and that necessarily moderate their demands encourage stability. As I discuss in this book, catch-all parties are better for democracy; sectarian parties can lead to polarization, isolation, and loss of electoral support. Similarly, parties that are active during electoral periods but virtually disappear between elections obstruct the working of democracy because they fail to represent and service their constituencies and to hold their elected officials accountable. Finally, parties that rely mainly on patronage and clientelism to maintain their bases of support face enormous difficulties in democratic environments, for they often lack the flexibility to adapt to changing conditions, and thus they often fail to represent their constituencies and respond to their concerns. The PRI, a party that depended heavily on patronage and clientelism to maintain its hold on power, lost its ability to compete with other political parties when the electoral arena became more democratic.

In this book, I discuss the challenges the PAN faces as a governing party. As an opposition party, the PAN was able to institutionalize a set of internal rules for affiliating with the party, selecting candidates, and organizing for political action, which allowed it to survive in an extremely hostile electoral and political environment. While these rules were crucial to maintaining the PAN's cohesion and ideological consistency, they also turned the party into a sectarian organization.

Now that the PRI has been defeated at the national level, the major ideological cleavage that defined the PAN—opposition to an authoritarian regime—has been eliminated. As a governing party, the PAN has to come up with more programmatic proposals, distinguish itself from its rival parties, gain a reputation for what it accomplishes in office, and entrench itself in the electorate on a permanent basis. To that end, it needs to leave behind its sectarian tendencies.

From Martyrdom to Power

Unlike many other opposition parties in Mexico that languished and disappeared over the years, the PAN has been remarkable in its ability to survive. Although for many years the PAN could not win a significant election, it never ceased to participate in the electoral arena. This became one of the central puzzles for the party, for participating in elections that were virtually impossible to win contributed to the legitimation of the very political regime it so fiercely criticized. However, its persistence and survival eventually won it credibility as the most independent and consistent opposition party in the country (Loaeza, 1999). Moreover, although participation in rigged elections helped to legitimate the regime, for panista activists, participation also became a proof of sacrifice and goodwill. They not only wanted to prove how undemocratic the regime was because it did not allow even the possibility of victory by another party; they also wanted to demonstrate that they were motivated by higher principles, that power was not their ultimate concern. Defeat, in other words, was a sign of martyrdom. And more important, for many years defeat was an important cohesive mechanism.

Panistas believed that their struggle was long-lasting. Electoral defeat was not incidental to this party but became central to its existence. Whereas the PRI was born out of power and was not expected to exist without it, the PAN was born as an opposition party. The PAN's founders were not expecting electoral victories. Realistic about their limited electoral opportunities, the PAN's founders believed in the importance of educating the public, disseminating their doctrine, and eventually contributing to the "moral rehabilitation of politics" (Lujambio, 1994, 51). They believed they could make people aware of the nature of the regime that governed their lives, offer an alternative, and ultimately persuade people to defeat that regime with their votes.[4] Although sixty years after the PAN's founding this is exactly what happened, the path was not exactly what panista founders envisioned. They believed panista voters would be those who had been convinced by the PAN's doctrine, not those who were disenchanted with the regime and attracted by a charismatic figure who did not fit the traditional panista profile of a leader.

Although the PAN started to win local elections during the mid-1980s, at the national level it was still regarded as an "opposition party." By winning the presidency—a central pillar of the "old regime"[5]—in 2000, the PAN has shed its identity as an opposition party, an identity that shaped its internal life and organizational dynamics. The future of the PAN as a governing party thus depends on its ability to adapt. This involves not only leaving behind a mental attitude akin to martyrdom but also changing its internal rules and organizational structure to maintain its electoral competitiveness without losing its political identity and unity in the process.

Some of these challenges became obvious as soon as the PAN started to win elections at the local and state levels. Once in power, the party could not afford to be a mere critic of the regime; it had to develop more programmatic proposals. Moreover, it had to "distribute" the spoils of victory among the rank and file, something that created enormous tension and division among its militants.

Other, more serious challenges began to emerge when the PAN had to organize for new elections in those places where it controlled the government. Unlike the past, when becoming the party's candidate was regarded as a sacrifice, candidacies now became highly contested as political ambition, rather than martyrdom, attracted a greater number of office seekers. The selection of candidates became a contested and often divisive process. The party's traditional mechanisms for selecting candidates, however, were anachronistic and became increasingly incapable of settling disputes and, above all, of producing the most attractive candidates. Furthermore, the PAN started to confront serious problems with maintaining its electoral coalitions in subsequent elections.

As I elaborate in this book, although during the past two decades the PAN has significantly enlarged its electoral presence, it has also experienced declining support in many places where it controls the government. While the PAN was successful in mobilizing people for elections against the PRI, it has failed to devise new mechanisms to maintain its links to the electorate on a permanent basis. In the state of Chihuahua, one of the most important strongholds of support for the PAN during the 1980s and most of the 1990s, the PAN was defeated in the 1998 gubernatorial elections. In the state of Jalisco, another crucial stronghold, the party won the gubernatorial elections for the second time in 2000 but by an extremely narrow margin and with high rates of abstention. Although the PAN has been able to win consecutively in two other states, Baja California and Guanajuato, its electoral success stems largely from the collapse of the PRI, the main opposition party, rather than from its successful entrenchment in these states' electorates. At the municipal level, the PAN's electoral performance has been more volatile, as it loses most of the municipalities it controls in consecutive elections. On average, during the decade 1991–2001, the party lost seven out of ten municipalities it already controlled. With Vicente Fox's declining popularity, in the 2003 midterm elections the PAN might have enormous problems expanding and maintaining the levels of electoral support it achieved in the 2000 presidential elections.[6]

It is a truism that political parties in democratic environments seek to win office (Downs, 1957; Sartori, 1976; Schlesinger, 1994). However, and paradoxically, for a political party long used to living in the opposition, electoral victory can be unsettling. Contrary to the PAN, the PRI could not conceive of itself without power, which it controlled uninterrupted since its founding in 1929. Access to the government's resources was crucial for distributing patronage and maintaining political support. The PRI could preserve internal discipline and coherence as long as it controlled the government. The PAN is experiencing the opposite problem. If unity was preserved as a result of electoral defeat, victory creates divisions within party ranks; once the party wins elections, panistas start to fight for positions in the new administration. Moreover, some panistas fear that the party's ideology will be compromised once the government confronts problems that require practical—not ideological—solutions. Winning the presidential election thus confronts the party with the most important challenge—maintaining unity while exercising power. More important, being the spearhead of the new regime, the PAN needs to play the lead role in the consolidation of democracy.

In analyzing the expansion of the PAN in the electoral arena and discussing the tensions between the party's internal rules and organizational structure and its new responsibilities as a party in government, this book brings a novel theoretical approach to the study of party organization and change. Most studies of political parties in Mexico have analyzed their reactions to the political and electoral environment and, in particular, their responses to the incentives generated by the various electoral reforms introduced since the 1970s (Molinar, 1991; Valdés, 1994; Crespo, 1995; Lujambio, 1995b; Prud' Homme, 1996; Loaeza, 1999; Chand, 2001). I turn the focus of my research to the party's internal rules and organization and analyze how a changing environment affects the party's internal life. I also explore how the party's rules and organization influence its relationship with the environment.

Organization of the Book

Chapter 1 gives a brief overview of Mexico's political system. It analyzes why the PRI was able to maintain its hegemonic position for more than seven decades and how the PRI's longevity shaped the structure of opportunities for opposition parties. After a brief analysis of the PAN's origins and ideological profile, the chapter discusses the strategies devised by the PAN to survive and expand its presence in an adverse electoral and political environment.

Chapter 2 analyzes the importance of a party's internal rules and organization for its capacity to adapt to changing electoral and political environments. A party's capacity to adapt profoundly influences its electoral performance. Drawing on an extensive theoretical literature on party organization and the relationship between parties and their environments, I propose a typology of political parties along two dimensions: the types of links parties establish with their constituents (the degree of territorial entrenchment and penetration into broader sectors of the electorate) and the degree of autonomy potential candidates enjoy to seek their nomination (the rules regulating intraparty competition and in particular candidate selection).

Chapter 3 analyzes the rules the PAN drafted to organize its internal affairs. Based on party documents and secondary literature, I argue that these rules allowed the party to survive in an extremely hostile electoral and political environment, but they also made the PAN sectarian, that is, an inward-looking party, preoccupied with the consistency of its philosophical and doctrinal principles and isolated from the rest of the world. I describe the party's electoral performance during its first thirty-five years, when it existed merely as an opposition party.

Chapter 4 discusses the movement away from sectarianism during the 1980s, when the PAN started to win elections at the local and state levels. It discusses the crucial role small and medium-size entrepreneurs played in strengthening the PAN in the electoral arena after 1982, when President José López Portillo nationalized the Mexican banks. This chapter, based on interviews with entrepreneurs and panista leaders, explains why entrepreneurs decided to support the PAN, why the PAN decided to welcome them into its ranks, and the challenges they encountered as political activists.

Chapter 5 examines the experience of the PAN in government. It discusses the PAN's styles of governing, which are profoundly influenced by the entrepreneurial origins of many of its public officials. It also discusses the many dilemmas the party faces now that it is the party in government. I explain why the PAN has resisted substantial reforms of its internal rules and structure and discuss why a governing party with sectarian rules encounters serious constraints for maintaining and expanding its electoral coalitions in competitive electoral environments. In the last part of the chapter I examine the experience of the PAN in three states, Chihuahua, Guanajuato, and Baja California. I explore the different strategies the PAN and the government used in these states to maintain their hold on power as well as the outcomes of each attempt.

Chapter 6 moves beyond an analysis of the PAN as an organization to examine the impact of political parties' rules and organizational structures on public perceptions and attitudes. Using survey data, I explore how the public evaluated the PAN and the PRI in three states: Chihuahua and Guanajuato, where the PAN controlled the government; and Puebla, where the PRI has never lost an election. The main goal of this chapter is to analyze the determinants of electoral preference in states controlled by different political parties and, in particular, to analyze whether the electorate's evaluations of government performance influence their votes. Contrary to what many panistas believe, I demonstrate here that government performance evaluations, while important, are not such critical determinants of electoral behavior. I also examine the relationship between evaluations of government performance and partisan identity, that is, whether or not positive evaluations of government performance translate into greater partisan identification with the incumbent party. Again, contrary to what many panistas believe, I show that evaluations of government performance, while important, do not exert a decisive influence on partisan identification. Party identity, still one of the strongest determinants of voting behavior, depends to a much greater extent on what parties, not only their governments, *do* as political organizations. And this in turn is related to the party's rules and organizational structure. In the case of the PAN, a party used to an opposition existence, a fundamental transformation of its internal organizational structure and rules is required in order to adapt to its new condition as a governing party.

The conclusion analyzes why Vicente Fox succeeded in winning not only the presidential elections but also the nomination of his own party. I summarize the main arguments presented in this book and discuss the challenges President Fox faces as the leader of the first "democratic" government in more than seventy years of priísta hegemony. I then examine the party's strategies and internal debates as it prepares for the midterm congressional elections of 2003 in a structurally different electoral environment from that which previously marked its existence.

C H A P T E R   O N E

The Paradoxes of Electoral Success

Unlike many Latin American countries that experienced political crises and fell victim to highly repressive military dictatorships, Mexico remained politically stable for much of the twentieth century. Although it was clearly not democratic, Mexico's political system was not as overtly authoritarian and repressive as were the regimes in other Latin American countries. But the very conditions that ensured political stability in Mexico delayed the transition to democracy. Unlike most of Latin America, where the transitions to democracy were national political events that occurred abruptly and that are generally commemorated on a particular date, in Mexico the transition to democracy began at the local, not the national, level, and the process lasted more than twenty years. More important, this transition was conducted through elections and political parties played a crucial role in this process.[1]

It is a matter of debate in Mexico when the transition to democracy actually began. Some argue that the process started in 1968, after the student movement was violently repressed and the government was pressed into liberalizing the regime. Others argue that it did not start until 1977, when substantial electoral reform was introduced that increased the share of representation of opposition parties at the National Congress. Yet others argue that the transition started after 1982, when President López Portillo nationalized Mexico's banks, a decision that eroded the traditional alliance between entrepreneurs and the government. Finally, others argue that it started in 1988, when the PRI was seriously challenged at the polls by Cuauhtémoc Cárdenas (Loaeza and Segovia, 1987; Molinar, 1991; Medina Peña, 1994; Bruhn, 1997; Lujambio, 1997; Woldernberg, Salazar, and Becerra, 1997). Regardless of when the transition to democracy began, what is clear is that it was a gradual, piecemeal, and peaceful process.

The "Ancien Régime": The Endurance of One-Party Rule

The PRI, which was finally defeated in 2000, was the centerpiece of the political regime that emerged after the Mexican Revolution of 1910. Since it was founded in 1929, it controlled the presidency uninterrupted, and until 1989 it also controlled all state governments and the overwhelming majority of local governments. Notwithstanding the introduction of numerous electoral reforms that, since 1963, gradually allowed opposition parties to gain greater representation in Congress, with the partial exception of 1988 when the PRI lost its absolute majority in the lower house, the PRI controlled both chambers of Congress until 1997.

As its official name denotes, the Institutional Revolutionary Party institutionalized the rules of the game for gaining access to office and surviving in the political arena after the revolution. Its hegemonic position, its internal discipline, and its total subordination to the president afforded the executive an extraordinary concentration of power. The "Imperial Presidency," as Krauze (1997) called it, became one of the most distinguishing characteristics of Mexico's political system. Although the president changed every six years, during his term in office, he became the most important (and only partially constrained) decision maker in the country. His powers included not only the definition and implementation of his program during his term, but also the nomination of a wide array of candidates for various offices, including his successor.[2]

In large part, the broad discretionary powers enjoyed by the president were formally and explicitly codified in the 1917 Constitution. The framers of the Constitution believed that a strong executive was required to pacify and unite a deeply fragmented country (Córdoba, 1988, 94–95; Weldon, 1997, 2). However, by themselves these constitutional provisions do not fully explain why the president in Mexico became such a vital centerpiece of the regime. The latter did not effectively take place until the founding of the Partido Nacional Revolucionario (PNR), the PRI's ancestral political organization, in 1929. More specifically, the concentration of power in the executive was consummated after President Lázaro Cárdenas (1934–40) expelled from the country former President Plutarco Elías Calles, a founder of the PNR who until 1934 still retained control of the party. Once Cárdenas managed to consolidate his power and win control of the "official party" during his term in office, the executive became the leader of the state, the government, and the party (Aguilar Villanueva, 1994, 40).[3]

The PNR was created to overcome the deep political divisions that were tearing the country apart after the Mexican Revolution. After the assassination of Alvaro Obregón, president-elect of Mexico, in 1928, President Elías Calles addressed the National Congress and summoned the remaining revolutionary leaders who still enjoyed local bases of support throughout the country to come together to form a political party. It was time to "relinquish the rule of personal leaders [*caudillos*] and to create a nation of institutions and laws" (Garrido, 1982, 67; see also Knight, 1992). The PNR would create an institutional mechanism to allow for the peaceful transition of power among the so-called Revolutionary Family.

The PNR was a pact among the revolutionary elites; its basic documents, as Knight (1992) demonstrates, were drafted in haste, with scant discussion and very little popular participation. The Catholic Church, the private sector, and non-Callista leaders who had at first supported the Mexican Revolution were excluded from the PNR (Knight, 1992).[4] The politics of this elite pact, as Knight (1992, 127) argues, "were national, centralized and incestuous, but in order to make the settlement stick its authors needed popular support." Thus, although it was a pact among elites, the PNR was committed to representing the popular demands that had originally inspired the revolution.

The official party was central to Mexican politics. It became not only an "electoral arm" of the government (Meyer, 1990) but also, and fundamentally, the vital institution for recruiting political leaders, gaining access to power, ensuring the advancement of politicians' careers, and maintaining political discipline. Although formally prohibited, the official party adopted the colors of the national flag and eventually came to be identified with the nation at large. For many Mexicans, being priísta was part and parcel of being Mexican.

After President Cárdenas took control of the party and managed to subordinate it to the office of the executive, it became the institutional arm of the presidency and a fundamental mechanism to maintain control over the other branches of government. As Weldon (1997, 3) argues, the enormous discretionary powers vested in the Mexican president depended on the existence of a highly disciplined political party, the subordination of this party to the executive, and its ability to maintain a hegemonic position in Congress.

In 1938, during Cárdenas's presidency, the PNR was reformed in a corporatist fashion, incorporating workers, peasants, the so-called popular sector,[5] and the military into its organization (Collier and Collier, 1991). With these reforms, the PNR changed its name to Partido de la Revolución Mexicana (PRM). Although the private sector was not formally included in the party, entrepreneurs established friendly, fluid relations with the government. As I elaborate in later chapters, entrepreneurs were obligated to organize into industrial and commercial corporatist organizations and refrained from participating overtly in politics. In exchange, the government guaranteed them a profitable and stable business environment.

Discipline became the golden rule of Mexican politics and one of the official party's most distinctive characteristics. Discipline was rewarded with access to positions of power. Lack of discipline was punished with the threat of expulsion from the party. In a noncompetitive political regime, the latter was tantamount to political death (Langston, 2000).[6]

The hegemonic position of the official party (PNR-PRM and then PRI) in Mexican political life was assured through a series of electoral laws that crucially restricted opposition parties' access to power. The first and most fundamental was the law of 1946, which "maximized the requirements and minimized the rights of political parties" (Molinar, 1991, 27–28). This law prohibited independent candidates from participating in elections; it also established that no political organizations other than registered political parties could participate in elections. Moreover, to discourage the proliferation of parties with local bases of support, the 1946 electoral law required parties to obtain "official registration" from the government. The requisites for obtaining this registration were exclusionary and restrictive: parties had to become national organizations, with political representation in the majority of the states. Parties also needed to adopt a centralized organization similar to that of the PRI and to have an official monthly publication. In addition to these highly exclusionary electoral laws and the frequent manipulation of elections and recurrence to election fraud, the PRI's hegemony was ensured through the organization of a vast political machine that distributed state patronage to the remotest regions of the country, through the widespread use of corruption, and through the implementation of an efficient system of co-optation to "include" a wide variety of dissidents or potential adversaries.[7]

Lacking an ideological commitment beyond its revolutionary rhetoric, the PRI was extremely flexible in adapting to a range of economic and political pressures. Priísta governments were at once advocates of free enterprise and staunch defenders of labor rights, supporters of the collectivization of agriculture and promoters of export-oriented farmers and small property holders, and advocates of neoliberalism and supporters of the poor.

The PRI's hegemonic position critically shaped the opportunities for opposition parties. If access to power was the main concern of non-priísta leaders, the latter had greater incentives to become included in the ranks of the official party. This actually happened in many cases; for example, several 1968 student leaders were later incorporated into the government (de Mauleón, 1998). If, on the other hand, opposition leaders regarded the promotion of certain ideological principles as more fundamental than mere access to power, then they were tolerated but condemned to political ineffectiveness. This was clearly the case for the PAN.

Unlike many opposition parties that languished and disappeared over the years or that decided to collaborate with the PRI,[8] the PAN survived as an independent political party under a hostile political regime. As Loaeza (1999) argues, the PAN gained credibility for having survived and for having consistently opposed the PRI and the regime for which it stood.

Origins of the PAN

The Partido Acción Nacional was founded in 1939 as a response by a group of conservative intellectuals, professionals, businessmen, and Catholic activists to the allegedly socialist and state-led policies introduced by President Cárdenas.[9] Cárdenas's vast land distribution, nationalization of the oil industry and the railroads, and creation of numerous state-owned enterprises and his decision to turn over to workers key administrative posts in these enterprises alienated important sectors of the upper and middle classes. Furthermore, Cárdenas's educational policies and particularly his endorsement of "socialist education" angered large sectors of the Catholic Church.[10] Finally, his decision to reform the official party in 1938 by incorporating the labor and agrarian sectors into its ranks angered a group of conservative intellectuals and professionals who had supported the 1910 revolution against the dictatorship of Porfirio Díaz. They were disappointed with the radical turn the revolution seemed to be taking and believed that Cárdenas was responsible for institutionalizing a heavily centralized and presidentialist political system that threatened the very foundations of capitalism and democracy.

Because of the deep economic crisis the country was experiencing during the last year of the Cárdenas administration, Cárdenas's opponents were uncertain about the future. The presidential election scheduled for 1940 convinced them of the need to found a new political party. Such a party, they believed, not only would provide them with a vehicle to voice their concerns and ideals in a more organized fashion; it would also enable them to compete for power and challenge what was becoming an official party. The latter hope was to prove illusory once the PRI managed to consolidate its power and exert a virtual monopoly on the political life of the country.

The PAN was an opposition party in a literal sense; being effectively barred from office, its task was to stage a permanent opposition against the regime. As one of its founders eloquently put it, the party's mission was "not a day's fight, but a struggle for eternity [*una brega de eternidad*]" (Gómez Morin, 1946).[11] These circumstances of its birth had enormous consequences for the party's future.

The PAN was created primarily on the initiative of Manuel Gómez Morin, a prominent lawyer, academic, financier, and politician from the northern state of Chihuahua. Gómez Morin was able to bring together a loose coalition united by their opposition to President Cárdenas and their fear that his successor would be equally radical (Mabry, 1973, 15). But while the PAN's founders shared antisocialist leanings, they disagreed about the role of government in society, the type of party they wanted to create, and the strategies for achieving their goals.

Gómez Morin had supported the revolution against the Díaz dictatorship and in the 1920s participated in several postrevolutionary governments. He was appointed undersecretary of finance by President Alvaro Obregón (1920–24) and later served as financial adviser to President Elías Calles (1924–28). During Elías Calles's presidency, Gómez Morin played a crucial role in drafting some of the most important economic laws: the organic law of the Banco de México (1925), the agricultural credit law, and the first Mexican income tax law (1926) (Mabry, 1973, 32). From 1934 to 1935 he was rector of the National University, which gave him important contacts with the intellectual community. As a corporate lawyer and financial adviser, Gómez Morin also had extensive connections with bankers and entrepreneurs who, like many professionals and intellectuals, played an important role in the party's founding.

Gómez Morin's experience in public office led to his disenchantment with the government and with the type of regime the revolutionary leaders were consolidating.[12] In his view, the postrevolutionary governments were consumed by naked ambition for power and lacked a set of principles and ideas to guide their actions (Loaeza, 1999, 115). Far from realizing the democratic ideals that had inspired the Mexican Revolution, these governments limited individual freedom and failed to create the conditions for the emergence of a participatory civic spirit, which Gómez Morin believed was indispensable to the construction and consolidation of a democratic regime (Wilkie, 1969).

As early as 1927, Gómez Morin thought about founding a political party as a means of forging a "civic spirit in Mexico" (Wilkie and Wilkie, 1969, 157). In 1929 he supported the candidacy of José Vasconcelos, a conservative intellectual who ran as an independent candidate against the PNR's candidate, Pascual Ortíz Rubio.[13] Convinced that the election had been rigged and that the PNR would not tolerate any opposition, Gómez Morin distanced himself from the bureaucracy and went into self-imposed exile in the United States (Reveles, 1996).

During the late 1930s, Gómez Morin began to travel extensively around Mexico, contacting old friends and acquaintances and gathering support for his idea to build a political party. It was not until President Cárdenas came to office, however, that this idea gained momentum. In Gómez Morin's view, Cárdenas constituted a serious threat to the democratic principles espoused by the Mexican Revolution.

Gómez Morin's most serious criticisms of the Cárdenas administration were its class-based policies favoring workers and peasants and disfavoring landholders and business interests and its strengthening of the state at the expense of civil society. The expansion of the state's participation in the economy through the creation of numerous state-owned industries and above all the incorporation of workers and peasants in what was becoming the official party discouraged individual initiative and restricted freedom of choice. In his view, the reform of the PNR along corporatist lines revealed Cárdenas's "fascist inclinations" (Yañez Maldonado, 1990, 41). By creating a permanent and captive clientele for the official party, Cárdenas was building a mechanism of political control that undermined the organization of other political options (Yañez Maldonado, 1990).[14]

Gómez Morin also disagreed sharply with Cárdenas's agrarian policy. He believed it was impossible, unrealistic, and demagogic to distribute land to all peasants. There was simply not enough arable land to distribute, and Mexico could not properly develop with more than half of its population living in the countryside. More important, Gómez Morin thought that the process of land distribution had been conducted without adequately defining and protecting the legal right to landownership. The expansion of the *ejidos,* collective landholdings, left peasants without adequate incentives to become responsible for the production of their land (Wilkie and Wilkie, 1969, 155).[15] Further, Gómez Morin opposed the organization of peasants into a huge corporatist organization controlled by the official party, as well as the imposition of a uniform agrarian policy without consideration for regional diversity (von Sauer, 1974, 57). Gómez Morin supported an agrarian regime based on small property owners, which in his view granted peasants the legal safeguards and freedom to become more productive.

Finally, although he was not a Catholic activist, Gómez Morin strongly opposed Cárdenas's educational policies. In his view, Cárdenas's efforts to weaken the church's influence in education and strengthen the state's was counter to freedom of expression and undermined the rights of parents to decide how to educate their children.

Gómez Morin's ideas finally materialized in 1939. According to Mabry (1973), an authoritative historian of the PAN, on September 16, 1939, approximately one thousand delegates gathered at the Frontón México in Mexico City to found the new political party. The founders were drawn from essentially three distinct groups.

The largest group consisted of young Catholic activists who opposed the enforcement of the anticlerical provisions of the Mexican Constitution and above all President Cárdenas's socialist and antichurch leanings. Many of these Catholic founders were middle-class intellectuals and professionals who had fought anticlericalism at the National University, when Gómez Morin was its rector in the 1930s. They were also active members of several Catholic movements, such as Acción Católica Mexicana (ACM), Asociación Católica de la Juventud Mexicana (ACJM), and Unión Nacional de Estudiantes Católicos (UNEC). The most prominent leader of this group, who later became a leading political thinker in the PAN, was the intellectual Efraín González Luna.[16] Although all these Catholics were deeply inspired by the church's Social Doctrine calling for active involvement of the state in support of the poor and underprivileged, they staunchly opposed the intervention of government in religious affairs. According to them, Cárdenas's 1934 amendment to Article 3 of the Constitution, which required the inclusion of socialist values in public education, revealed the government's intention to enforce the most radical aspects of the Mexican Constitution, which until then had existed only on paper. The construction of a socialist state threatened to weaken the position of the Catholic Church and to undermine its values. Given the constitutional restrictions on the church's involvement in politics,[17] these Catholic activists believed that their interests could be more effectively expressed through a political party, an organization that could play according to the formal rules of the game.

The second group of founders comprised middle-class professionals and conservative intellectuals who had played important roles in the National University (as directors, chairmen, and rectors) and in previous government administrations (in government ministries and the foreign service). The most prominent leader of this group was of course Gómez Morin. But other important members of this group were Valentín Gama, Ezequiel A. Chávez, and Fernando Ocaranza, all of whom had been rectors of the National University; Manuel Bonilla, secretary of commerce under the Madero administration (1910–11); Miguel Alessio Robles, secretary of industry in the Obregón administration (1920–24), and Bernardo Gastelum, secretary of health, undersecretary of education, and diplomat (Mabry, 1973, 35). These founders regarded Cárdenas's statist and corporatist policies as an assault on the market, on an effective system of checks and balances, and on political freedom. Although they also opposed Cárdenas's plans to include socialist values in the school curriculum and to weaken the Catholic Church, they objected most strongly to his policies that increased state intervention in the economy and strengthened the presidency at the expense of the other two branches of government. They particularly opposed the administration's collectivization of agricultural land through the creation of ejidos, its incorporation of laborers and rural workers in the official party through corporatist organizations,[18] its commitment to workers' demands, its support of labor in labor-management disputes, and its populist rhetoric. The president's decisions to grant political asylum to Spanish refugees and to Trotsky were seen by these activists as clear signs of his socialist leanings. To them, the creation of a political party on the right of the ideological spectrum was crucial for fostering a democratic version of the Mexican Revolution and preventing the consolidation of a regime based on a single hegemonic party.

The third group of founders consisted of entrepreneurs and landholders who had either been affected by Cárdenas's land distribution policies and the strengthening of worker and peasant organizations or feared their interests could be harmed by his radical and socialist leanings. The majority of these entrepreneurs were well connected in the financial sector. The most prominent members of this group were Miguel Estrada Iturbide (General Hipotecaria), Manuel F. Escandon (Banco de Comercio), and Carlos Novoa (Banco Internacional and then leader of the Mexican Bankers' Association) (Mabry, 1973, 35–36).

The entrepreneurs' opposition to the Cárdenas administration was effective in pressing President Cárdenas to choose a more overtly pro-business candidate to succeed him in office. Although he was committed to the poor, Cárdenas understood that the industrialization of the country, the generation of wealth, and, in the end, the economic and political stability of the country required the cooperation of the private sector. Thus, although Francisco J. Múgica, secretary of communication and public works, was ideologically more akin to the president, he chose General Manuel Avila Camacho as his successor. Avila Camacho's moderation seemed better suited to work with the private sector and to consolidate Cárdenas's reforms (Garrido, 1982, 271; Hamilton, 1982, 269).

After Avila Camacho (1940–46) came to office, many of the entrepreneurs who had originally supported the PAN left the party. The president's conciliatory attitude and above all his efforts to win back the confidence of the private sector in Mexico encouraged these entrepreneurs to work closely with the administration and to refrain from overt participation in politics.[19] This inaugurated the so-called alliance for profits, a working arrangement between entrepreneurs and the government that institutionalized a pattern of cordial and cooperative relations between the private and public sectors that lasted for more than thirty years. The entrepreneurs adopted a low political profile and tolerated the government and the PRI's revolutionary and antibusiness rhetoric in exchange for a profitable and stable economic environment.

The exodus of the entrepreneurial sector from the PAN during the 1940s had important implications for the party's internal life, for it strengthened the position of Catholic activists, who came predominantly from the central states of the country and who already represented the most numerous faction inside the party. Catholic intellectuals were to play a vital role in defining the party's ideological profile and in designing and drafting its internal rules.

The PAN's Ideology

Although Catholic activists constituted the largest bloc of delegates at the party's constituent assembly, the PAN adopted a nonconfessional position due in large part to the decisive influence of Gómez Morin, who became the party's president during its first ten years (1939–49). Gómez Morin, himself a devout Catholic, was convinced of the importance of separating the religious and political spheres.[20] Catholic activists had a strong presence in the party's top administrative positions, however, and exerted considerable influence on the party's ideological profile and the "messianic" vision (which conceived political participation as a sacrifice) that the party adopted since its creation.

According to Gómez Morin, Mexicans had never been trained in the art of citizenship (Wilkie and Wilkie, 1969, 176). An independent political party was vital if a pluralist society in Mexico were to emerge and if citizens were to participate in political life without the tutelage of the official party. These civic goals were cast in an ideology deeply inspired by the Social Doctrine of the Catholic Church.

Given the separation of church and the state and the prohibition on political activity by the church, the PAN could not call itself a Christian Democratic party. But like Christian Democratic parties elsewhere, the PAN's doctrine rests on two papal encyclicals, *Rerum Novarum* (1891) and *Quadregesimo Anno* (1931). In these, the church defined the responsibility of the state as the attainment of the "common good," called for the search of a "third way" between free-market liberalism and communism, advocated in favor of policies to help the poor, and established a commitment to democracy and private property (Mabry, 1973).

Also, like other Christian Democratic parties, the PAN draws its philosophy from Aristotelian and Thomist political thought, which conceives of society as a harmonious organization based on the individual (the person's dignity) and informed by deep moral values (the common good). According to this philosophy, which rejects the notion of class struggle, the state should have as its most important goal the "realization of the common good, which implies at one and the same time attaining justice and safety, defending the interests of the collectivity, and respecting and protecting the individual" (PAN, *Principios de doctrina*). Thus the state should intervene in economic and social matters only to the extent that its actions do not violate the capacity of individuals to obtain their own goals.

The PAN's doctrine defines two other important political principles: *subsidiarity* and *solidarity*. Subsidiarity is an "ordering principle" between the state and civil society.[21] It rests on the idea that the state should participate only in those matters that civil society cannot accomplish by itself. In the party's words: "As much society as possible, as much government as necessary" (PAN, *Principios de doctrina*). Since, according to this philosophy, the family is the most important social institution, the government should intervene only in matters that the family cannot manage by itself. Thus education, for example, should be regarded as a matter for which the family, not the state, has primary responsibility. Parents should be given the freedom to decide how to educate their children.[22]

The logic of subsidiarity also applies to the various levels of government. Thus municipal authorities, the closest to the community, should function largely without intervention by the state and federal authorities. The latter should intervene only in those matters that exceed local government's capacity. The emphasis on local government made the PAN a strong advocate of federalism, which was particularly notable in a highly centralized political regime such as Mexico's.

The other central principle of the PAN's ideology, solidarity, rests on the idea that the state has the moral responsibility to help the poor and those who cannot help themselves (Loaeza, 1999; López, 1999).[23] The state should protect people against economic destitution, but private initiative should constitute the core of the economy. Private property "dignifies" the individual. The state should assist rather than substitute for private initiative. Thus the PAN traditionally has been opposed to the collectivization of agriculture in the form of the ejido because it violates the right of peasants to own their land.

On social issues, the PAN is closely linked to the ideas endorsed by the Catholic Church: it opposes abortion, it is against sexual liberty (for example, in matters related to homosexuality and birth control), and it supports strong family values. Following these ideological principles and confronted with a political regime that severely limited their opportunities to gain access to office, the PAN's central mission was conceived not as attaining power but rather as inserting morality in politics, educating the people, and inculcating a set of principles that would guide their political actions. The ultimate goal of politics was visualized as the attainment of the "public good," a harmonious social environment in which the "human being" would be able to develop to his or her full potential. Politics was considered a service to the community, not a self-serving activity driven by political ambition. Panistas saw themselves as "political missionaries who derived psychological satisfaction from proselytizing and martyrdom" (Mabry, 1973, 187). Without a solid ideological foundation, political power could have a strong corrupting effect. The PAN's members were actively involved in politics because they wanted to "serve," not because they had political aspirations.[24] And they conceived of their political involvement as a sacrifice without expecting an imminent reward.[25] Indeed, from this moralistic approach to politics, being in the opposition became for panistas a chance to "remain pure," to participate in politics without being contaminated by the ambitions concomitant with power.

The Rewards of Sacrifice: The PAN's Electoral Performance

For many years, PAN activists and supporters knew that their vote for the PAN would not bring about a significant change in Mexico. They nevertheless continued to vote for the party. They understood this was a long battle; voting was part of their "service" and an expression of their "democratic" commitment to change.

Given the hegemony of the PRI, the centralization of political power in the hands of the president, and the consequent subordination of Congress to the executive, PAN legislators also knew that they were virtually impotent to effect political change. They became the "moral voice" of the opposition to the regime. The most they could aspire to was to condemn the authoritarian aspects of the regime and challenge the subordination of Congress to the executive.

By the beginning of the 1960s, however, the strength and dynamism of the PAN's moral voice was languishing as a result of the overwhelming and overt recurrence of election fraud. The 1958 presidential elections, in particular, were condemned by the PAN for fraudulence. The PAN demanded that its six elected deputies resign their positions and threatened to abstain from participating in subsequent elections.[26] Faced with this serious challenge to the very legitimacy of the government and the PRI, the government agreed in 1963 to introduce a partial system of proportional representation in Congress. Opposition parties could gain a maximum of twenty seats in Congress, a considerable improvement in the party's electoral representation as until then, the party had not been able to win more than six seats.[27]

As Lujambio (1994, 49) argues, the 1963 electoral reform inaugurated a series of additional electoral reforms that progressively increased the electoral opportunities for opposition parties and eventually contributed to the opening of Mexico's political regime. In 1977, after the PAN failed to field a presidential candidate in 1976 because of serious internal divisions, a new and more comprehensive electoral reform increased the size of Congress and introduced a system of proportional representation for electing members of Congress. Since 1977 the PAN has substantially increased its presence in the lower chamber of Congress, from 20 seats in 1976 to 43 in 1979 to 101 in 1988.

After the heavily contested elections of 1988, President Carlos Salinas de Gortari was pressed for additional electoral reforms. Indeed, during his term in office, the government introduced three reforms. Although they allowed the opposition to have greater electoral presence, until 1993 they still confined the opposition to a marginal position in Congress.[28]

At the municipal and state levels, the PAN's political presence was also extremely limited. Until the mid-1980s the party controlled a very small number of municipalities (never more than seventeen) and no state governments. Although, compared to the 1960s, the PAN's electoral presence had increased substantially, it was still too marginal to challenge the hegemony of the PRI.

The turning point for the PAN was President López Portillo's decision to nationalize the banks in 1982. Angered by the arbitrary and unilateral manner in which this decision was taken and concerned about the dangers of an unaccountable and unlimited executive, a significant number of entrepreneurs decided to organize in opposition to the PRI and gave their support to the PAN.

By the presidential elections of 1988, the most seriously contested elections in Mexico since 1958, the PAN had begun to adopt a new political profile. Its presidential candidate, Manuel J. Clouthier, former president of the Confederación Patronal de la República Mexicana (COPARMEX), one of the most radical and outspoken business organizations in the country (Mizrahi, 1994a; Tirado, 1987; Luna, Tirado, and Valdés, 1990) and a newcomer to the ranks of the PAN, staged an unparalleled aggressive and widely publicized electoral campaign. Although the PAN did not receive a significantly larger share of the total vote at the national level, at the local and state levels it increased its electoral presence substantially. In 1989 the PAN won its first state governorship in the northern state of Baja California. Just ten years later, in 1999, the PAN controlled six state governments and more than three hundred municipalities, including important capital cities.

During the 1990s, the PAN significantly strengthened its electoral position at the state and local levels. In contrast to the center-left PRD, which adopted a radical political position and challenged the PRI and the government at the national level, the PAN decided to take a more conciliatory stance toward the PRI and the regime at the national level while organizing aggressive electoral campaigns at the state and local levels.

Knowing that they did not have the electoral strength or sufficient political and organizational infrastructure to mount an all-out attack against the PRI, the PAN's leaders decided to adopt a gradual and piecemeal political strategy. During the administration of President Carlos Salinas de Gortari (1988–94), the PAN collaborated with the PRI in Congress by passing important presidential initiatives, such as the electoral reform of 1989 and several constitutional amendments in 1993.[29] In exchange, the government was more prepared to tolerate panista victories at the state and local levels.[30] By the time President Ernesto Zedillo came to power in 1994, the PAN had become a significant electoral force in the country. Although the PRD had not been as successful, it also constituted an important political force. By the end of the Zedillo administration, the PRD controlled six state governments and 263 municipalities.

Pressed by this new configuration of influence, the Zedillo administration finally introduced a significant electoral reform in 1996. It granted independence to the electoral institutions in charge of organizing elections and allowed the Supreme Court to intervene in electoral matters.[31]

The PAN's gradualism was born out of both ideology and opportunity. The PAN leaders knew that the PRI and the government would be more willing to accept electoral victories at the local and state levels than one at the national level. As Lujambio (1995a) argues, in a presidential system, there is too much at stake in a presidential election. Losing elections at the municipal or state levels allowed the PRI to share power with the opposition without actually losing power (Lujambio, 1995a). Moreover, the PAN's organization was still weak at the national level. It could concentrate its resources in those few places where it was strongest. Finally, in contrast to the PRD, the PAN did not have major differences with the government's economic policies.[32]

Ideologically, the PAN justified its gradualism as a reflection of its federalist conviction and its commitment to fight against an overcentralized state by revitalizing the smallest political unit in the country, the municipality. Democracy, according to the PAN's founders, needed to be constructed from the bottom up. Gaining control of municipalities allowed the party to experience the art of governing at the local level and to gradually become a more viable national political option. Eventually, in 2000, the strategy paid off.

From Opposition to Power: The Challenges of Governing

Notwithstanding the PAN's indisputable electoral growth during the past fifteen years, the road has not been smooth. While the PAN has been successful in organizing attractive electoral campaigns and mobilizing large and heterogeneous sectors of the electorate in opposition to the PRI, it has been less successful in supporting its governments, maintaining its ties with the electorate, and winning consecutive elections. Accustomed to living in the opposition, the PAN tends to contract and to become virtually paralyzed once it wins elections. In part, the problem stems from the weakness of its organizational infrastructure and the lack of sufficient personnel. Confined to the opposition and with scarce opportunities to gain access to office, the party attracted very few militants and lacked financial and professional resources. For decades, the PAN had an extremely small, weak, and fragmented structure.

During the 1980s, when the PAN started to win elections at the local level, most people who had joined the party and worked with the candidates during elections moved to the administration, leaving the party as weak and fragmented as it was before. As a former president of the PAN once remarked, "the party tends to weaken as an organization when it wins an election."[33]

But the PAN's weakness as a governing party has deeper roots. Having forged an identity as an opposition party, it has failed to design a blueprint for action once it gains access to government. Panista leaders were used to criticizing the regime and organizing elections; victory confronts them with the need to define a more programmatic position and to forge a new political identity based on their accomplishments in office.[34] Moreover, victory often generates serious tensions among the panista rank and file. Although for many years traditional panista activists claimed they were not interested in attaining power, once power is within reach, they fight for the spoils of victory.

Traditional panistas often feel displaced by the new panista activists who since the mid-1980s have been more successful in the electoral arena.

Finally, while the PAN has been successful in mobilizing a broad electorate disenchanted with the government and willing to organize against the PRI, it is still an ideologically compact organization. Its internal rules reflect its preoccupation with preserving its ideological purity and almost mystic devotion of its activists. Beyond its commitment to democracy, federalism, and a fight against corruption, the PAN has not been flexible enough to articulate the interests and general concerns of a large number of its voters. Thus once in office the PAN has not been able to devise a strategy to maintain its ties and serve its constituencies on a permanent basis.

A recent survey of panista activists and voters shows that a gap exists between the PAN as an organization and its supporters. According to Magaloni and Moreno (2000), at the elite level the PAN is a relatively coherent and ideologically compact party, but at the mass level the PAN supporters are more dispersed ideologically and define the party as a catch-all party. That is, despite their ideological differences, in 2000 panista voters saw the party as capable of defeating the PRI.

On the ideological spectrum, the PAN traditionally has been regarded as a conservative, or right-wing, party in Mexico. This is due to the support it received from Catholic activists at its founding and to the party's position on abortion, sexual liberty, and family values. But if we analyze the PAN from the perspective of its supporters, a different picture emerges.

Although most Mexicans are in general rather conservative with respect to religiosity and moral values, the socially most conservative electorate tends to support the PRI, not the PAN. The latter receives support from voters scattered all along the conservative-liberal dimension (Magaloni and Moreno, 2000, 20). Moreover, according to Moreno (1999a), during the 1990s, Mexicans consistently identified the PAN as a "centrist" political party, to the *left* of the PRI and to the *right* of the PRD.[35]

While the "centrist" position of panista supporters may be regarded as an electoral opportunity for this party, as the majority of the electorate is located at the center-right of the ideological spectrum,[36] it also poses a difficult dilemma. Panista leaders fear losing ideological consistency if they attempt to reach this larger electorate and build stronger and more permanent electoral coalitions.

This gap between the party as an organization and its constituencies affects the party's governing styles and has profound consequences for the party's electoral future. Being more concerned with the preservation of its ideological principles, PAN leaders, both in Congress and in the party's headquarters, often obstruct and oppose its own elected officials. This has already been apparent at the national level, where differences between the PAN and President Fox have led to serious tensions. Moreover, once in power, panistas often refuse to accept more members into the party's ranks, for they fear that an expansion of the PAN's active membership will necessarily reduce traditional panistas' chances to benefit from the party's new electoral opportunities. Finally, the PAN's weak and inconsistent political presence beyond electoral

Table 1.1   The PAN's Rate of Repetition in Municipal Elections, 1983–2001

Year	Total of Municipalities Won by the PAN	Number of Municipalities Where the PAN Won Consecutively	Rate of Repetition (percentage of consecutive victories with respect to the previous election)
1983	17		
1984	3		
1985	3		
1986	12	2	11.7
1987	1	0	0
1988	13	1	33.3
1989	21	4	33.3
1990	12	0	0
1991	44	4	30.7
1992	37	3	14.2
1993	16	4	33.3
1994	89	7	15.9
1995	118	28	75.6
1996	37	8	50.0
1997	144	44	49.4
1998	86	31	26.2
1999	19	1	2.7
2000	224	94	65.2
2001	172	30	34.8

Source: Partido Acción Nacional, Office of Electoral Affairs.

Mayors are elected for a three-year term and there is no reelection. The percentage of consecutive victories refers to the number of municipalities retained by the PAN in the next consecutive election. Since each state has a different electoral calendar, any given year only represents the number of electoral victories obtained by the PAN in those states holding municipal elections. Thus, for example, in 1986 the PAN won a total of 12 municipalities in states that were up for elections, but only in 2 municipalities was this a consecutive victory. That is, the PAN retained 11.7 percent of the municipalities it controlled in 1983.

periods prevents it from establishing permanent ties with the electorate. The latter greatly explains the PAN's difficulties in maintaining its levels of electoral support in consecutive elections.

As Table 1.1 shows, while the PAN's success in elections at the municipal level has increased considerably between 1983 and 2001, the party loses the majority of municipalities it already controls in consecutive elections. In 1994, for example, the PAN won a total of 89 municipalities but won consecutively in only seven cases—that is, it won in 15.9 percent of the municipalities it held in 1991. In 2000, due largely to the charisma of Vicente Fox, who was running for the presidency that year, the PAN had an exceptional electoral performance; it retained power in 65.2 percent of the municipalities it controlled in 1997. But the next year the rate of repetition declined to 34.8 percent, a number closer to the historical trend. On average, from 1991 to 2001, the PAN's rate of repetition was 36 percent; that is, the PAN loses seven out of ten municipalities it controls.[37]

In a country ruled by a hegemonic political party for more than seventy years, forging new political identities becomes a major challenge. Parties can entrench themselves in society and maintain their political presence as long as they are capable of aggregating interests and representing and serving their constituencies. But the latter requires permanent work, not just the organization of elections. For the PAN, this represents a major challenge and entails a radical transformation. The PAN's tendency to contract between elections thus fails to create an electorate that can identify with it. The latter seriously affects the party's future electoral fortunes, for partisan identity, as I discuss below, is still one of the most important determinants of electoral preference.

Political Parties as Organizations

A Typology of Parties

One may be puzzled by the longevity of the PAN in a political system such as Mexico's that until recently was dominated by a single party. How did the PAN survive in such an environment? How did this environment affect the internal life of the party? And to what extent is this party, born in a noncompetitive and authoritarian framework, able to adapt to an increasingly more competitive electoral and political environment?

Until the 1980s the PAN had a marginal electoral presence in Mexico. In presidential elections, the party's share of the total vote was less than 15 percent, and in congressional elections, it could not overcome the threshold of twenty seats to which any party with more than 2.5 percent of the total vote was entitled.[1] More important, between 1943, when the party participated in elections for the first time,[2] and the 1980s, the PAN did not win a gubernatorial election or a seat in the Senate. Until the 1980s, the party's presence in municipal elections was equally marginal.

Most scholars and journalists have explained the recent electoral victories of the PAN as the result of important changes in the political and economic environment. Since the early 1980s the country has experienced a series of severe economic crises. In the eyes of many voters, the PRI lost its capacity to articulate and represent their interests. These crises, coupled with a series of corruption scandals, led a growing number of voters to withdraw their support from the governing PRI. Indeed, as can be seen in Charts 2.1 and 2.2, since 1976 the vote for the PRI in presidential and congressional elections decreased consistently. At the same time, the introduction of several electoral reforms since the 1960s significantly increased the electoral opportunities for the opposition (Molinar, 1991; Crespo, 1995; Nacif, 1996; Loaeza, 1999).[3]

Chart 2.1   Presidential Elections, 1964–2000

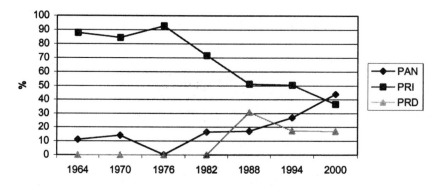

Chart 2.2   Congressional Elections, 1964–2000

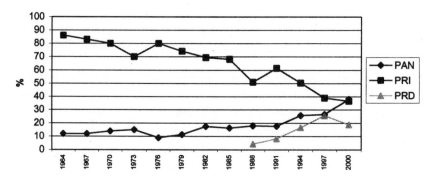

Although all these factors certainly had an important role in strengthening the opposition, no party grew electorally as much as the PAN. The PAN's electoral performance cannot be fully understood without taking into account the strategies the party adopted to respond to these factors. These strategies are constrained by the party's internal organization, in particular, by two critical aspects: (1) its rules governing intraparty competition and the process of candidate selection; and (2) the types of linkages the party establishes with the electorate. These aspects condition the party's flexibility to adapt to changing contexts and its stability in new electoral and political environments. They also define the distinctive characteristics of political parties: who they represent and to whom they are accountable.

I argue that a party's performance in the electoral arena depends crucially on its internal organization. And this structure is in turn shaped by the objectives and strategies party leaders choose.[4] Thus if a political party is, as Aldrich (1995, 4) argues, the "creature of politicians," it is to a large extent an endogenous institution, one that is shaped by the decisions of political actors.[5]

Exogenous change in the political, economic, social, or electoral arenas confronts parties with new sets of opportunities and constraints. But not all parties are equally capable of seizing these new opportunities and overcoming these constraints. An effective response often involves important internal reforms that redefine the relationship among leaders, activists, constituents, and the electorate at large. And as is the case with any other process of change, reforms inevitably upset established power structures within the organization and confront parties with numerous dilemmas and trade-offs they need to resolve to ensure their permanence and observance, that is, their institutionalization. Thus analyzing the decisions party leaders make when they confront changing environmental conditions is crucial for explaining a party's electoral performance.

Taking this analytic perspective, I argue that although the PAN's internal rules allowed the party to survive as an organization in a hostile electoral environment, these same rules—which have been only partially changed since the party's creation in 1939[6]—severely limit its degree of stability and flexibility to adapt to a more competitive environment. While during the 1980s the PAN's leaders were able to adopt innovative responses to a changing environment, without reforming the party's rules, these innovations cannot be fully institutionalized, and therefore they can easily be lost in future electoral contexts. The future of the PAN as a governing party thus greatly depends on the capacity of its leaders to modify its internal rules and structure to attract larger electorates and take advantage of greater opportunities to gain access to power.

This chapter develops a set of theoretical tools for analyzing the interaction between political parties and their environments and for understanding the internal mechanisms that condition a party's ability to adapt and endure in changing environmental conditions.[7] I propose a typology of parties that can be used to understand the PAN's political development during the past twenty years as well as to examine the multiple dilemmas it faces as its electorate grows and the electoral arena becomes more competitive.[8]

Political Parties as Organizations

In his most influential book on party organization, Panebianco (1982, 107) argues that like any other organization, political parties are structures that constantly evolve, reacting to the environment in which they are immersed. But a party's response to changing political and electoral environments is by no means automatic. It is mediated by the decisions party leaders make as they seek to accommodate environmental conditions. The environment thus shapes the range of opportunities and constraints available to political parties, but it does not determine whether and to what extent they change.

From this analytic point of departure, one must acknowledge the importance of *agency* and *choice* in explaining political parties' performance. Parties adapted to authoritarian settings may be ill suited organizationally to surviving in more competitive environments. Whether they prosper depends on the strategic decisions their leaders make.

In the case of Mexico, this is already evident in the official party, the PRI, which controlled the presidency from 1929 to 2000. Faced with stronger opposition parties, more independent electoral authorities, and a growing disenchantment with President Zedillo's administration, the PRI was pressed to alter its internal rules and organizational structure.[9] In the process, the party has encountered multiple dilemmas as it has had to redefine significant aspects of its identity as well as attack the political interests of many who profited from the traditional rules.[10]

But what is perhaps less evident is that opposition parties also confront enormous challenges and dilemmas as they seek to adapt to an electoral environment with increased opportunities to gain access to office. Opposition parties (both on the left and the right) devised a set of internal rules that allowed them to survive in a noncompetitive electoral environment. They could maintain their identity and ideological coherence while playing a game they knew was almost impossible to win.[11] Being accustomed to criticizing the government and organizing against the PRI, these parties gained their credibility by being in the opposition. Once they started to win elections and become parties in government, they confronted enormous difficulties that threatened their future electoral success and eventually their very survival as political parties. Their ability to hold on to their constituents and prosper as political organizations thus depends on the ability of their leaders to introduce reforms designed to seize the opportunities created by the new electoral environment.

Kitschelt (1994, 2) argues that "parties' rejuvenation depends on their capacity to go beyond the parties' programmatic, organizational, and electoral legacies." What this means is that party leaders have to make difficult choices when they confront change. And these choices have important consequences for the party's electoral fortunes.[12] The centrality of these choices cannot be understated.

For a country like Mexico that has experienced a tortuous transition to democracy, overcoming the legacies of the authoritarian past is essential for the consolidation of democratic practices. The latter crucially depend on the strength of political parties. More than winning a single election, what is at stake is the ability of parties to participate successfully in a competitive electoral field. Strong parties are those that are able to maintain and expand their electoral coalitions, that are able to define a set of issues that identify and distinguish them from other political parties, and that endure as political organizations, whether they are in government or in the opposition.[13]

Thus as political parties in Mexico have greater opportunities to gain access to power, the question is, how can they continue to win elections without disintegrating as political institutions?[14] How can parties transform themselves without losing their identity? How can they maintain party unity when internal competition for power increases? And how can they strike a balance between their more complex role as both opposition and governing parties?

A Typology of Political Parties

In the literature on party organization and change a trade-off is often recognized between flexibility and stability, and this trade-off in turn is related to the party's degree of institutionalization (Panebianco, 1982, 107; Levitsky, 1998, 453; Kitschelt, 1994, 207). By "institutionalization," I mean, following North (1990), the existence of routinized rules and a system of enforcement that guarantees that these rules are obeyed. An institutionalized party thus means a party in which rules are entrenched and are regularly obeyed by its members and whose violators are effectively sanctioned.

Institutionalized parties tend to have strong bureaucracies and a set of regulations that limit party leaders' capacity to introduce strategic innovations. Conversely, weakly institutionalized parties tend to have fragile bureaucracies and a more fluid set of rules for decision making that reduce the costs of change and give party leaders greater opportunities to innovate. Thus a party with lower levels of institutionalization is more flexible when confronted with new environments but may also encounter greater problems in maintaining its constituents and surviving as an organization. Alternatively, a party that is more institutionalized tends to become more rigid and inflexible when confronted with changing environments but might nevertheless be able to endure both electorally and as an organization if it has strong and entrenched bureaucratic organizations.

Although this argument seems convincing, the relationship between flexibility and stability does not necessarily involve a zero-sum game: parties can be both flexible and stable or inflexible and unstable. The critical element in explaining a party's degree of flexibility and stability is not necessarily its degree of institutionalization or the existence of a bureaucratic apparatus but rather the type of rules regulating intraparty competition and the nature of the ties that parties establish with the electorate.

One need only think of political parties in the United States, which are highly institutionalized—they have both routinized and entrenched rules, and they have both a stable and a permanent staff working for the party—and yet they also have high degrees of stability and flexibility (Schlesinger, 1994). These parties have the strategic capacity to incorporate new issues into their agendas, target new electorates, define new strategies, and select new and attractive candidates for office. Moreover, both of the dominant parties in the United States maintain their ties with the electorate by serving their needs between elections.[15] As a result, both parties retain a strong presence in the electoral arena. Indeed, after the introduction of important reforms in candidate selection during the 1970s, parties in the United States managed to institutionalize flexibility.[16]

While bureaucracies tend to develop a vested interest in the preservation of the status quo, and that is an important fixed cost limiting the parties' flexibility, I argue that flexibility critically depends on the rules regulating the party's internal competition for power and in particular the candidate selection process. Parties whose rules restrain ambitious office seekers in their pursuit of candidacies have lower degrees of flexibility to define new strategies and priorities than parties that grant office seekers greater room to maneuver. As Schattschneider (1942, 64) argued long ago in his study of political parties, the candidate selection process is crucial to determining the nature of the party: "He who can make nominations is the owner of the party."

When the party apparatus controls the process of candidate selection, potential candidates need to mobilize support within the party and obey a plethora of rules of party discipline that in the end curtail the party's capacity to react to new public concerns and electoral agendas. In selecting their candidates, these parties are inward looking: potential candidates appeal to the party's militants (or leaders), and the nomination process reflects the accommodation of different groups within the party. As a consequence, the candidate becomes accountable first and foremost to his party militants (or leaders). These parties privilege the preservation of ideological coherence over indiscriminate vote-getting strategies.

On the contrary, when party rules allow ambitious politicians to independently organize and mobilize support in pursuit of their nomination as party candidates, the party acquires higher degrees of flexibility to adapt to new and increasingly more complex electoral arenas. In such a party, the process of candidate selection is outward looking; that is, candidates appeal to the public at large in their quest for the nomination.[17] The candidate, consequently, becomes accountable to the electorate at large and can take some actions independently of his own party. These parties privilege vote-getting strategies over the preservation of ideology.[18]

The growing importance of candidates over their parties in the United States—and sometimes in spite of them—has led many scholars to believe that parties are declining as political organizations (Polsby, 1983; Crotty, 1984). But as Aldrich (1995) persuasively argues in his analysis of political parties in the United States, in the era of mass media and candidate-centered elections, parties have become stronger organizations, better financed and with larger and more professional staffs. Candidates with any serious hope of gaining access to power need the support of their party. Furthermore, once elected, officeholders remain partisans. Finally, partisanship has remained stable and enduring for most adults and is still the strongest predictor of voting preference (Aldrich, 1995, 15).

As argued above, political parties play a critical role in reducing uncertainty and minimizing voters' decision-making costs. Parties "provide candidates a 'brand name.' In advertising, successful brand names convey a great deal of information cheaply" (Aldrich, 1995, 49). The parties' role, however, has changed. Rather than control their candidates, as was true in the past, parties now offer important "services" to their ambitious office seekers, staying in the background while candidates take the lead (Aldrich, 1995, 272–73). And this has been achieved by the implementation of a series of reforms that substantially transformed the party's candidate selection mechanisms.

The introduction of reforms geared to increase candidates' room to maneuver and enhance the party's flexibility of course involves great risk. In searching to expand the party's electoral appeal by going beyond its programmatic and electoral legacies, it may lose its original ideological profile. Traditional party militants may feel increasingly underrepresented and alienated from the party's candidates and platforms. More important, the party may fall prey to political opportunists who seek power without any interest in the preservation and promotion of the party's ideology or traditional platform. Finally, the introduction of reforms also usually upsets many party officials and leaders who benefit from existing rules and cling to the status quo.

Lack of flexibility, however, entails a much bigger risk: if the party sticks closer to its original ideological profile, defends the status quo, and limits the freedom of its candidates to mobilize electoral support, it may lose touch with a rapidly changing electorate and eventually fail to win elections. By deciding to represent its core constituency, the entire party, not only its traditional leaders and militants, is at risk.[19]

The transformation of its rules of political competition thus confronts the party with the challenge of striking a balance between ideology and pragmatism. And this also frequently entails striking a balance between the party's traditional core or dominant coalition—who are more interested in ideological consistency—and its peripheral electoral coalitions—who might be interested in the expansion of office opportunities or the promotion of particular benefits for their constituencies (Gibson, 1997).

Like flexibility, the stability of political parties (i.e., their capacity to remain in power and to endure as organizations) does not necessarily depend on their degree of institutionalization or on the size of their bureaucratic apparatus. Rather stability depends to a much larger extent on the types of linkages the party establishes with its constituencies and with the electorate at large. By "linkages," I mean the extent to which the party establishes a presence among the electorate and becomes a relevant actor in the affairs of the community. Parties that maintain weak links to their electoral base, that do not service their constituencies, and that do not aggregate their interests are electorally more unstable than parties that develop stronger links. The former typically confine their mobilization to electoral periods but refrain from doing casework and servicing their constituencies between elections.[20] As we shall see below, these parties can be highly institutionalized, and yet they might not have the capacity to continue in power or to ensure their cohesion as organizations when they win elections or when the electoral or political environment changes. In contrast, parties strongly rooted in the electorate are more service oriented and typically engage in community organizing and casework activities on a more permanent basis. In general, these parties are more able to maintain (or increase) the loyalty of their followers, particularly during periods of change.[21] This explains why some parties are better able than others to maintain a cushion of support among their constituencies, even when party policies might run counter to their interests.[22] Similarly, these parties are less vulnerable to a dwindling of support or to internal fragmentation when they win or lose an election. In general, these parties tend not to be totally out of government. They might lose the presidency but retain ample representation in the legislative branch or in local and state governments.

Thus a party that has strong roots in the electorate not only has larger bureaucracies but also and more important has a decentralized organization that allows party officials to penetrate and work closely with their communities on the ground.[23] Such a party distributes patronage, provides legal or medical assistance, helps people to obtain scholarships, pulls the right strings in government to help people solve specific problems, helps people to organize to make demands on the authorities, and "educates" members of the community to increase their awareness of a particular situation that affects them. Beyond their ideological principles, such a party relies to a large extent on the distribution of selective, nonideological incentives to maintain the loyalty of its base.[24]

Parties with looser ties to the electorate have smaller and more centralized bureaucratic apparatuses and tend to confine their activism to electoral periods. These parties have a less permanent presence among their voters and do not necessarily rely on the distribution of selective incentives. They can mobilize electoral support by appealing to their ideological principles and/or by presenting themselves as the best alternative when widespread discontent with the status quo exists. While these parties may be successful in mobilizing new electorates, they have a more difficult time securing voter party loyalty. Thus while these parties may be able to win elections, they are less able to remain in power.

However, as is the case with flexibility, changing the party's internal organizational structure to increase its electoral stability also entails a serious risk: the expansion of the bureaucratic apparatus tends to give party officials a stake in preserving their office, regardless of their effectiveness. Moreover, fostering a bureaucratic structure that has more permanent links to the electorate may be extremely costly for a party since that requires hiring a staff that stays active between elections (Ware, 1992). But more important, for the party's core constituency, the expansion of the party's bureaucratic apparatus and the reliance on selective incentives to maintain loyalty among the electorate runs the risk of eroding the party's cohesion on commonly shared ideological principles. Thus, confronted with a changing electoral arena, political parties face the challenge of striking a balance between appealing to ideological principles and relying on selective benefits to maintain—or increase— their bases of support.

My argument so far is that a party's degree of flexibility and stability depends on the rules regulating intraparty competition and on the types of links that parties establish with their electorates. By combining these two dimensions, as shown in Figure 2.1, we obtain a typology with four ideal-typical parties.

Figure 2.1   Typology of Political Parties

LINKS TO THE ELECTORATE

		STRONG Party offices through- out the country Electoral entrenchment	**WEAK** Party offices mainly at the center Lack of electoral entrenchment

	HIGH
	
	Candidates organize their
	campaigns and mobilize
	suport by appealing to the
	public at large
		Catch-all Parties
		
		· Flexible
		· Stable (solid
		  electoral
		  coalitions)
			Electoral Parties
			
			· Flexible
			· Unstable (fragile
			  electoral
			  coalitions)

AUTONOMY
OF
CANDIDATES
	LOW
	
	Candidates depend on their
	parties for their nominations
	and the organization of their
	campaigns
		Bureaucratic Mass Parties
		
		· Inflexible
		· Stable (solid
		  electoral
		  coalitions)
			Sectarian Parties
			
			· Inflexible
			· Unstable (fragile
			  electoral
			  coalitions)

If we consider first those parties whose candidates do not have autonomy to pursue their nominations and organize their campaigns, we obtain two types: sectarian parties and bureaucratic mass parties. Sectarian parties have weak links to the electorate at large but strong links to a core of supporters who are committed to the preservation of certain ideological and programmatic principles. The latter are reflected in the rules for selecting their candidates.[25] Strict rules of affiliation, candidate selection, and campaigning restrict potential candidates' room to maneuver to mobilize electoral support. These parties are *inflexible:* they are both unwilling and unable to introduce strategic innovations when confronted with a changing environment. Sectarian parties are typically marginal in the electoral arena and remain virtually inactive between elections.[26] If for exogenous reasons—such as an economic or political crisis that leads many voters to seek a viable alternative for expressing discontent with the status quo—the vote for sectarian parties increases, this expansion tends to be ephemeral: sectarian parties are highly inefficient in maintaining their electoral coalitions.[27] While sectarian parties have a stable core of supporters, their electoral coalitions are *unstable,* and thus they are too fragile to remain in power. Since ideological consistency is privileged over electoral attractiveness, these parties appeal to their convinced followers. While they may survive as organizations, they are less able to maintain their internal cohesion and endure as governing parties. Among these are several communist and radical right-wing parties in Latin America, Europe, and the United States. As we shall see below, for many years the PAN also belonged to this category.[28]

Bureaucratic mass parties develop strong ties with the electorate but also limit ambitious office seekers' freedom to mobilize support for their nomination. The party's control over the nomination process subjects potential candidates to numerous filters and rules (both formal and informal) of political mobilization that instill conformity and subordination to party discipline. Although these parties are rigid and sluggish in responding to change, their deep entrenchment in society makes them electorally *stable:* they can maintain their electoral coalitions, retain office, and survive as organizations during times of change. While these parties are not necessarily concerned with preserving their ideological purity, they are nevertheless *inflexible* in adopting new electoral agendas or in welcoming new leadership styles. They resist change largely because they enjoy a cushion of support among the electorate, which gives them few incentives to change. But this cushion critically depends on the party's ability to continuously provide its electorate with patronage or selective benefits. Bureaucratic parties thus greatly benefit from being in office and tend to develop higher stakes in the preservation of the status quo. Examples of these parties are the PRI in Mexico, the Acción Democrática (AD) and Comité de Organización Política Electoral Independiente (COPEI) in Venezuela, and Alianza Popular Revolucionaria Americana (APRA) in Peru (Graham, 1992; Coppedge, 1994).[29]

If we consider now those political parties in which candidates enjoy a considerable degree of freedom to mobilize support for their nomination and to organize their campaigns, we obtain two types, electoral parties and catch-all parties. Electoral parties have weak links to the electorate but grant their potential candidates high degrees of freedom to mobilize support for their nomination. These parties are sensitive to the pulse of the electorate and are *flexible* in adapting to changing electoral agendas and public concerns. But their weak linkages to the electorate make them highly *unstable* in retaining power.[30] Furthermore, since these parties become active mainly during electoral periods, they tend to contract and sometimes disappear after the elections are over.[31] These parties are more concerned with enlarging their electoral appeal than with the preservation of their ideological profile.[32] When they are in the opposition, electoral parties typically benefit from existing discontent with the status quo. They eagerly seek to attract protest voters, whether or not they agree with the party's doctrine and regardless of their future loyalty and commitment to the party. Examples of these parties abound throughout Latin America. They include parties organized by a charismatic leader to run for a particular election but which languish and disappear after the elections, particularly if they are out of office. They also include opposition parties that remain quite inactive during nonelectoral periods, such as the PRD in Mexico (Bruhn, 1997) and the Partido dos Trabalhadores (PT) in Brazil (Keck, 1992).

Finally, catch-all parties have strong roots in the electorate and yet maintain high degrees of flexibility because they grant potential candidates ample room to maneuver to mobilize support for their nomination. These parties remain active between elections and have permanent staffs of activists who maintain their presence in the community by servicing their constituencies. While the latter gives these parties high degrees of *stability* in maintaining their electoral coalitions and holding on to their office positions, catch-all parties are also *flexible* to adapt to changing electoral and political environments. Candidates in these parties organize their campaigns and appeal to the electorate at large in seeking their parties' nomination. That allows them to incorporate new issues, adopt new strategies, and react to changing electoral agendas. Catch-all parties have high stakes in retaining office, because being in power gives them greater access to the various resources they distribute among their constituents. However, these parties cannot entirely disregard concern for ideological consistency. Because they are often simultaneously in government and in the opposition, they require a minimum degree of ideological consistency to maintain their distinctiveness in highly competitive electoral arenas. This means that these parties need to focus on issues, not only on selective benefits, to mobilize the electorate. Moreover, as governing parties, catch-all parties need to be able to translate their ideological principles into effective public policies to maintain their credibility. The Democratic and Republican Parties in the United States belong to this category. Both parties grant ample maneuvering room to their candidates, and both parties have a permanent staff working with constituents.[33] Other examples include the Peronist Justicialista Party in Argentina, a party that allows presidential candidates ample room to maneuver to organize their campaigns and that maintains strong and permanent links to its constituents (Levitsky, 1998).[34] The Socialist Party and the Christian Democratic Party in Chile can also be placed in this category, for both grant candidates freedom to organize their campaigns and are "vote getters" in the sense that they are willing to seek alliances and relax their ideological agendas for the sake of winning office (McDonald and Ruhl, 1989; Roberts, 1994).

So far, the discussion has centered on the party's degree of flexibility and stability when confronted with changing electoral and political conditions. However, as Figure 2.2 shows, if we take a particular electoral environment as a given, we can say that the rules and organizational structure of sectarian and bureaucratic political parties make them better adapted to noncompetitive electoral environments. Catch-all and electoral parties, on the other hand, are better adapted to competitive electoral environments.

Figure 2.2   Political Parties and Electoral Environments

| | | TYPE OF ELECTORAL SYSTEM | |
		COMPETITIVE	NONCOMPETITIVE
PARTY'S STATUS	GOVERNING	**Catch-all Parties** • Concerned about the preservation of office, votes, and ideological consistency • Electorally competitive parties	**Bureaucratic Parties** • Concerned about the preservation of office • Electorally dominant parties
	OPPOSITION	**Electoral Parties** • Concerned about winning votes • Electorally significant, may win	**Sectarian Parties** • Concerned about ideological purity • Electorally marginal parties

When the electoral arena is not competitive, bureaucratic parties greatly benefit from being in government. Their extensive linkages to the electorate allow them to cater to their constituencies—albeit in a highly unequal and selective manner.[35] Because these parties do not need to compete for votes, their lack of flexibility does not hamper their ability to retain their grip on power. Moreover, their control over the candidate selection and nomination process allows these parties to enforce strict party discipline and to preserve unity among their activists.

On the other hand, opposition parties in noncompetitive electoral arenas have little choice but to attempt to survive in an environment of limited possibilities. They may try to expand their electoral appeal, but if the environment is not conducive to that end, remaining close to their ideological principles and criticizing the regime becomes a crucial survival strategy.

Catch-all and electoral parties, on the contrary, find more suitable playing fields in highly competitive electoral environments. Their flexibility to respond to changing electoral preferences enables them to compete for votes more effectively. However, while electoral parties find greater opportunities when they are in the opposition, catch-all parties benefit more when they are in government. Electoral parties are typically more efficient in mobilizing discontent but less efficient in maintaining their electorates. Catch-all parties, on the other hand, find greater opportunities to engage in casework and pork barrel politics when they control the government.

When an electoral party wins office, it may end up being ill suited to its new role. Its lack of organizational entrenchment in the electorate makes it difficult for it to win in consecutive elections. More important, it often fails to articulate new issues for electoral mobilization. As a governing party, it can no longer mobilize people on the basis of discontent with the status quo. Similarly, when a bureaucratic party loses power, it may find it difficult to operate and survive as an opposition party in a more competitive environment. These parties depend on their access to government resources for maintaining their electorates.

As I argue below, when parties confront changing environmental conditions such as losing or winning an election, the introduction of electoral reforms, or the outbreak of a severe economic or political crisis, they need to respond in order to survive. But how they respond and to what extent they are able to adapt to the new environment largely depends on the ability of party leaders to alter the rules and organizational structure of the party. This in turn depends on the configuration of power inside the parties.

The Process of Change

The typology of parties developed above does not of course exist in pure form. Political parties often combine different attributes: they may resemble more a bureaucratic type at the local and regional levels and a catch-all type at the national level.[36] A party may also introduce certain changes in some states and not in others. Parties are not static organizations. At one point in time they might resemble one type of party, and at another they might change and resemble yet a different type.

Parties can evolve and transform themselves as the environment in which they operate changes. But, as I argue above, this process is not automatic. A transformation requires a decision to change the party's rules and organizational structure, whether in a formal or an informal manner. Party leaders might indeed decide to resist change altogether or to introduce reform in a piecemeal fashion. These decisions (or nondecisions), however, have important electoral consequences. Party leaders may attempt to resist change for a while, but if the party loses its electoral grip as a result, they might become convinced that change is necessary. Alternatively, leaders who resist change might lose control of the party apparatus, giving way to a new generation of reform-oriented leaders. Finally, some parties may overreact when confronted with changing environments. A hasty or excessively radical reform might disturb the party's internal balance of power and prove equally unsuccessful in the electoral arena.

The question therefore is, what motivates change? In great part, party change can be triggered by exogenous factors. The electorate might shift over time due to either severe economic crises or to stable periods of prosperity.[37] A change in public concerns may convince some party leaders of the need to respond and attend to those concerns if they want to win elections. Similarly, the introduction of electoral reforms confronts both governing and opposition parties with new sets of opportunities and constraints in the electoral playing field. And winning or losing elections might thrust parties into new political environments.

Exogenous change, however, only affects the nature of incentives political parties face. Whether and how parties respond to changing environments depends on the decisions their leaders make. And this depends in turn on the internal balance of power between leaders of different factions or groups. The introduction of party reform does not necessarily benefit all party members equally. Some party members develop a stake in the preservation of the status quo, while others clearly benefit from change. While a party may benefit in the electoral arena by transforming its internal rules and organizational structure, it may fail to do so if party reform is extensively opposed.

Like any other organization, a political party is not a homogeneous or unitary institution. Political parties harbor complex relationships between leaders and party activists who have different goals and who do not always agree on the party's strategies or tactics. More important, as Mair (1994) suggests, political parties are composed of at least three organizational elements that for analytic purposes can be disaggregated: the party in government (its relationship with the state), the party on the ground (its relationship with the electorate), and the party in its central office (party headquarters). Because public officials in government do not necessarily share the same interests or professional profiles with activists on the ground or with officials at the party's headquarters, conflicts often arise between these different elements or "faces" of political parties.

The introduction of party reform presumes the existence of a constituency for change inside the party. Whether these reformers succeed depends on their ability to convince other party leaders (or potential leaders) of the benefits of party reform as well as on their success in reducing the costs for those who stand to lose from change.

Some groups within the party may have a stake in the preservation of their offices, regardless of whether the party grows in the electoral arena. These groups can be working both in government (in Congress or in the executive's cabinet) and in the party's headquarters. Other groups might regard preserving the party's ideological consistency as a more important goal than increasing the party's electoral appeal. These groups are usually associated with the party headquarters and with many of its activists on the ground. Finally, for other members of the party, increasing the total vote, rather than gaining a particular office or preserving the party's ideological consistency, might be a higher priority.[38] These members are usually activists working on the ground but tied to a particular candidate. In reality, of course, these goals are related, just as much as the party's different organizations interact with one another.

For analytic purposes, however, it is possible to identify the goals that tend to dominate in each type of party. In a sectarian party, activists and leaders are more interested in preserving the party's ideology than winning votes or gaining access to office. In these parties, party headquarters predominates over the party on the ground or the party in government.

In an electoral party, leaders are mainly vote seekers, regardless of whether voters agree with the party's principles. In these parties, the party on the ground—and particularly those members related to a particular candidate—acquires greater importance than party headquarters or the party in government.[39] When electoral parties contain a core of ideologically motivated activists, they often face enormous internal divisions, because these activists typically reject seeking voters indiscriminately.[40]

In bureaucratic parties, in contrast, leaders develop a vested interest in the preservation of their offices, because the latter give the party access to resources needed for maintaining their electoral bases of support through patronage. In these parties, public officials who have greater access to resources gain more power in the party's decision-making process than activists do on the ground or officials at the party's headquarters.

Finally, in catch-all parties, leaders and activists need to reach a difficult equilibrium among these three goals, although vote seeking becomes a pivotal concern for leaders. Without winning votes, the party can assure neither office positions nor the effective introduction of public policy that reflects the party's ideological positions or the satisfaction of their constituencies. In these parties, accordingly, both activists working on the ground and public officials gain more strength and power than do officials at the party's headquarters.[41]

When a change in the environment modifies the structure of incentives facing parties, party reformers need to convince leaders and activists who support the status quo—and who might lose with change—how the party as a whole may benefit from the introduction of reforms. Too often, this is far from a smooth and peaceful process; it entails a power struggle inside the party. And the most important challenge then becomes managing to maintain party unity in the face of change. Some parties are destroyed in the process. Other parties survive but with weakly institutionalized reforms that may not endure. In other cases reforms are introduced but in a piecemeal or gradual fashion.

Successful introduction of reforms (i.e., a change in the party's rules) usually involves the reorganization of the party's internal balance of power. This in turn confronts parties with numerous and costly trade-offs between continuity and change, between pragmatism and ideology, and between flexibility and stability. The path that each party takes, however, cannot be theorized a priori. It is something that must be analyzed through empirical research.

To grasp analytically this complicated process of change, we need to conceive the typology of political parties developed above in more dynamic terms. That is, instead of classifying parties in fixed categories, we can define our two independent variables as dimensions along a continuum. Candidates' degree of autonomy to organize and define their campaigns varies in a range from high to low autonomy. Similarly, the party's tie to its constituencies varies within a range of strong ties to weak ties. This dynamic perspective also allows us to analyze the intensity and breadth of a party's ties to its constituencies. For example, a sectarian party might have weak ties to

the electorate at large but strong ties to a small group of ideologically motivated party loyalists. Alternatively, a catch-all party may have broad but super-
ficial ties to the electorate at large.

If we plot these two dimensions in a graph, as Figure 2.3 shows for Mexican political parties, we can analyze parties as they evolve over time. Thus as
parties introduce reforms, they may not suddenly jump to a different category
or type of party. Rather they can move along a continuum, introducing
reforms that eventually transform the party organization and rules altogether.

Figure 2.3   Political Parties' Trends in Mexico

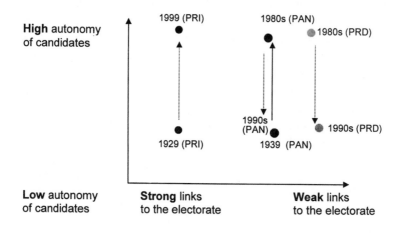

Political parties can introduce far-reaching reforms to increase the autonomy of their candidates and yet move at a slower rate to reorganize their
linkages with their constituencies. Similarly, in particular circumstances,
parties can grant candidates greater degrees of autonomy to organize their
campaigns without formally changing the rules. As I show in the following
chapters, this was the path taken by the PAN during the 1980s, when it received an important influx of supporters, primarily from the business community. The PAN moved from a sectarian to an electoral position without
formally changing its rules of candidate selection. Moreover, in the vast
majority of places where the PAN is in government, the party has not been
able to expand its organization, penetrate the community, and thus entrench
itself more firmly in the electorate. After the presidential elections of July
2000, some leaders in the PAN openly acknowledged the need for substan-

tial statutory reforms to adapt to the new electoral environment. They believed that as a national governing party, the PAN needed to promote the growth of its base of activists and above all modify the candidate selection mechanisms to allow the party to select more attractive candidates for office. In their view, the party rules were too restrictive to maintain its constituency, which they knew was extremely heterogeneous and fragile, for the only thing it had in common was its distaste for the PRI.[42] Although a reform committee was established that proposed a statutory reform in the November National Assembly, most of the proposal was rejected and only minor changes were made in the party's statutes.[43] Thus even as a governing party, the PAN continues to adhere to sectarian rules.

Political parties may also change when confronted with a particular problem and then return to their original positions when the contingency that brought about the change disappears. In the case of the PRI, for example, the party leadership decided to institute open primaries as a new method for selecting its candidates. While this method helped to legitimize the candidate selection process, in the case of the nomination of the presidential candidate in 2000, for example, the process was manipulated to ensure that the candidate favored by the president won the nomination. Although an open primary actually took place, the process seemed to cover up the more traditional method of selecting the presidential candidate. Thus, during President Zedillo's term, the PRI seemed to move away from a bureaucratic to a catch-all position. However, having lost the presidential elections and thus the most important resource for benefiting its constituents, it is quite uncertain whether and how the PRI will be able to retain its constituencies. If it is unable to do so, the PRI may move to a more electoral position, particularly in those states where it is in the opposition.

With respect to the PRD, the greatest challenge is precisely to move away from its electoral position of the 1980s. During the 1990s, the PRD seemed to adopt an increasingly sectarian form. Since it was ostracized by President Salinas de Gortari, the PRD radicalized its political discourse and refused to negotiate any congressional bills introduced by the executive. The PRD also wanted to distinguish itself from the PAN, which took a more conciliatory and negotiating attitude with the government. In some cases, however, particularly in the Federal District, which it has controlled since 1997, the PRD seems to have adopted a more catch-all position. The party has been able to expand its organization and, using the organizational infrastructure of a vast number of preexisting social movements in Mexico City, to maintain its presence at the community level (Bruhn, 1998b; Wuhs, 2002).

Following this analytic perspective, the rest of this book examines how the PAN has reacted to changing environmental conditions during the past twenty years and evaluates the extent to which the PAN has been able to transform its rules and organizational structure as it increasingly becomes a governing party.

CHAPTER THREE

The PAN as a Sectarian Party

Since its foundation in 1939, the PAN was the most consistent opposition party in postrevolutionary Mexico. Its capacity to survive as an independent political party and to actively participate in elections that were virtually impossible to win has conferred unparalleled political credibility and legitimacy throughout the years (Loaeza and Segovia, 1987; Loaeza, 1999). Yet this willingness to participate in fraudulent elections generated serious tensions inside the PAN. The dilemma of whether or not to participate in the elections haunted the party for nearly forty years but did not lead to serious divisions until 1976, when a dispute over the extent to which it should participate in the electoral arena almost tore it apart.[1] As we shall see in chapter 4, by 1978 the conflict between those who advocated a more aggressive electoral position (the "pragmatists") and those who favored a more restrictive electoral role as a means of safeguarding the party's ideological principles (the "doctrinaires") was largely resolved in favor of the pragmatists. But the doctrinaires continued to occupy important positions in the party and to exert significant influence on its affairs, especially after the party began to expand its electoral support dramatically during the 1980s.[2]

The party's survival in a hostile electoral system can be attributed in large part to the introduction of a set of electoral reforms that beginning in the mid-1960s gradually increased the party's electoral opportunities.

The government and the official party, the PRI, needed an opposition party in order to legitimate its own electoral victories. Although the government was not prepared to share power with this opposition, it also did not want to weaken opposition parties to the point of extinction or encourage them to boycott elections altogether. The PRI considered nothing more dangerous than running without competitors (Crespo, 1995).

Although these reforms were extended to all opposition parties, not all of them were able to endure and preserve their political independence. As I argue here, the PAN was able to persevere because it institutionalized a set of internal rules designed to preserve its central ideological principles and safeguard it against political opportunists. While these rules allowed the party to survive as an independent opposition party in a noncompetitive regime, they became a source of weakness as the electoral environment became more competitive and the PAN gained greater access to power. These rules restrain the growth of party militants, curtail the party's flexibility to respond effectively to a changing and more demanding electorate, and hinder the PAN's entrenchment among broader sections of the population. Indeed, once it became a governing party, these rules were too rudimentary to allow the party to play a more constructive role in a more consolidated democratic political regime. These rules affect not only the party's electoral performance in consecutive elections but also and more important its capacity to aggregate, articulate, and represent its constituents. In short, they affect the quality of democracy that emerges as a result of the transfer of power.

The PAN's Rules and Organization

The Federal Electoral Law of 1946 established the requirements political parties needed to fulfill to obtain official registration, without which they could not participate in elections. The law's major objective was to discourage the proliferation of local and regional parties based on the leadership of military or political caudillos. To participate in federal elections, parties were obliged to become *national* political organizations and to centralize their decision-making bodies, with a national assembly, a national executive committee, and a directive committee in every state where the party participated in elections. In effect, the parties were forced to adopt a structure similar to that of the PRI (Mabry, 1973, 114).[3]

According to Article 17 of the PAN statutes, the supreme authority of the party rests in the National Assembly. Article 21 states that the assembly is to meet at least every three years and is the only body of the party entitled to modify or reform the party's statutes, merge it with other political organizations, or dissolve it, as well as other decisions of vital importance. The National Assembly selects the members of the party's National Council, the party's central overseeing and decision-making body, which in turn selects the members of the National Executive Committee and the president of the party.[4]

The National Assembly is composed of delegates appointed by the State Directive Committees and of those sent by the National Executive Committee. Active members of the party may also participate in the assembly, although they do not have the right to vote (Article 22). Votes are weighted according to the electoral results obtained by the party in each state. The National Executive Committee has an important presence in the National Assembly: it has an equivalent number of votes to the average votes of the delegates to the assembly (Article 29). Decisions of the National Assembly are taken by majority vote and are definitive (Articles 33 and 34). The party's statutes stipulate that state and municipal assemblies can be organized to draft complementary norms following the general party principles and statutes. However, the National Executive Committee can veto decisions taken by the state and municipal assemblies if they are deemed contradictory to the principles or general objectives of the party.

The PAN's National Assembly, National Council, and National Executive Committee are at the top of the decision-making process. This structure is reproduced at the state and local levels, although state and local organizations may not contravene decisions taken by the national bodies of the party. Accordingly, in every state there is a state assembly, a state council, and a state directive committee and in every municipality, a municipal assembly and a municipal committee.

Although formally the PAN's structure resembles that of the PRI, there are important differences. First, the PAN's state and local organizations were granted considerable autonomy to decide their own affairs. For example, they are responsible for deciding whether the party should participate in local and state elections. They are also responsible for selecting candidates for the offices of municipal president, governor, and local deputy. The local party organization, the municipal committee (Comité Municipal), is also the most important institution for the recruitment of new party members, and, together with the national-level organizations, state and local organizations are responsible for sanctioning or expelling disaffected members.[5]

The PAN's founders were advocates of political and economic decentralization. Gómez Morin, in particular, believed that political life begins at the municipal level and that the party should be organized from the bottom up (Lujambio, 1995a). This contrasts with the practice of the PRI, where until recently local and state organizations lacked any authority to decide their own affairs. Moreover, unlike the PRI, the PAN recruits on an individual and voluntary basis; it is a party of citizens, not a sector- or class-based party.[6] Further, the PAN restricted membership to a select number of people who subscribed to the party's principles. Finally, in contrast to the PRI, the PAN censored political ambition, focused on the realization of higher goals, and structured its activities on a long-term schedule based on strong criticism of the regime.

The Party's Linkages to the Electorate

Since 1971 the PAN has acknowledged explicitly that gaining access to power through elections constitutes only one of the party's central objectives (Article 1). The party's statutes still list "the formation and strengthening of a democratic culture among Mexicans," the "diffusion of its principles, programs, and platforms," and the "education of its members" as fundamental objectives. Moreover, the statutes make clear that the ultimate goal of politics is the attainment of the "common good" and that individual action should be subordinated to this overall objective (Article 2).

According to Panebianco (1982), political parties are at once "voluntary associations" that share common goals and principles and "bureaucracies" that become interested in the continuity of the organization and the distribution of selective incentives such as power, status, or material benefits. As political parties evolve, different groups within them tend to develop contradictory interests: some become more interested in the preservation of ideology, while others become interested in the preservation of the organization. The survival of parties depends on how their leaders manage to balance the interests of these two groups (Panebianco, 1982, 42). In the case of the PAN, the limited opportunities to gain access to power tilted the balance overwhelmingly in favor of preserving the party's ideology. Holding on to the original ideals that brought the party into existence became the means to guarantee the party's survival.

This reliance on collective incentives to cement the organization led panistas to disdain the distribution of selective incentives as a method of mobilizing political support for the party. Thus patronage was considered reprehensible as a method of garnering support because it was driven by purely material, not ideological, concerns.[7] Even when panistas officially recognized that a central objective was winning elections, they did not want to win at any price: it was hoped that those who voted for the party did so out of deep ideological conviction.

The ideological bent of the party deeply affected the ways in which panistas understood their relationship to the electorate and structured their organization. Although the party's statutes acknowledge that the PAN should engage in political and civic activity on a permanent basis, this referred more to the party's "educational" role than to establishing permanent linkages to the electorate by actively engaging in the daily affairs of the community. This was considered a deviation from the original goals of the party and was associated with the PRI. As one top-level party official said,

> In Mexico, the central functions of political parties have been perverted. Parties should not engage in casework activities and in community organizing. This is what the PRI has done for years. The PAN is different. Besides organizing elections, the party's central tasks are to formulate proposals, train its militants, reflect on its principles, and create new party offices in places where the PAN still lacks any political presence.[8]

For many decades, the PAN refused to build a professional party bureaucracy that would allow it to mobilize the electorate on a continuous basis. Lack of resources constituted a significant limitation. But more important, the PAN's activists feared that if they built a bureaucratic structure, "the PAN could lose its mysticism and encourage the formation of a *bureaucracy of mediocrities,* that is, people living off the party and without any interest other than the preservation of their jobs."[9]

The PAN relied on a core of spirited and enthusiastic activists for the organization of its campaigns. As a result, the party was active mainly during electoral periods. Between elections the party concentrated on publicizing its criticisms of the government—which had a limited impact because of government control of the media—and carrying out its educational tasks among its select activists.

Until the end of the 1970s, the PAN had an extremely weak and fragile organizational structure. It operated with volunteers, many of them lacking administrative experience, had limited resources, and in many municipalities did not have an office.[10] Although the PAN was a "national" party, its presence was confined to the Federal District and to a few other states: Guanajuato, México, Michoacán, Puebla, Jalisco, and Veracruz (von Sauer, 1974, 102). Most of the panista electorate was urban, educated, religious, and middle class (Mabry, 1973, 170).

The absence of a professional staff often led to improvisation, to poor coordination among the organizations inside the party, and to a lack of continuity. As Luis H. Alvarez, the PAN's president during the 1980s, stated, "We had our statutes, our principles of doctrine, our National Executive Committee and our party secretariats, but these existed merely on paper. We did not have the capacity or the resources to implement any of our decisions."[11]

In sum, the PAN operated more like a spirited fraternity than as a political party. However, for many years, this weakness did not constitute a serious problem for the party. If anything, it had some advantages: during electoral periods, the PAN could build up its organization, and afterward, it could contract without having to face the costs of sustaining a political machine.

Recruitment of Members

Not unlike a religion-based organization, the PAN devised strict rules of party affiliation. The PAN's founders wanted to prevent the infiltration of political opportunists who could use the party as a political platform to promote their own interests. Until a modest reform of the party's statutes in 2001, to become a member of the party, a person had to apply in writing, and the application had to be supported by an active member. Although the latter is no longer required, applicants still need to prove they have "an honorable mode of living" (Article 8). Aspiring PAN members are required to attend a course on the party's doctrine and must formally subscribe to the party's principles. The application process usually takes at least six months, but sometimes applications are simply not acted on. As one high-level public official in the Chihuahua administration complained, "My son applied to the PAN a long time ago, and the party simply hasn't responded. This is quite common and I don't understand why this is the case."[12] Similarly, the former governor of Baja California complained, "The PAN makes it extremely difficult for people to become members of the party. There are applications that have been submitted three years ago, and the party has yet not processed them."[13] The sluggishness in the party's processing of membership applications demonstrates party activists' reluctance to include a heterogeneous and ideologically diverse population in its ranks.

The party recognizes two forms of membership: "active" members and "adherents." The former have the right to participate in the party's internal affairs, become delegates to the party's assemblies and conventions, and run as candidates. The latter are those who have applied to the PAN but have not been formally admitted. The statutes also recognize as an adherent member anyone who supports the party intellectually or financially (Article 9).[14]

In accordance with the party's conviction that the municipality is the basic political organization, where the individual begins his political involvement, the PAN's municipal committees were given considerable authority to recruit new members. An individual seeking to become a member of the PAN has to submit his or her application to the municipal committee. This method of recruitment was regarded by party founders as an effective means of encouraging people to become involved in local politics and to move inside the party organization from the bottom up (Delhumeau, 1970, 195).

The PAN was not interested in attracting large numbers of members. Panistas considered themselves a "select group that did not want to be confused with the multitude."[15] One leader of the party expressed this even more clearly: "We prefer quality over quantity."[16]

Until the end of the 1980s, the PAN's leaders felt they did not need a registry because they were very few and "everybody knew each other."[17] In 1989, when the PAN first recorded its membership, it had a total of 58,209 active members throughout the country. Membership has since increased significantly, although the PAN still has a notably small base of militants. By 1995 there were 145,500 active members and by 2001, 170,000. Even with this expansion, however, the rules for recruiting new active members have not changed significantly since the party's creation in 1939.

Nomination of Candidates

Until 1999 all PAN's candidates for office were selected at party conventions. The National Convention was responsible for nominating the presidential candidate as well as candidates for the upper and lower houses of Congress elected by proportional representation.[18]

In 1999, before the presidential election of 2000, the PAN decided to select the presidential candidate through a primary election in which *both* PAN's active members and its adherent members had the right to vote.[19] In 2001, after the presidential election, the party expanded this candidate selection mechanism to governors and senators.[20] However, the 2001 reforms restricted voting in primary elections to active members.[21]

National conventions are still responsible for elaborating the party's platform, which all candidates are required to endorse.[22] These conventions are attended by state delegates and by a national delegation chosen by the party's National Executive Committee. The State Directive Committees are responsible for selecting the state delegates to the National Convention. These delegates are chosen from lists of active members drafted by the municipal committees in each state.[23] The votes of each state delegation to the National Convention are weighted according to the party's number of active members and electoral strength in the state. If a state delegation does not vote unanimously, the minority is given a vote if it represents 10 percent or more of the total vote (Articles 22–30).

When candidates were chosen through party conventions, the party apparatus had virtually complete control over the selection process, for it was the party's State Directive Committee that decided who was sent as a delegate to the party convention. Moreover, as some panistas used to complain, the party leadership could actually bias the decisions adopted at the party conventions by selecting delegates who they knew would vote in favor of a particular candidate.[24] Now that candidates are selected through primary elections the party apparatus has lost this direct control over candidate selection. However, by restricting the right to vote in primary elections to active members, candidate selection still remains an internal party affair, and in a way it is still controlled by the party leadership, for to obtain registration, candidates need the approval of the National Executive Committee. Moreover, candidates are still elected by a narrow vote of active members, which by 2001 reached an all-time record of 182,000. The party has consistently refused to expand its base of active members.

At the state level, candidates for the local congress are still selected through party conventions.[25] Decisions at state conventions are also taken by municipal delegates who are selected by the municipal committees. As in the case of the National Convention, the president of the municipal committee has enormous discretion in the selection of delegates for the convention. Mayoral candidates are selected at municipal party conventions.

For many years, national and state party conventions were small affairs. As one longtime member of the party said, "I used to meet all my friends during the national party's conventions."[26] The party did not pay its delegates to come to the national conventions, so only those who could afford the trip to the Federal District participated. As the party base of militants expanded, these conventions became too large and difficult to administer. According to one of the presidents of the PAN, in 1994 the National Convention was attended by more than ten thousand people.[27] This situation encouraged party leaders in 1999 to amend the rules for the selection of the party's presidential candidate and of the federal congressional candidates elected through proportional representation.[28]

In the past, the nomination of candidates at the state and local levels sometimes did not even go through party conventions. Given that few people registered to run for the party's nomination, the party leadership "often had to appoint its candidates."[29] The rules for the nomination of candidates were clear, but they could not be implemented because of the small number of candidates.

Since the selection of candidates is an internal party affair, those seeking nomination need to appeal to the core of the party and thus have little opportunity or incentive to define their agendas for the public at large independently of the party. According to a 1999 survey of PAN activists, the majority still believe in the importance of ideological coherence for voting in support of the PAN. Consequently, they prefer to appeal to traditional panista voters rather than to the broader electorate.[30] Even more revealing, a survey of the PAN's activists conducted by the party itself shows that 81 percent of those interviewed explicitly said that they prefer to lose an election rather than lose their ideological identity.[31]

The Sectarian Subsistence: The PAN's First Forty Years

The presidential elections of 1940, the first elections in which the PAN participated as a registered political party, confronted panistas with the dilemma of participation. The differences among panistas concerning the role of the party in the upcoming elections became explicit. Gómez Morin, along with a group of intellectuals and professionals, advocated participation, as the PAN could not be considered a genuine political party if it did not participate. Gómez Morin was realistic; he knew that conditions were not ripe for the PAN to be elected to office, but he believed that the PAN should continue to challenge the regime until the party became a significant political force. He viewed this as a long-term project and one that was essentially gradualist and incremental. His famous phrase, "Let there be no illusions so that you don't become disillusioned,"[32] referred to his call for realism and his belief that through its perseverance, the party would one day become a strong political force, able to challenge the regime in the electoral arena. History proved him right, although he did not live to see it.

Efraín González Luna, along with the Catholic activists, on the contrary, believed the party should abstain from the elections. In his view, it was important for the party to elaborate its doctrine and concentrate on its principles rather than participate in an electoral process that was biased in favor of the governing party. Since the conditions were not ripe for democracy, the main goal of the party should be to "save the nation" by educating people and disseminating the party's ideals. That implied concentrating on the party's ideology and isolating it from the pressures and demands of the electorate at large (Loaeza, 1999, 174).

Because of his enormous influence as president of the party, Gómez Morin's perspective prevailed, and the party decided to participate.[33] But the question of whether the party should participate in the electoral arena was discussed before every subsequent election at the party's National Assembly, its most important deliberative body.

For many years, the divisions inside the party between the doctrinaires and the pragmatists did not cause serious conflicts. Because the party had little chance of winning power, it did not risk compromising its ideological profile by participating in the electoral arena. The PAN could seek the support of convinced voters rather than appeal to the electorate at large. Moreover, although the party's participation in elections contributed to the legitimation of the regime, campaign organizations became effective vehicles for propagating the party's ideology. The PAN could thus fulfill its educative mission through the electoral arena (Delhumeau, 1970, 172, 193; Yañez Maldonado, 1990).

By the time Gómez Morin stepped down as president of the PAN in 1949,[34] the party had a well-established set of rules governing its internal life but still had an extremely fragile bureaucratic structure. It had few militants and meager resources and had not been able to establish its presence throughout the country (Reveles, 1996, 17).[35]

Furthermore, Gómez Morin's retirement freed the party's Catholic activists to increase their presence and influence inside the party (Mabry, 1973, 187). During the 1950s, a number of young Catholic activists joined the party, many of them former Sinarquistas, the most fanatically religious and conservative Catholic activists (Mabry, 1973, 52), and over the next three decades, they gained significant access to its decision-making bodies, beginning with the presidency of the PAN itself (Lujambio, 1994).[36] Since the PAN could not realistically compete for power, it adopted an increasingly confessional and doctrinal position and isolated itself from the rest of the world.

Although it continued to participate in the electoral arena, until the late 1970s the PAN was a marginal political force, both in terms of its elected positions and in terms of its capacity to influence the decision-making process in Mexico. Effectively barred from office, panistas viewed their political participation in ethical terms—purifying political life of corruption and naked ambition—and shielded themselves behind their principles; the PAN became a sectarian political party.[37]

The emphasis on ideology and the disinterest in electoral politics discouraged panista leaders from taking steps to expand and strengthen their political organization. The PAN had not been able to establish party offices throughout the country, and in many electoral districts it failed to present candidates. The party was active only during the periods leading up to elections and virtually disappeared between them. The fragility of the organization made the PAN look more like a club of friends than a political party. It did not seek to increase the number of its activists and, much like a sect, recruited people through a strict process of indoctrination. According to Loaeza,

> [L]eaders of the party believed that the best recruiting strategy was person-to-person proselytism, accomplished through small meetings in people's houses which were attended by between three and twelve persons. For panistas, this personal and voluntary mode of affiliation contrasted with the PRI's massive and collective means of affiliation, which made it look more like a totalitarian party. (1999, 242; my translation)

By the end of the 1950s, a number of prominent panista leaders started to question the party's inclination to participate in elections. Adolfo Christlieb Ibarrola, one of the strongest critics of the party's position, argued that participating in fraudulent elections and accepting three or four seats in Congress only contributed to legitimating an undemocratic regime. He claimed that until the electoral system was reformed, the opposition should abstain from participating in elections (Lujambio, 1994, 53).

This abstentionist position gained strength after the 1958 presidential election, which was condemned for its fraudulent practices.[38] Participating in such elections was becoming increasingly costly for the PAN. The party was not contributing to "moralizing" politics; quite the contrary, by participating in an electoral process that was overtly unfair and rigged, the PAN faced the danger of losing its integrity. It not only legitimated an authoritarian political regime; it also drained the party's scarce resources, further weakening it.

In 1962 Christlieb Ibarrola became president of the PAN. Although like previous PAN presidents he was a devout Catholic who had participated in Catholic organizations, Christlieb Ibarrola shared Gómez Morin's belief in the separation of church and state and felt that the party's close association with the Catholic Church and Christian Democracy was a mistake. During his term as president, Christlieb Ibarrola expelled a number of radical Catholic activists who insisted on identifying the PAN with the Christian Democratic movement and reformulated the doctrinal principles of the party (Mabry, 1973, 72).[39]

Christlieb Ibarrola was convinced that opposition parties needed greater incentives to participate in the electoral arena. He advocated for the introduction of an electoral reform that would increase minority parties' representation in Congress. Confronted with the threat of abstention, in 1963 the government enacted a bill that incorporated most of Christlieb Ibarrola's proposals.[40]

The new electoral law provided for "party deputies." Parties could obtain five seats in Congress if they won at least 2.5 percent of the total vote. For every additional 0.5 percent of the vote, they won another seat up to a maximum of twenty seats (Medina Peña, 1994, 166). This reform ensured the PAN at least twenty seats in Congress, from a previous high of six seats under the old provisions (See Tables 3.1 and 3.2).

Table 3.1   Percentage of Votes for the PAN in Federal Elections, 1943–1973

Year	Congressional Federal Elections (%)	Presidential Elections (%)
1943	5	
1946	2	
1949	6	
1952	8	7.82
1955	9	
1958	10	9.42
1961	8	
1964	12	11.07
1967	11	
1970	14	11.93
1973	16	

Sources: Lujambio (forthcoming); Rocío Rodríguez, Información Electoral del PAN, Dirección de Relaciones Nacionales del CEN del PAN, Mexico, 1997.

Although the 1963 law increased the incentives for political participation, the recurrence of fraud, particularly in the 1968 elections, and the reluctance of the government to hear the oppositions' concerns convinced Christlieb Ibarrola that his strategy, in the end, had not been fruitful. Nevertheless, the opportunities to gain greater access to positions of power had one important consequence for the party: the PAN began to expand its organization, train new cadres, and increase its presence in regions of the country where the party had never penetrated before (Lujambio, 1994, 68; Lujambio, 1995b).

Overall, however, the party as an organization was still extremely fragile. Since it refused to accept public funding, it operated with limited resources drawn primarily from voluntary contributions, and it relied entirely on volunteers. The party did not even remunerate its president. However, some local

Table 3.2   Number of Elected Positions Won by the PAN, 1946–1975

Year	Municipalities	Deputies Total
1946	1	4
1948	1	
1949	0	4
1950	2	
1952	6	5
1955	1	5
1956	3	
1958	0	6
1959	1	
1961	0	5
1962	1	
1963	1	
1964	0	20
1965	3	
1966	2	
1967	10	20
1968	2	
1969	1	
1970	0	20
1971	2	
1972	2	
1973	5	25
1974	7	
1975	1	

Source: Ana María León, *Puestos de elección popular que ha tenido el Partido Acción Nacional en toda su historia* (Mexico, D.F.: Dirección de Relaciones Nacionales del CEN del PAN, 1997).

and state party organizations, particularly in the northern state of Nuevo León, began to expand their organization and to acquire a new and more combative political profile. This was mainly the result of the mobilization of a new generation of party activists with strong links to the private sector and profoundly hostile to President Luis Echeverría (1970–76), whom they regarded as a populist supporter of a state-led economy based on irresponsible financial policies.[41] These activists pressed the party's national leadership to abandon the party's excessive doctrinal profile. They were convinced that the party had to come out of the "electoral desert" in which it had lived for more than three decades. To become a more effective electoral force, they believed the PAN needed to adopt a more pragmatic line, to become more flexible in order to appeal to the electorate as a whole. In their view, that required the introduction of an open door policy that welcomed anybody who wanted to work for the party. The PAN could attract disaffected voters, but to do that, it needed to implement a more aggressive electoral strategy and leave its sectarian tendencies behind.

This pragmatist position gained considerable support during the 1970s. In 1971 the party statutes were amended in ways that reflected the pragmatists' concerns. One of the most important changes was the explicit recognition that winning elections was a central objective. The reforms also stipulated that the party could enter into coalitions with other organizations that shared its principles.[42] The pragmatists' leader, José Angel Conchello, an entrepreneur from Nuevo León, became president of the PAN in 1972. By 1973 the "electoral strategy" of the party seemed to be paying off. In the legislative elections of that year, the PAN obtained an unprecedented two million votes, 16 percent of the total vote (Reveles, 1996, 23). Given an electoral reform in 1973, which increased the maximum number of "party deputies" from twenty to twenty-five, the PAN obtained twenty-five seats in the Chamber of Deputies that year. Conchello adopted a more radical antigovernment rhetoric, hoping to move the party away from its longtime sectarian position.

As the pragmatists strengthened their position inside the party, the resistance of the doctrinaires increased. Led by Efraín González Morfín, they argued that the pragmatic faction threatened to undermine the party's identity, giving way to the entrance into the party of political opportunists with no interest in the party's doctrine. They maintained their traditional position that the party should only seek the vote of convinced supporters. In their view, it was better to preserve the party's ideology even if it damaged the party electorally (Loaeza, 1999, 307). As González Morfín said, "[T]he goal of the party should not be reduced to the mere quest for power, undermining those aspects that give meaning to this quest and that provide it with a doctrinal and programmatic conception" (*La Nación*, April 2, 1975).[43]

As I discuss more fully in the next chapter, the confrontation between these two factions increased as the party was preparing to nominate its presidential candidate. By 1976 the conflict reached a climax: the party deadlocked and failed to nominate a candidate for the presidency. By 1978 the conflict in the PAN had been resolved in favor of the pragmatists, a number of important members of the doctrinaire faction had left, and the party had adopted an open-door policy. Yet the internal rules and organization of the party remained virtually unchanged.

The Journey through the Electoral Desert

Forty years after its creation, the PAN was the strongest opposition party in Mexico. While it certainly did not constitute a serious electoral threat to the PRI, its strength came primarily from its ideology, its consistency, and its perseverance. The party had become a staunch critic of the PRI regime: it condemned the lack of effective political representation and participation; the overly centralized and presidentialist political system that granted virtually unlimited powers to the executive; the absence of the rule of law and political accountability; the widespread corruption that pervaded all levels of the government; and the failure of the government to adhere to basic ethical principles in the conduct of public office. In sum, the PAN criticized the PRI regime for violating the principles of citizenship and for obliterating any sense of civic culture in the country.

From this moral perspective, the criticism was impeccable. But as an electoral force, the PAN was too distant to be able to put to work any of its principles. Panistas who ran for office were considered "martyrs" who despite knowing they could not realistically win elections, still devoted their time and efforts to the pursuit of a higher principle. Political participation was a calling, not an ambition. It was led by idealism, not pragmatism.

During the first twenty-five years of the party's life, the PAN was able to win between four and five seats in the lower house of Congress. In 1943 the party presented candidates for elections for the first time, nominating candidates for the office of federal deputy in twenty-one out of two-hundred federal districts. The party won 5 percent of the total vote and did not win any seats in Congress. In 1944 the PAN presented candidates at the municipal and gubernatorial levels. But it was not until 1946 that the party gained its first electoral victories. Even though the party did not present a candidate for president, it nominated fifty-eight candidates for seats in the federal Congress and was able to win four seats with 2 percent of the total vote. Also in that year, the PAN won its first municipal election, in Quiroga, Michoacán. By 1948 the PAN was nominating candidates in eighty municipalities and won its second victory in a small municipality in the state of Jalisco (see Tables 3.1 and 3.2).

When Gómez Morin left the presidency of the party in 1949, the party was a consolidated but powerless political institution. Although the panista federal deputies were active in initiating legislative proposals, these often never even made it to the congressional commissions to be discussed.

In 1952, the PAN nominated its first presidential candidate, Efraín González Luna, one of the main political thinkers and a cofounder of the party. In this election the PAN obtained 8 percent of the total vote. Also in 1952, the PAN nominated 143 candidates for Congress and won 5 seats. The PAN's electoral presence seemed to be growing slowly but steadily. However, after the widespread irregularities of the 1958 elections, the PAN lost confidence in the readiness of the PRI to accept even this meager electoral growth. After the PAN withdrew its elected deputies from Congress, the PRI was left practically alone. Since that was precisely what the government and the PRI sought to avoid, they became more willing to introduce an electoral reform that would increase the incentives for opposition participation (Crespo, 2000, 1).

The results of the 1963 electoral reform produced the desired results. The PAN continued to participate in elections, and its electoral presence in Congress increased considerably. Still, in terms of political influence, the party continued to be marginal.

The electoral presence of the PAN remained stable until the end of the 1970s. By 1976, however, when the PAN failed to nominate a presidential candidate, the PRI and the government confronted a situation similar to that of 1958 but with graver political implications. For the first time since the PRI was founded in 1929, the PRI candidate ran unopposed. The threat of the opposition's abstention in presidential elections dangerously exposed the undemocratic nature of the regime. The government considered it imperative to significantly increase the opposition's electoral opportunities. While the government's intentions were to preserve the illusion of democracy, the 1977 electoral reform eventually contributed to the erosion of the PRI's long-held hegemony. The new electoral opportunities, coupled with the PAN's more pragmatic style of leadership and the influx of a new breed of activists, pushed the party out of its sectarian position during the 1980s.

CHAPTER FOUR

The PAN as an Electoral Party

The unprecedented mobilization and expansion of the PAN during the 1980s is surprising not only because of the contrast with the party's previously weak electoral performance but also because in 1976 the party confronted an internal crisis so severe that it threatened its very existence. What accounts for this spectacular growth when the party was so fragmented and seemed weakest? How did it emerge from its sectarian position? And how sustainable was the movement away from sectarianism?

Undoubtedly, a large part of the PAN's success at the polls stems from a series of electoral reforms—one enacted in 1973 and another, more significant one enacted in 1977—that considerably expanded electoral opportunities. However, the PAN was able to capitalize on these reforms to a far greater extent than other opposition parties, allowing it to break out of its previous marginal position. I argue that the party started to grow after the nationalization of the banks in 1982, when a new wave of party activists who came predominantly from the business sector decided to organize against the PRI and the government by supporting the PAN. Due in large part to the party's weaknesses, both financial and organizational, these entrepreneurs had significant room to maneuver and were able to organize wider, more aggressive, and more effective opposition to the PRI. The entrepreneurs' decisive role in the party's affairs greatly contributed to strengthening the party in the electoral

67

arena. However, the PAN's increased electoral strength was not matched by reform of its internal rules and organizational structure, which could have enabled the party to consolidate its new coalitions and sustain its electoral victories in the long run. As a result, once the PAN gained access to power at the state and local levels, it tended to fall back into its sectarian position and, in many cases, lost significant electoral support in consecutive elections.

The Evolution of Mexico's Business Community: The Roots of Discontent

One of the most striking characteristics of the political regime that emerged after the Mexican Revolution of 1910 was not only its longevity but also its ability to maintain political stability. Compared to other Latin American countries that fell victim to extremely repressive military regimes and to recurring cycles of political and economic crisis, the Mexican case indeed appeared a "miracle," as it was called during the 1960s and the first half of the 1970s. As many scholars have long argued, the incorporation (and control) of workers and peasants into the ranks of the PRI largely explains this political outcome (Brandenburg, 1964; Reynolds, 1970; Hansen, 1971; Reyna and Weinert, 1977; Collier and Collier, 1991). Yet the unparalleled stability of Mexico's political regime could not have existed without an alliance between the government and entrepreneurs. Despite the government's "revolutionary" commitment to workers and peasants and the use of populist and often aggressive antibusiness rhetoric, entrepreneurs found an extremely profitable environment in which to do business. Although not formally incorporated into the ranks of the PRI (a party that explicitly excluded business as a sector in its organization), entrepreneurs succeeded in establishing informal channels of communication with the highest levels of government to protect and promote their interests. Unlike their counterparts in other Latin American countries, Mexican entrepreneurs were not motivated to resort to the military or organize in opposition to the PRI to protect themselves against the government.[1] After the reformist and populist government of Lázaro Cárdenas, who was distrusted by the business community, Mexican entrepreneurs and the government were able to devise a cordial and conciliatory relationship that lasted for more than four decades.

President Cárdenas's confrontation with the business community was part of a broader strategy of consolidating and institutionalizing the power of the presidency after the Mexican Revolution. Cárdenas expelled former president and party chief Plutarco Elías Calles, a personalistic leader who wielded enormous political power behind the scenes. Cárdenas also appealed to the popular classes, distributed vast amounts of land, expropriated the oil industry, and nationalized the railroads. More significantly, he promoted significant reform in the official party, the Partido Nacional Revolucionario (PNR), transforming an elite-based party into a mass-based party organization, which included workers and peasants as its most important sectors.[2] These measures, harshly criticized by the business community at the time, proved crucial in establishing a solid coalition between the government and the popular sectors, an essential element for the stability of Mexico's political system. All that was left after Cárdenas left office was to regain the confidence of the business community.

In an effort to recover this confidence and to stimulate private investment, which was regarded as a crucial catalyst of economic development, the government of President Avila Camacho offered entrepreneurs a series of attractive economic incentives. It devised a set of protectionist policies that included import licenses, tariffs, and tax exemptions, as well as cheap credits, subsidies, and basic infrastructure. In addition, the government maintained an extremely low tax structure and guaranteed the existence of a cheap and acquiescent labor force through its control of the unions.

The favorable economic conditions and attractive opportunities offered to entrepreneurs soon paid off. After the Cárdenas administration, the business community and the government were able to reach a tacit agreement whereby business would not participate in politics in exchange for the government's protection of their interests. The so-called alliance for profits[3] was premised on the separation of the economic and political arenas and the willingness to resolve any differences between business and government out of public view. Although conflicts between business and the government did emerge, they never became a concern for the PRI. Entrepreneurs were able to lobby the government behind closed doors and could threaten government officials with shipping their capital out of the country.[4] Supporting an opposition party and organizing against the PRI was not an option until the 1980s.[5]

However, the incentives and benefits granted to entrepreneurs were not distributed evenly among all sectors of the business community or among all regions of the country. The government privileged large industrial and financial entrepreneurs, particularly those living in the state of Mexico, the Federal District, Guadalajara, and Monterrey (Hansen, 1971; Tello, 1979; Jacobs, 1981; Jacobs and Pérez Núñez, 1982; Cordero, Santín, and Tirado, 1983). These entrepreneurs not only benefited most from the many concessions granted by the government. They also had privileged access to the authorities. Large entrepreneurs were consulted on most important matters of economic policy and exerted a powerful influence over the selection of people for the highest offices, including that of the president (Luna, 1992, 10; Mizrahi, 1994b).

Although entrepreneurs were formally excluded from the PRI and they tacitly agreed to abstain from expressing their views in public, they were formally required to organize in corporatist business organizations, which were also controlled by the largest and most powerful entrepreneurs (Shafer, 1973, 117; Camp, 1989, 156–70).[6] However, most important negotiations between entrepreneurs and the government were not conducted through the business organizations; they were conducted in private. Moreover, two small, exclusive business associations had the most privileged (and informal) access to government authorities: the Asociación de Banqueros de México (ABM), the bankers' association, and the Consejo Mexicano de Hombres de Negocios (CMHN), a business group that represents the most prominent entrepreneurs in the country.[7]

Notwithstanding the advantages enjoyed by the largest entrepreneurs in the country, for many years, small and medium-size entrepreneurs did not complain openly. In part, this was because of the lack of adequate channels to government. But in great part it was due to the perception prevalent within the business community that in the end the interests of the entire business community were compatible. As one medium-size entrepreneur said,

> We used to think that the interests of large entrepreneurs were compatible with those of small and medium-size entrepreneurs and that therefore the latter did not need to act in defense of their interests. Large entrepreneurs were going to defend themselves first if the government threatened their interests, so small and medium-size entrepreneurs did not have to worry. This was a cheap strategy.[8]

By the end of the 1970s, this situation started to change. On the one hand, throughout the 1970s, particularly during the oil boom of the second half of the decade, domestic capital was concentrated in even fewer hands. This was largely the result of the liberalization of the financial system and increased economic integration into international financial markets.[9] Multisector conglomerates (the so-called Economic Groups) benefited disproportionately from the flow of international capital and their privileged access to low-cost foreign credits. They were able to expand, finance investment, speculate with foreign exchange, and lend in the high-cost national market.[10] The largest corporations experienced rapid growth and saw their power and influence increase, while small and medium-size enterprises, without access to low-cost credits, were increasingly squeezed financially (Maxfield, 1990, 97).

On the other hand, and despite the adverse financial conditions, during the 1970s, the number of small and medium-size businesses grew considerably (Hernández Rodríguez, 1991, 449). This was particularly the case in northern Mexico, which experienced higher rates of economic growth, triggered primarily by the dynamism of the maquiladora industry (Tamayo and Fernández, 1983; Tamayo, 1985; Stoddard, 1986; González Aréchiga and Barajas Escamilla, 1989). The increasing numerical and economic importance of small and medium-size entrepreneurs strengthened their bargaining power in the business community, making them less tolerant of their inability to influence economic policy. They were also less ready to accept their perceived disadvantage vis-à-vis the largest entrepreneurs. Moreover, many regarded themselves as "self-made" individuals who did not depend on the government's protection, concessions, contracts, credits, and subsidies, and consequently they felt they owed little to the government and the PRI (Mizrahi, 1994a).

Since the mid-1970s, small and medium-size entrepreneurs started to demand a bigger role in their business organizations. The selection of business representatives became an increasingly controversial matter as provincial entrepreneurs fought to obtain leadership positions in some business organizations and national confederations. They believed this was necessary so that the business organizations could become political and ideological training platforms. In some states, the strategy of these entrepreneurs succeeded. They were able to gain leadership positions in the local chapters of their business organizations.[11]

During the 1980s, small and medium-size entrepreneurs also supported the creation of new business associations that attempted to overcome the problems of representation. However, these associations lacked access to the executive and thus had no power to influence the decision-making process (Shadlen, 2000).[12]

By the time President López Portillo decided to nationalize the banks, the ground was ripe for a violent reaction. López Portillo's unanticipated and unilateral decision detonated an unprecedented reaction within the business community, and it did not subside, despite the efforts of the following administration of Miguel de la Madrid (1982–88) to regain the confidence of the private sector.

Many of the entrepreneurs who had managed to gain leading positions in their local business organizations believed they still lacked sufficient power to fight what they perceived was an overcentralized, arbitrary, and corrupt political system.[13] To become more effective, they needed to seek alliances with other sectors of the population and mobilize them for political action. In the north, the fight against authoritarianism was also articulated as a demand for greater regional autonomy and a struggle against centralization.

Small and medium-size entrepreneurs realized that the apathetic political attitude that had characterized the business community was no longer adequate to protect their interests. More important, they realized that democracy provided the necessary institutional mechanisms to check the power of government officials and make the government more accountable and predictable. In their view, the authoritarian character of Mexico's political regime, which for many years was not only tolerated but endorsed as a critical component of prosperity, threatened the interests of business in the long run. By leaving government officials unchecked and unbound by the rule of law, they could actually turn against business with greater ease than in more democratic regimes. This was all the more evident to those entrepreneurs who lacked personal connections with government authorities and who could not effectively threaten the government with shipping their capital out of the country. For these entrepreneurs, it thus became imperative to actively become involved in politics and to adopt a more independent political profile by challenging the PRI in the electoral arena.

Many of the entrepreneurs who took a leading role in the PAN previously had served as president of COPARMEX.[14] The most notable case is Manuel J. Clouthier, an entrepreneur from the northern state of Sinaloa who in 1978 became national president of COPARMEX and in 1988 was nominated as the PAN's presidential candidate.[15]

Unlike the entrepreneurs in the central region of the country, northern entrepreneurs shared a common educational path. Most of them were trained at the Instituto Tecnológico de Monterrey, a private university oriented to business and economics and deeply inspired by social Christian principles of "social responsibility."[16] Many entrepreneurs from the north were also trained in the United States and were influenced deeply by the democratic practices of this country, which they see as a source of values and ideas. Finally, given their proximity to the United States, many entrepreneurs from the northern states developed ties with their American counterparts, particularly through civic associations such as the chamber of commerce, the Rotary Club, and the Lions Club.

From their experience in business organizations, these entrepreneurs gained valuable leadership skills and organizational resources that were later put to use in their political activities. In fact, these business organizations became training grounds of future leaders and springboards to the electoral arena in support of the PAN. As leaders of business organizations, entrepreneurs also gained recognition, visibility, and respect in their own communities. They were consulted periodically by the media and regarded as legitimate opinion leaders. Entrepreneurs were not viewed with the contempt and skepticism usually accorded traditional politicians. Their legitimacy as social leaders enhanced their capacity to appeal to and mobilize wide sectors of the population in support of the PAN.[17]

Many entrepreneurs believed that to gain enough influence to change government policies, they needed to organize a broader political opposition front. And this could only be accomplished by supporting a political party. As one entrepreneur said,

> I became convinced that the business organizations were inadequate to bring about political change. Business groups have not been able to fire a corrupt police chief, remove a governor, or prevent the authorities in the Ministry of Public Works from doing dirty business. On these respects, the business groups are totally ineffective. This is why I decided to join the PAN.[18]

The PAN welcomed these entrepreneurs into its ranks and gave them free rein to organize the campaigns and define the party's electoral strategies and tactics.[19]

Bank Nationalization: The Spark of the Rebellion

When President López Portillo nationalized the banks, he not only affected economically one of the most powerful sectors of the business community; he also eliminated, at least temporarily, the business community's privileged group of negotiators and mediators with the government. For many years and until the nationalization of the banks, bankers "operated as sophisticated influence peddlers, brokers between politicians and the private sector" (Camp, 1989, 175). As a former president of the Mexican Association of Bankers said, "Bankers performed a moderating role between entrepreneurs and the government. Bankers always negotiated with the government in private and softened policies that affected entrepreneurs. At the same time, they negotiated with entrepreneurs and moderated their demands against the government."[20]

The centrality of Mexican bankers as financiers of the private and public sectors explains why they adopted such a moderating role. Bankers had close alliances with high-level government officials and with the most prominent entrepreneurs in the country. By nationalizing the banks, López Portillo altered the balance within the business community. As bankers sought to defend themselves against this measure, rather than try to prevent an escalation of conflict between the private sector and the government, the more radical and belligerent entrepreneurs found greater freedom to voice their criticisms against the government and organize in opposition to the PRI.

Although the nationalization of the banks largely affected the interests of bankers and of large entrepreneurs closely associated with the banks, the latter did not adopt a politically belligerent attitude. In the past, these entrepreneurs, particularly the leaders of the biggest holdings, or Economic Groups, had been the most outspoken members of the business community whenever they felt threatened by the government.[21] But in 1982 they had a great deal at stake in negotiating the value of their banks and their assets. They preferred to remain loyal to the PRI, adopting a more accommodating position and deciding to resolve their differences with the government behind closed doors. Although they were angered by the president's decision, large entrepreneurs were afraid of "provoking the beast," and as an official of one of the private sector's think tanks said, "Large entrepreneurs and bankers were afraid that if they reacted vociferously, then the government could start expropriating more enterprises."[22]

Small and medium-size entrepreneurs, on the other hand, particularly from the northern states, took a more confrontational approach. Unlike the large entrepreneurs in the country, small and medium-size entrepreneurs were economically more autonomous from the government and thus had more freedom to voice their concerns and demands. They had comparatively little to lose by organizing openly against the PRI and the government (Mizrahi, 1994b).[23] In contrast to large entrepreneurs, who had direct access to decision makers and could exert direct pressure on the government, small and medium-size entrepreneurs had to find a more positive threat and thus decided to organize against the government and resort to the use of their "voice" (Hirschman, 1970).

Thus, although nationalization of the banks did not affect the interests of small and medium-size entrepreneurs in particular, they regarded it as a unilateral and arbitrary measure that clearly demonstrated the dangers of an unchecked president in an unaccountable political system. A political system based on the supremacy of a president who was not really constrained either by Congress or by strong opposition parties could eventually behave "irresponsibly" and turn its back on the interests of business. As one entrepreneur from Chihuahua said, "The nationalization of banks was a powerful blow for us. The bankers were a symbol; they were the most powerful sector of the business community. If the government was capable of attacking them, who knows what could happen to the rest of us."[24] Francisco Barrio, an entrepreneur who later became governor of Chihuahua in 1992, offered a similar response: "The nationalization of the banks did not affect my pocketbook; it affected me psychologically."[25]

The political participation of these entrepreneurs revived an old opposition party that since its creation in 1939 had not competed effectively in the electoral arena. They brought to the PAN not only much-needed financial resources, leadership styles, organizational capabilities, and new advertising and marketing techniques drawn from their own business experience. More important, entrepreneurs took a leading role in the organization of campaigns and in many cases became the party's candidates. They also organized massive postelection mobilizations when an election was suspected of having been fraudulent. For the first time in Mexico's postrevolutionary history, entrepreneurs took a leading role in a popular and electorally centered rebellion against authoritarianism.

The influx of entrepreneurs into the party would not have been possible without the party's adoption of an open door policy, which, as I argued above, was the outcome of the conflict between the pragmatist and doctrinaire factions in the party. Yet had PAN's internal organization not been as weak and fragmented to begin with, these entrepreneurs would not have been able to exercise such a decisive influence without much interference from the leaders of the party.[26] Yet, however much the entrepreneurs contributed to expanding the electoral base of the PAN, they did not contribute to strengthening the PAN as an organization. Because their interest was mainly to defeat the PRI, they confined their political participation to the electoral arena, often creating parallel structures that they used to organize the party's campaigns. After the elections were over, the entrepreneurs lost interest in party affairs and made no serious attempts to help the party penetrate into broader sectors of the population.

Where the PAN won an election, entrepreneurs were frequently asked to serve in the administration. Where the party lost, entrepreneurs typically returned to their businesses and dropped their party's activities. Thus while the PAN was effectively propelled out of its sectarian position, organizationally it remained as weak as it had been before. One of the most evident signs of this weakness was the contraction of the party to the point of virtual paralysis after an election. Eventually, some party officials began to perceive this sluggishness as a problem. In Guanajuato, for example, an elected PAN official said that "the PAN almost disappeared when they won the elections."[27] Similarly, in Chihuahua, the former secretary general of the party said, "When the campaigns came to an end, the party virtually fell apart."[28] Perhaps no one expressed this more eloquently than Carlos Castillo Peraza, former president of the PAN: "The PAN seems to lose when it wins."[29]

The organizational weakness of the PAN did not seem of much concern to its leadership. On the contrary: not having a permanent party machine with vested interests in the preservation of the organization gave the party more flexibility to expand and contract with the electoral cycle, to select ad hoc candidates with roots to their communities, and to address issues of interest to each region. However, once the PAN became the governing party, this organizational fragility turned increasingly into a major weakness. The party lacked the capacity to work with and service its constituencies on a permanent basis and to entrench itself more deeply in the community. It was also unable to transcend its oppositional role by formulating feasible policies and continuing to appeal to the electorate on issues other than mere opposition to the PRI.

Laying the Groundwork: The Legacy of the Pragmatists' Victory

The presidency of José Angel Conchello (1972–75)marked a turning point in the life of the PAN. Conchello, a businessman from Nuevo León, was a fierce opponent of President Echeverría. Along with many other entrepreneurs throughout the country, Conchello believed that Echeverría's fiscal policies were irresponsible and that the expansion of the state's role in the economy was detrimental to the market and to private property. For Conchello and his entrepreneur supporters, Echeverría's populist rhetoric, his openness to socialist countries such as China, Cuba, and the Soviet Union, and his support of Salvador Allende in Chile were all proof that the president was flirting with socialism. Given the serious economic problems the country was then confronting[30] and the tense political environment after the repression of the student movement in 1968, Conchello and the new leaders of the PAN believed they needed to mount a more serious political offensive. It was time to move away from the party's traditional position as loyal opposition, they believed, and become a more effective and radical alternative (Loaeza and Segovia, 1987). But this would require important internal changes in the PAN.

Conchello and his pragmatist supporters believed that the PAN's position was overly doctrinaire and that this weakened the party and limited its political significance in the country. In their view, the party needed to relax its emphasis on doctrinal purity, abandon its intransigent position, adopt new electoral tactics, and seek new electoral allies. This was essential if the party wanted to become a more influential political player capable of constraining the president, who had hitherto appeared to act without restriction. While Conchello was far from supporting a revision of the party's doctrine or statutes, he did believe that the party should "simplify its truths [and] express the doctrine in terms more understandable *and* easier to comprehend by the general public."[31]

The 1973 electoral reform encouraged Conchello to refocus the PAN's strategies for pursuing power. While Conchello never believed that this reform constituted a real democratic opening, he nevertheless supported the adoption of the open-door policy geared to accepting all those who wanted to work for the party.[32] In his view, the party had to seek out the support of discontented voters, regardless of whether they agreed with the PAN's ideological principles. Electoral growth needed to take precedence over indoctrination (Yañez Maldonado, 1990, 109).

As I argued in chapter 3, Conchello's pragmatism elicited strong opposition from many panistas who feared that the quest for power would undermine the party's ideology and doctrinal identity. The doctrinaires considered the PAN unique, because unlike other political parties, it was driven by higher political and philosophical goals than the mere pursuit of power. Efraín González Morfín, leader of the "doctrinaire" faction,[33] and his followers believed that the party's goal—to create a new civic culture shaped by strong ethical principles—could be reached without participating in elections and that seeking electoral victory was a means, not an end in itself. In sum, they did not want the PAN to become an "electoral party," attracting the support of an electorate that had little concern for the party's ideological positions (González Morfín, quoted in Yañez Maldonado, 1990; La Nación, February 12, 1973, 10–13).

The conflict between the two factions escalated in 1975, when elections for party president were held. Conchello ran for reelection but was challenged by González Morfín. After six rounds of voting, González Morfín was finally able to win the required majority and was elected the PAN's president. But Conchello and his faction remained united and continued to exercise significant influence over the party's decisions. In fact, González Morfín and his followers accused Conchello of organizing a parallel party, with its own loyalties, organization, and funding (Loaeza, 1987, 88; Reveles, 1996, 23).

In 1976 the conflict between the doctrinaires and the pragmatists finally burst into the open as the party prepared to nominate its presidential candidate. Neither of the two main contenders—Pablo Emilio Madero, representing the pragmatists, and Salvador Rosas Magallón, representing the doctrinaires—received the required majority of 80 percent of the delegates' vote. The divisions between the factions were so deep that no agreement seemed possible. The convention was unusually confrontational, quite different from the peaceful and polite conventions of the past. Even after seven rounds of voting, the party was unable to nominate a presidential candidate. Although the party participated in the congressional elections, its total vote collapsed in 1976. Compared to the 1973 elections, the PAN lost more than

40 percent of its voters (from 2.3 million votes in 1973 to 1.4 million in 1976) (Yañez Maldonado, 1990, 126; Loaeza, 1999, 308–10).

Given the weakness of the opposition and particularly alarmed by running unopposed,[34] President López Portillo promoted a new and more substantial electoral reform soon after taking office. The president was convinced of the need to stimulate opposition parties and prevent them from withdrawing altogether from the electoral arena. To ensure its hegemony and at the same time maintain a "democratic façade," the PRI needed competition from the opposition (Crespo, 2000, 18).

A new electoral reform in 1977 significantly increased the number of elected positions available to the opposition, but it also punished parties that did not participate in the elections. The Ley Federal de Organizaciones Políticas y Procesos Electorales (LFOPPE) enlarged the National Congress from 200 to 400 seats, increased the number of electoral districts from 200 to 300, and introduced a system of proportional representation to allocate the 100 extra seats. But it also canceled the registration for parties that failed to participate or reach a minimum of 1.5 percent of the vote (Molinar, 1991, 97).[35]

Conchello believed that boycotting the reforms and abstaining from participation was tantamount to committing "political harakiri" (Yañez Maldonado, 1990, 135), but González Morfín argued that the reform would transform the PAN into a mere "electoral party" and that it was better if the party concentrated on swaying public opinion by propagating the party's ideology (Yañez Maldonado, 1990; Loaeza, 1999, 319). In the end, Conchello and his faction won more support inside the PAN and González Morfín and other doctrinaire leaders decided to leave the party in 1978.

The departure of the doctrinaires resolved the internal conflict but weakened the party significantly. In many regions the PAN was virtually dismantled as most of its activists left. Nevertheless, largely as a result of the new electoral rules, in the 1979 elections the PAN made significant electoral progress, winning forty-three seats in Congress (4 by winning the majority of votes in a district and 39 through proportional representation). Since then, and with the partial exception of the elections in 1985 and 1991, as Table 4.1 shows, the PAN's presence in Congress has increased consistently.[36] However, the PAN was still a marginal political player, with little capacity to influence the decision-making process or to serve as a counterweight to the power of the PRI and the president.[37]

The electoral expansion of the PAN did not really take off until after 1982, when a considerable number of northern small and medium-size entrepreneurs decided to throw their support behind the PAN after the nationaliza-

Table 4.1   Percentage of Votes for the PAN in Federal Elections, 1976–2000

Year	Congressional Elections (%)	Presidential Elections (%)
1976*	9	
1979	12	
1982	18	15.62
1985	16	
1988	18	17.07
1991	18	
1994	27	26.69
1997	26	
2000	38.1	43.8

*There was no PAN presidential nominee in this election.

Source: Lujambio (forthcoming); Rocío Rodríguez, *Información Electoral del PAN,* Dirección de Relaciones Nacionales del CEN del PAN, 1997. For the year 2000, see www.cidac.com.mx.

tion of the banks.[38] In virtually all regions where the PAN currently enjoys a strong base of support, entrepreneurs played a pivotal role.[39]

The entrepreneurs who supported the PAN knew that they had an uphill battle, for they expected that elections would most likely be fraudulent. They believed that organizing a strong campaign, ensuring the participation of a large number of voters during the elections, and mobilizing against fraud after the elections was essential in pressing the government to tolerate opposition victories. However, fraudulent elections also had a deterrent effect, for the perception that the PRI was impossible to defeat gave way to a growing disenchantment with electoral mobilization. After fraudulent elections, many entrepreneurs and opposition voters abstained from participating in further elections. Eventually, however, the strength of the opposition in various states and the mounting pressure for clean elections forced the government to tolerate opposition victories at the local and state levels.

In Chihuahua, for example, one of the most important strongholds of the PAN during the 1980s, the government of President Miguel de la Madrid tolerated the victories of the PAN at the local level in 1983. This was part of the government's strategy to regain legitimacy after the nationalization of the banks. However, the strength of the PAN in these elections scared the PRI and the government. Consequently, in the federal congressional elections of 1985,

they resorted to fraud to win all the districts in the state. By 1986 the government had turned its back on its promise to bring about a "moral renovation
of society" and relied on massive fraud to ensure the hegemony of the PRI.
Although these elections were hotly contested and the postelectoral mobilizations against fraud attracted enormous national and international media
attention, the PRI was able to assume power. By the presidential elections of
1988, the entrepreneurs who had supported the PAN had returned to their
businesses, and a large number of opposition voters refrained from participating in elections. The PRI was able to win overwhelmingly with abstention
rates of more than 60 percent.[40] The PAN had lost its electoral strength, and
it remained weak until 1992, when Francisco Barrio decided to run as the
PAN's gubernatorial candidate.

At the national level, however, the pressure for clean elections began to
mount, as state and local elections attracted larger numbers of opposition voters. Eventually, elections became too destabilizing for the regime, as larger and
stronger mobilizations against fraud exposed the PRI and the government's
strategies to maintain power.

By the time President Salinas de Gortari took office in 1988, the time was
ripe for tolerating more opposition victories, albeit selectively.[41] He came to
power after a contested and controversial election. To attain legitimacy, he was
prepared to demonstrate his commitment to democracy by tolerating an
opposition victory at the state level.

In 1989 the PAN won its first governorship, in Baja California. This victory
set off a wave of unprecedented victories at both the state and the municipal
level. During Salinas de Gortari's term (1988–94), the PAN increased its share
of the vote significantly, even though elections continued to be besieged by
accusations of fraud and in many places electoral results continued to be contested. In 1982 the PAN controlled 22 municipalities; by 1990 it controlled 35,
and by 1999, 284. In 2000, the PAN controlled more than 300 municipalities.
(See Table 4.2 and Chart 4.1.) In addition, the PAN won the governorship in
Guanajuato in 1991, in Chihuahua in 1992, in Jalisco and Baja California in
1995, and in Nuevo León, Querétaro, and Aguascalientes in 1997.[42]

The Influx of Entrepreneurs into the PAN

When entrepreneurs decided to support the PAN, they encountered an extremely small and fragile political party. The party's insignificant electoral
presence, the scarcity of financial resources, and the inability to appeal to and
attract more people because of years of internal conflict convinced many

Table 4.2   Number of Elected Positions Won by the PAN, 1976–2001

Year	Municipalities	Deputies			Senators	Governors
		Total	Majority	Proportional Representation		
1976	3	20				
1977	5					
1978	1					
1979	7	43	4	39		
1980	8					
1981	3					
1982	10	51	1	50		
1983	17					
1984	3					
1985	3	41	9	32		
1986	12					
1987	1					
1988	13	101	38	63		
1989	21					1[a]
1990	12					
1991	44	89	10	79	1	1[b]
1992	37					1[c]
1993	16					
1994	89	119	20	99	24	
1995	118					3[d]
1996	37					
1997	144	121*	64	57	33	2[e]
1998	86					1[f]
1999	19					
2000	224	156	86	70	46	3[g]
2001	172					1[h]

*One Federal Deputy resigned in 1997.

Sources: Ana María León, *Puestos de elección popular que ha tenido el Partido Acción Nacional en toda su historia* (Mexico, D.F.: Dirección de Relaciones Nacionales del CEN del PAN, 1997). The 1998–2000 data come from Remes (2000). The data for 2001 were obtained from the PAN's Electoral Office (Acción Electoral).

[a] Baja California
[b] Guanajuato (interim)
[c] Chihuahua
[d] Baja California, Jalisco, Nuevo León

[e] Nuevo León, Querétaro
[f] Aguascalientes
[g] Morelos, Guanajuato, Chiapas (coalition)
[h] Yucatán

Chart 4.1   Municipalities Governed by the PAN, 1960–May 1999

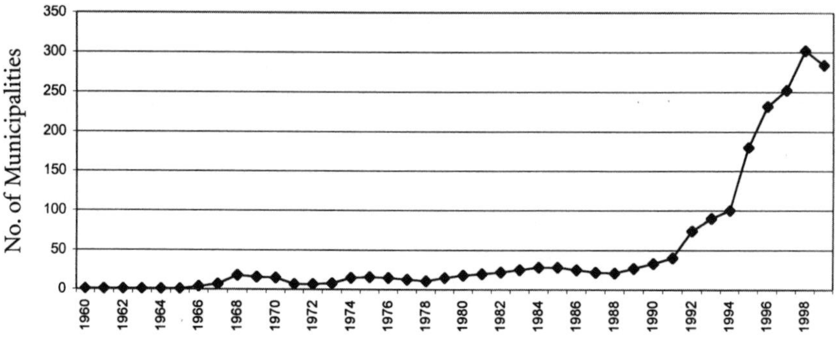

Source: Lujambio (2000).

panistas that they had little to lose in any case by welcoming entrepreneurs into their ranks. Although many panistas regarded these entrepreneurs with skepticism, they believed that closing their doors to new leaders with recognizable social prestige and isolating themselves ideologically threatened their very survival as a political party. As the general director of Francisco Barrio's campaign in Chihuahua recalled, "People in the PAN were wise enough to accept us and let us lead the movement. After all, we were nothing but intruders."[43]

The very weakness of the PAN was attractive to entrepreneurs, for it gave them greater room to maneuver to organize and impose their agenda. In many cases, particularly in the northern states, entrepreneurs explicitly demanded that the party apparatus refrain from interfering in the organization of the election campaigns.[44] The party leaders acceded to these demands in the belief that the entrepreneurs would increase the PAN's electoral strength.

During the 1980s and 1990s, the PAN acquired a new political dynamism, reflected in its candidates for office. The PAN was also able to tap significant new sources of financial resources that allowed it to run well-organized, aggressive, and innovative campaigns. It adopted a new rhetoric that was assertive and seemed more focused on winning. Rather than appeal only to those voters who subscribed to the party's principles, the PAN now appealed to the electorate at large. It portrayed its fight for democracy as a struggle against corruption, governmental inefficiency, and economic and political centralism. It also incorporated new tactics of social mobilization such as honking horns, covering cars with panista propaganda, and writing political messages on peso bills, which allowed people to show their support for the PAN without being recognized and consequently "punished" by the government. And finally, as part of a more general crusade for democracy, the new panista candidates were able to reach out and gain the support of a wide variety of civic organizations that monitored the elections.[45]

The PAN's new electoral strategies started to pay off. In the 1988 elections, the PAN obtained 17 percent of the total vote in the presidential election and won a total of 101 seats in Congress. (See Tables 4.1 and 4.2.) At the municipal and state levels, the PAN did not start to register substantial electoral victories until the 1990s, despite its unparalleled ability to mobilize greater sectors of the population during its campaigns. In large part this lag was a result of the persistence of election fraud and the government's refusal to recognize many of the PAN's alleged victories throughout much of the 1980s. In several important northern cities, such as Monterrey, Hermosillo, Chihuahua, Durango, and Mexicali, the PAN staged unusually aggressive campaigns and mobilized a large number of people against election fraud.[46] In most of these cases, entrepreneurs took the lead. They blocked streets and government buildings, went on hunger strikes, and took their grievances to international organizations such as the Organization of American States (OAS). A widely publicized case was that of Chihuahua in 1986, where the PAN claimed that the government (and the PRI) had committed serious election fraud to prevent the PAN from winning the governorship.[47]

Before the involvement of entrepreneurs in the PAN, the party had neither the resources nor the organizational capacity to appeal to and mobilize wide sectors of the population, give voice to the existing discontent with the government, and design and plan effective campaigns against the PRI. As the former governor of Baja California, himself an entrepreneur, openly admitted,

> Traditional panistas are more used to resisting fraud, to turn the other cheek; they come from a tradition that values martyrdom and that conceives electoral activity in mystical terms. Entrepreneurs brought fresh resources and strategies into the party. . . . Without the entrepreneurs, the PAN could not have won elections.[48]

Yet the entrepreneurs' mode of political participation did not lead to the strengthening of the PAN as an organization. While entrepreneurs participated actively in campaigns and provided financial resources and advice, their direct involvement with the PAN was limited. After the elections, the majority did not assume an active role in the day-to-day party affairs. Few of them agreed to run as candidates for office in the party apparatus (Guadarrama, 1987). Moreover, entrepreneurs did not believe they had a stake in institutionalizing the innovations they had introduced.

As leaders of the campaign committees, entrepreneurs assumed a crucial role in the definition of election goals and strategies. The campaigns were often run by parallel organizations relatively independent from the PAN. They had their own buildings, their own directors, treasurers, administrative staff, press managers, and logistics departments. The campaign committee, not the party bureaucracy, made most of the important decisions. Indeed, many of the staff working in the campaign organization were not even members of the PAN. This eventually caused serious problems between the "newcomers" (or, as they later were called, the "neo-panistas") and the longtime members of the PAN, who felt displaced and ignored. To this day the tensions between these two factions constitute one of the PAN's greatest sources of tension and were particularly evident in the organization of Vicente Fox's 2000 presidential campaign.

By supporting the PAN and becoming actively involved in electoral politics, entrepreneurs did not really attempt to become the party's new core constituency (Gibson, 1991), that is, a constituency that defines the party's agenda and ideological profile. Rather they used the PAN as a political platform to organize against the PRI. Their lack of interest in the party's internal affairs made traditional party leaders and longtime party activists less resistant to accepting their participation. After all, they did not challenge their positions inside the party. It was a marriage of convenience. However, and paradoxically, in the long run the success of this marriage created new challenges and sources of tension inside the party.

When the PAN actually won an election, entrepreneurs who had been closely involved in the organization of the campaign and who had close ties to the candidate filled government positions in the new administration. This eventually alienated the traditional panistas, who felt not just ignored but betrayed.[49]

The PAN's Organizational Response

As the panista electorate expanded and the PAN began to gain greater access to government positions, the weakness of the party became a matter of concern for many panista leaders. At the national level, party leaders introduced important reforms designed to catch up with the party's growing success in the electoral arena.

In 1987, when Luis H. Alvarez became national president of the PAN, the party decided to remunerate its officials so that they could work full time for the party. For the first time in its history, the PAN also agreed to accept public funding, arguing that the rules for distributing public resources to political parties had become clearer and more transparent. And finally, the party established the Secretaría de Estudios (Research and Training Secretariat) to train its public officials and design policy proposals and the Secretaría de Acción Electoral dedicated to monitoring and supervising elections throughout the country.[50]

The efforts to expand and reinforce the party's organization continued throughout the administrations of Carlos Castillo Peraza (1993–96) and Felipe Calderón Hinojosa (1996–99). To improve the quality of information about the party's performance in elections, Castillo Peraza launched a program to install computer centers that would be capable of conducting opinion polls and gathering election results faster than the government. This was regarded as a critical resource in the fight against election fraud. The party also created two new foundations, designed mainly to support the activities of the party in Congress.[51]

Although the party has expanded its organizational activities significantly since 1987, it has not been able to overcome many of its historic weaknesses and to respond effectively to the growing demands and problems it confronts. The PAN still has a shortage of well-trained professionals working for the party on a permanent basis. It has not yet been able to expand geographically throughout the country;[52] it has a reduced base of party activists, and at the state and local levels, the party continues to have a fragile political apparatus that becomes active mainly during election campaigns. More important, the internal life of the party still operates as if it were a small and ideologically tight opposition party. While these same rules did not obstruct the nomination of new and attractive candidates (the "intruders") when party activists perceived there was little to lose, these same rules become a major obstacle to the nomination of electorally attractive candidates once the party starts to win elections. Since the rules were designed to prevent the infiltration of political opportunists, they tend to benefit the more traditional and ideologically committed members, and not necessarily those most qualified to become the party's candidates. Moreover, these rules also undermine the party's capacity to maintain and increase its bases of support, to be active beyond elections, and to support its elected officials with feasible public policies.

During the 1980s and 1990s, the PAN became an electoral party with sectarian rules. These rules limit the PAN's potential to adapt to its new responsibilities as a party in government. They also undermine the party's ability to reach an internal consensus regarding its ultimate goals: winning elections or promoting its principles and educating the public. Perhaps nowhere was this more evident than during the 1994 presidential election, when the PAN's candidate, Diego Fernández de Cevallos, a longtime panista activist, refused to seize the initiative after he won the first nationwide televised presidential debate. Just after opinion polls showed the PAN had a good chance of winning the presidential election, Fernández de Cevallos became increasingly ambivalent and decided to slow down his campaign activities. According to a high-level party official who was close to the campaign, "Diego Fernández de Cevallos did not pull back from the electoral front, . . . but he did not push forward either."[53]

A party that weakens as a result of organizing and, above all, winning elections and that is still skeptical (or afraid) of power is ill suited to become a major player in a more democratic setting.

The Internal Balance of Power

The participation of entrepreneurs in the PAN created new sources of tensions and divisions inside the party. The pragmatists of the 1970s along with the longtime party activists felt increasingly displaced by the newcomers, who became the party's candidates for office. The nomination of the presidential candidate for the 1988 elections clearly revealed the differences between the long-term party supporters and the newcomers. Manuel J. Clouthier, an agricultural entrepreneur from Sinaloa, won the nomination by a wide margin against Jesús González Schmall, a member of the PAN since 1964 and a supporter of the pragmatist faction during the 1970s (Loaeza, 1999, 441). Like most of the entrepreneurs at the state and local levels, Clouthier conducted an innovative presidential campaign. He organized unusually large demonstrations against the PRI and adopted radical and aggressive political rhetoric. Clouthier conceived his campaign as a popular mobilization against the regime. But, as Loaeza argues, he did not "identify with the PAN, was not able to blend into its organization[,] . . . and on several occasions expressed his discomfort with the restraints that derived from his ties to the party" (Loaeza, 1999, 447).

With the unexpected strength of the left-wing opposition, led and organized by Cuauhtémoc Cárdenas,[54] Clouthier's rhetoric became even more radical and frequently diverged from the PAN's traditional ideology. Although many panistas eyed Clouthier with distrust, they had no choice but to defer to his charismatic leadership. After all, since the PAN was in the opposition and had no realistic chance of winning the presidency, Clouthier did not really represent a serious threat. If anything, he could help to increase the total vote for the PAN, strengthening the party both in Congress and at the state and local levels.

The 1988 elections were highly controversial and the official results widely contested by the opposition.[55] However, despite the allegations of fraud, what was unequivocal was that the FDN, led by Cuauhtémoc Cárdenas, received more votes than the PAN. The oldest and most consistent opposition party had been relegated to third place by a new coalition of PRI dissidents and left-wing parties.[56]

Nevertheless, the PAN became a pivotal party. Although the PRI won the presidency by a wide margin, it lost its absolute majority in the lower house of Congress. For the first time since it was created in 1929, the PRI needed the support of the opposition to pass its legislative initiatives. Since Cárdenas represented the most serious political threat to the PRI and there was an ideological affinity between the pro-business proposals of President Salinas de Gortari and the PAN, the PRI preferred to work more closely with the PAN and to find new grounds for reconciliation.[57] The PRI needed the PAN to govern (Barraza and Bizberg, 1991, 438). For its part, the PAN stood to profit greatly from the government's more accommodating position. If it collaborated with the PRI in the legislative arena, the PAN could increase its political leverage to press the government and the PRI into recognizing its electoral victories at the state and local levels. Moreover, by collaborating with the PRI, the PAN could present itself as a more moderate and less risky political opposition, effectively isolating Cárdenas and his newly founded political party, the Partido de la Revolución Democrática.

By 1989 the PAN voted with the PRI in the lower chamber of Congress in favor of a new electoral reform, which was heavily criticized by the PRD and even by an important number of panistas, including Clouthier.[58] The most controversial aspect of the reform was the modification of the so-called governability clause, which altered the formula for the allocation of seats on the basis of proportional representation in a way that assured overrepresentation of the majority party in Congress. Critics of this reform considered that this was in fact a "counterreform," for it increased the advantages of the PRI in Congress (Crespo, 1995).[59]

Alvarez, president of the PAN at the time, stated that the PAN did not have "the electoral weight to press further. . . . We did what we could at the time. We had to be pragmatic and realistic."[60] Moreover, he recognized that even though many of the PAN's original demands had not been incorporated into the new electoral law, the PRI had already accepted important concessions that could be lost if the PAN voted against the legislation.[61]

The PAN's moderation and its adoption of a gradualist political strategy soon led to a new internal conflict. A number of panistas who opposed the new electoral law and above all the pragmatism of the PAN's leadership founded an organization inside the party, the Democratic and Doctrinaire Forum (Foro Doctrinario y Democrático). The main goals of the Foro were to promote democratization within the party and to emphasize its doctrinal positions, which it believed had been sacrificed in the name of pragmatism. The Foristas included many longtime party activists as well as many of the pragmatists of the 1970s.[62] Much like the doctrinaires of the 1970s, the Foristas claimed that the party risked losing its identity in the mere pursuit of power.[63] Although this specific conflict was finally resolved in 1992 when the Foristas decided to abandon the party, the tensions between "traditional" panistas and "newcomers" remain. Perhaps nowhere were these tensions more evident than in the nomination of the PAN's presidential candidate in 1999. Vicente Fox, a "newcomer,"[64] won the nomination but with little enthusiasm and support from the party base and with the hostility of some of the most prominent leaders of the party.[65] Paradoxically, after winning the party's nomination, Fox still needed to convince members of his own party to support his nomination. Fox's electoral strength stemmed more from his ability to appeal to broader sectors of the population and from his success in building his own campaign organization (the Friends of Fox) than from his commitment to the PAN's traditional constituents and ideology.

While the tensions between the traditionalists and the newcomers intensify as the PAN strengthens its electoral position, they become potentially explosive particularly after the party wins an election. Distributing the spoils of victory becomes one of the most contentious matters for the party, for both the traditionalists and the newcomers feel they are responsible for the victory and believe they need to be compensated for their work. As we shall see in the next chapter, once the party is in power, the traditional activists organize to control the nomination process for the next election. And while these activists succeed, they often choose candidates that are unattractive to the electorate at large. As a result, the PAN often loses elections in places where it already controls power.

CHAPTER FIVE

The PAN in Government
Obstacles to Building a Catch-All Party

The victory of the PAN in Baja California in 1989 inaugurated a period of profound transformation in Mexico's electoral landscape. For the first time in sixty years, the PRI's uncontested hegemony at the state level came to an end. In 1992 the PAN obtained its second major electoral victory when it won the governorship in Chihuahua, a stronghold of the party during much of the 1980s.[1] By 1997 the PAN controlled seven state governments[2] and more than three hundred municipalities, including important capital cities.[3] In 2000 the PAN finally won the presidential election.[4]

In all these elections, the PAN was able to draw support from middle-class professionals, university students, large sectors of the working class, particularly those that are nonunionized, and even some peasants. Once in office, however, the PAN has been confronted with the challenge of designing a strategy to continue to appeal to this heterogeneous electorate. This greatly depends on the capacity of both the PAN and government officials to articulate a programmatic agenda that moves beyond the general commitment to democracy and honest government. Furthermore, to maintain its hold on power, the party must service its constituencies and become engaged in politics on a permanent basis rather than only during election periods. This requires a stronger organization that allows the party to penetrate in society, create stronger roots, and foster a greater partisan identification among its supporters.

Likewise, to respond to the many, sometimes contradictory demands of the electorate, the PAN needs to allow its candidates greater autonomy without losing ideological coherence. And finally, to remain competitive electorally, the party needs to expand its constituency and preserve its unity while acknowledging ambition as a driving force of politics. These challenges cannot be met without substantial change in the party's internal rules. But here is precisely where the PAN's leaders have exerted the greatest resistance—moving away from sectarianism and transforming the PAN into a catch-all party.

In this chapter I explore the paradoxes the party faces. I argue that the PAN's sectarian rules, which were designed to preserve its ideological principles and protect it from opportunists, are now out of sync with the electorate and constitute a serious obstacle to its development and ability to broaden its base of support. Indeed, the party as an organization is too anachronistic to respond effectively to the growing demands of its constituencies and to its new responsibilities as a governing party.

The gap between the party elites and its voters is crystallized in its internal rules. Indeed, these rules prevent the expansion of the party's base of activists and its entrenchment among wider sectors of society, obstruct the introduction of new forms of social mobilization and political participation, limit the party's flexibility to select more attractive candidates for public office, and vitiate the relationship between the party and the government.

One of the most serious consequences of this internal form of organization is the party's difficulty in maintaining and expanding its constituencies in places where it controls the government. Even in places where panista governments have been successful in introducing substantive and innovative administrative reforms, the party often fails to win consecutive elections. Chihuahua is perhaps the most dramatic case, where after its victory in 1992, the PAN lost every election in a state considered a traditional bastion of this party.[5] In the states of Baja California, Guanajuato, and Jalisco the PAN was relatively more successful: it won in subsequent elections and continues to control these states.[6] But the PAN's electoral success in these cases owes greatly to the failure of the PRI, the main opposition party in these states, to reorganize and maintain its unity after its electoral defeat. In Guanajuato and only partially in Baja California, the PAN was able to introduce some innovations in its state-level organization, even as the rules of the PAN at the national level remained unchanged. These changes, albeit limited in scope, were instrumental in further debilitating the PRI, thus also contributing to the electoral success of the PAN in these states.[7]

The disconnection between the party's elites and its voters also affects the quality and degree of tolerance of panista governments. Being too concerned with the promotion of the party's ideological agenda, the PAN's public officials have often lost touch with the general concerns of their electorate. Indeed, several local governments, like those in Puebla, Aguascalientes, and Monterrey, have censored art exhibits that in their view were "obscene." In Aguascalientes, a municipal official announced that homosexuals would be fired from the administration.[8] Other governments, like that of Guadalajara, have allegedly imposed a "dress code" and "forbidden" the use of vulgar language in public places (Shirk, 1999, 68). But perhaps the most revealing and alarming example of this gap between the party and its voters is the anti-abortion legislation introduced by panista legislators in Guanajuato and passed by the local Congress.[9] The most controversial feature of this legislation was that it prohibited abortion even in cases of rape. The passage of this legislation triggered a strong reaction among the public and soon became a national issue. Pressed with widespread opposition, the governor in the end was forced to veto it.[10]

The PAN's "New Managerialism": A New Style of Administration in Mexico

After years of PRI hegemony, the victory of an opposition party usually generates expectations of change among broad sectors of the population. Given that great expectations also tend to lead to great disillusionment, a challenge of new administrations is to deliver quick and tangible results. But herein lies one of the most difficult dilemmas of non-priísta governments. In most cases, change cannot be induced overnight. Moreover, many of the reforms introduced by new administrations, while significant, do not immediately bear fruit or become evident to the general public. Finally, and more important, public officials often realize that enhancing the government's efficiency and efficacy is not necessarily compatible with greater democratization and participation of society, particularly when most organized interest groups in society have a strong association with the PRI.

In the case of the PAN, these dilemmas become even more acute because of the entrepreneurial origins of many of its public officials. As good entrepreneurs, panista officials believe in the need to separate the administrative and political realms. Following the theory of "new managerialism" (Osborne and Gaebler, 1992), they tend to run the government as if it were a business; they place greater emphasis on "managing" the government in an honest and efficient way than on seeking political and electoral support. With few exceptions, panista officials are often better managers than politicians (Mizrahi, 1996).

In their campaigns, most entrepreneurs promise to combat corruption, reduce inefficiency and waste in the provision of public services, abolish cronyism in the allocation of government offices, and curtail the power of rent-seeking corporatist groups linked to the PRI. While these reforms seem attractive, once the party wins elections they are usually difficult to perceive by the general public and fail to generate electoral support in subsequent elections.[11] Now that the PAN controls the government at the presidential level, these difficulties have already become evident, as President Fox's rate of popularity dramatically declined after his first year in office.

Furthermore, unlike priísta government officials, panistas usually refuse to invest in visible, lavish, and costly public works projects as a means of generating political support. In their view, these projects undermine the overall efficiency of the administration because they are carried out on the basis of political, not technical, criteria.[12] In addition, panista officials usually do not advertise government projects, a practice they consider overly wasteful of resources and which they also associate with the PRI. According to a former president of the PAN, "People do not really know what their governments do for them because panista officials refuse to publicize their own achievements."[13]

The result is that once in government, panista officials are perceived by the people as efficient and honest but far too removed from the public and insensitive to their constituents' daily concerns (Guillén López, 1993; Ward and Rodriguez, 1995; Aziz Nassif, 1996).[14] As one high-level government official (himself an entrepreneur) in Chihuahua admitted after the PAN's poor performance in the 1995 elections, "We come from a school that promotes honesty and efficiency, but we have wrongly concentrated too much on the more administrative tasks of governing; we have stressed efficiency and have failed to become closer to the community."[15] Former governor Ernesto Ruffo of Baja California identified a similar problem:

> People perceive panistas as honest and efficient politicians, but that does not lead to greater political support. People dislike the rigidity of panista officials, their refusal to twist the law to help particular people. A good and efficient government does not guarantee public support.[16]

However, the distance between panista officials and the citizens they serve has deeper roots. To fight corruption and run the government in a more efficient manner, panista officials believe they need to isolate themselves from and protect the government against a wide array of corporatist organizations linked to the PRI. These organizations, panista officials contend, are not only led by corrupt leaders; they also place excessive demands on the adminis-

tration that undermine its capacity to plan and provide services more effi-
ciently and rationally. Most panista administrations have confronted and
in some cases successfully dismantled many of these organizations. Typically, panista officials at the state level have had major confrontations with
teachers' unions, bureaucrats, taxi and bus drivers, urban squatters, and
informal merchants (Guillén López, 1993; Espinoza Valle, 1996; 1997; Mizrahi, 1996).

Panista administrations believe rightly that destroying these corporatist
organizations is crucial to fighting corruption and eroding the traditional
bases of support of the PRI. The problem, however, is that they have largely
failed to construct new and alternative bases of political participation and
support more sympathetic or at least not opposed to the PAN. But this is a task
that administrations (and particularly those led by managers rather than
politicians) cannot accomplish themselves; they need the support of their parties if they want to maintain their electoral coalitions in a democratic electoral
arena. And here is precisely where the PAN has encountered the most serious difficulties.[17]

As an opposition party for so many years, the PAN does not always succeed
in adapting to its new role as a party in government. After an electoral victory,
the party typically contracts at the state and municipal levels to a point of virtual paralysis: it lacks a blueprint for political action that goes beyond organizing people in opposition to the PRI and consequently does not cater to its
constituencies between elections.

Moreover, many longtime panista activists are still wary of power and are
afraid of the party losing its ideological profile, especially when the candidates
who win elections are not traditional panistas but newcomers. As a former
president of the party said, "Panistas do not know what to do when they win.
They do not understand themselves as a governing party. They know how to
be in the opposition. Just as priístas are used to winning and feel they lose their
soul if they lose an election, panistas feel they lose their soul if they win."[18]

As I elaborate below, the PAN's sectarian rules benefit the most traditional
and ideologically driven factions of the party and obstruct a more collaborative relationship between the party and its administrations. In the end this
weakens the party's position in the electorate and hinders its capacity to organize alternative and long-lasting forms of political participation.

The Paradoxes of Victory: A Governing Party with Sectarian Rules

In contrast to the past, when the PAN's main problems were associated with
its inefficacy in the electoral arena, today the party confronts problems asso-

ciated with its electoral success. One of the most controversial issues the party has to confront after it wins an election is how to distribute positions of power among longtime party activists and newcomers. Although the former feel they deserve these positions, the latter believe *they* are better trained and prepared to take the responsibilities of government.[19]

Where entrepreneurs have run as party candidates and won elections, they have had a decisive influence in the integration of their cabinets. Usually first-level positions in panista administrations (secretaries and deputy secretaries) have been held either by businessmen who worked closely with the candidate during the campaign or by professionals who do not necessarily belong to the PAN. In some cases, governors have appointed priístas to their cabinets to ease the government's interaction with organized sectors of the PRI.[20]

While most of the administrations are generally staffed with newcomers, longtime party activists tend to remain in control of the party organization at the state and local levels. They occupy most of the positions in the party bureaucracy, and they also frequently run for congressional positions at the local and federal levels. Longtime activists in particular are rewarded with positions in the party's lists for congressional seats allocated on the basis of proportional representation.[21]

The differences between the longtime party activists and the newcomers, most of whom are entrepreneurs, tend to intensify after an electoral victory. The former not only feel ignored by the newcomers, they also fear that the newcomers' more pragmatic approach to governing will erode the party's ideological profile. Eventually, these differences tend to distance the party from its mass of supporters. But equally important, they also affect the relationship between the party and its own administrations: PAN government officials complain that the party fails to support them; panista activists complain that the government ignores them, treats them with contempt, and disregards their ideological concerns.

Divisions and competition among different political factions besiege most political parties in democracies. As Joseph Schlesinger (1994) points out in his seminal work on political parties, to ensure their organizational cohesion, political parties need to be able to distribute different types of benefits to their various supporters. In his view, parties are *teams* of individuals working together and cooperating to achieve a shared goal: winning office.

In this team effort, there are different individuals with different types of goals. Some members of the team are "office seekers," that is, candidates who want to gain access to a particular office. These are, in Schlesinger's view, the party's entrepreneurs (Schlesinger, 1994, 19). Other members are "benefit seekers," that is, people who obtain certain benefits as a result of the party's electoral success. Unlike office seekers, who gain immediate satisfaction by winning office, benefit seekers have to await the decisions made by the office-holders (Schlesinger, 1994, 146).

The benefits sought by benefit seekers can be collective (benefits derived from adherence to ideological principles and endorsement of certain public policies, which the candidate promises to introduce) or private (gaining a position in the administration, a favor, a contract, access to the decision-making mechanism, or other type of promotion). While the first type of benefits gives the party its ideological and programmatic coherence, they are not enough for preserving its organizational cohesion. As Schlesinger argues, there are political "purists" who derive purposive benefits from their participation. "But political parties must also produce, as a side product, private goods and provide private benefits" (Schlesinger, 1994, 18). This analytic perspective recognizes that the motivational force underlying the behavior of office seekers and benefit seekers alike is *ambition* and that the rules and institutions of democratic regimes must therefore stimulate and direct this political drive (Schlesinger, 1994, 33).

While the pursuit of political ambition seems ordinary in well-established democracies, it can become politically explosive when it appears in a political party that traditionally questioned its legitimacy as a driving force of politics and whose very rules were designed to protect the party against its feared effects. As the PAN gains access to office, political ambition is bound to appear regardless of whether the party's doctrine recognizes its legitimacy. The challenge for the PAN as a governing party is thus not only to accept ambition as a natural driving force of politics but also to reform its internal rules and organizational structure in order to ensure that it does not destroy the party's unity or commitment to its guiding ideological principles.

Perhaps no one put it more clearly than Felipe Calderón Hinojosa, the PAN's former president, when he said that "the challenge for the PAN was to win elections without losing the party,"[22] that is, to build a stronger political organization, to gain and above all retain power, without losing the party's identity in the process. It is not surprising that after the PAN won the presidential elections in July 2000, a growing number of panistas, particularly those closely associated with President Fox, advocated in favor of a reform of the party's internal rules, particularly those regulating party affiliation and candidate selection mechanisms.[23]

As is the case with any process of reform, reforming the party's sectarian rules is bound to create tensions inside the party, as well as between the party and its governments and the party's core constituencies and the general electorate. Below I analyze the dilemmas the party confronts as it gains access to power, in particular the dilemmas that result from the party's recruitment mechanisms, its candidate selection procedures, and its organizational structure.

Restrictive versus Inclusive Membership: The PAN's Recruitment Mechanisms

Although the PAN mobilizes vast sectors of the population (above and beyond its core constituencies) during electoral campaigns, it does not make any effort to expand its membership, particularly after winning an election. The party's tendency to contract after the electoral periods is instigated by its own rules for recruiting new members.

As I argued in chapter 3, the party's recruitment procedures are strict. In an effort to discourage political opportunists and those with no interest in the party's ideology, the PAN has refrained from relaxing its membership requirements. But the problem goes further. Once the party wins an election, "[p]anistas begin to perceive membership as a privilege; they close down the access for new members. Panistas recognize as legitimate party members only those who were already there before the party started to win elections."[24]

An expansion of party membership entails sharing the spoils of victory with an increasing number of people. Although many longtime party activists feel that panista government officials do not "reward" them with positions in the new administrations, they believe that they are the ones who stand to profit from the party's future victories. The problem is that although traditionalists tend to become candidates for subsequent elections, in many cases the party fails to win.

More important, many longtime activists distrust the newcomers in government and fear losing control of the party. Although they welcomed these newcomers when the party had nothing to lose, now that the party is gaining access to power, they do not want to accept new members who approach the party only when it begins to win. As a former leader of the PAN in Guanajuato said,

> The "neo-panistas" have taken over our party. . . . At first they presented themselves simply as collaborators, like Manuel Clouthier in Sinaloa, Eugenio Elorduy in Mexicali, Francisco Barrio in Chihuahua, Carlos Medina and Vicente Fox in Guanajuato. . . . "Neo-panistas" are pragmatists, they are concerned with efficiency. For them everything is understood in terms of numbers: More is good, less is bad. They are interested in neither the ethics nor the history of a party that was created to promote the common good.[25]

As we saw earlier, the party's municipal committees are responsible for recruiting new party members. As these organizations are led mostly by long-time party members, the latter virtually control the recruitment process. Not only are they quite selective in recruiting new party members; they can also manipulate the recruitment process to influence the nomination of particular candidates in upcoming elections. Newcomers often complain that the party fails to accept professionals or businesspeople, that is, people who resemble them and who may not be indoctrinated into the party's ideology. They also complain that the party recruits people who they know can vote in the party's conventions and primaries in favor of particular candidates.[26] For example, in Chihuahua, several government officials complained that in 1998 the traditionalists' candidate for governor had far more delegates than the candidate supported by the governor and his cabinet. This, they argued, was in large part the result of the PAN's failure to affiliate people they knew would not vote for their preferred candidate at the convention.[27] Similarly, in Guanajuato, the newcomers' preferred candidate for governor (an entrepreneur) also complained that the party leadership had manipulated the convention by recruiting members who they knew would vote for the traditionalists' preferred candidate.[28] The party's resistance to recruiting new members can also be explained by the ideological differences between the PAN's activists and the PAN's voters.

As I argued above, according to a survey conducted by Magaloni and Moreno (2000), panista supporters are heterogeneous and ideologically dispersed and define the PAN as a catch-all party, whereas panista activists are a more ideologically compact and coherent group. For example, in the "liberal-conservative dimension," which categorizes voters according to their position on moral issues such as abortion, homosexuality, and family values, panista voters are not only less conservative than party activists but also *less* conservative than priísta voters.[29] Similarly, the PAN's supporters are not clearly defined as "rightist" in terms of the "left-right economic dimension," which basically considers the role of the state in the economy. The survey demonstrates that the PAN seems to receive support from people positioned across the left-right dimension. In the words of Magaloni and Moreno,

> The higher the level of education, income and social class, the more liberal and rightist PAN supporters are. Conversely, the lower the social class, education levels, and income, the more leftist and conservative PAN voters get. . . . Given these results, *the disconnection between PAN elite and supporters seems to be particularly striking.* PAN elite is positioned on the lower

right quadrant (rightist and conservative), an empty space in terms of PAN's own mass support. (2000, 20–21; my emphasis)

Panista activists, in other words, are much more ideologically concerned than panista supporters and thus fear losing the party's ideological coherence by incorporating a growing number of activists.[30] The problem for the PAN is that many of the voters who supported this party as a way to express their opposition to the PRI and the government do not necessarily stay loyal to the PAN in later elections.

In an effort to overcome the municipal committees' resistance to affiliate new members with the party, in 1998 the PAN's national president tried to introduce an innovative recruitment mechanism. Without reforming the party's affiliation rules, he organized the so-called national affiliation week, whereby anybody could register to become a party member, without necessarily going to the party's municipal committees. This was designed primarily to recruit members in the Federal District, where the PAN has only about three thousand active members. The party, however, decided to include these new members as "adherents," not as "active" members, and, consequently, they could not immediately enjoy the privileges that active members have, such as becoming delegates to the party's conventions or voting in the party's primary elections.[31] Since 1998 the number of adherents has increased substantially. As of 2000, the PAN had more than 600,000 adherent members throughout the country.

In 2001 the party introduced a statutory reform establishing that adherent members could become active members after six months. These adherents, however, still must take the party's doctrinal course and comply with all the prerequisites for becoming a member of the party, such as "having an honest way of life" and "endorsing the party's principles" (Article 8). Furthermore, some of the adherents' applications to become full members are not processed rapidly by the party's bureaucracy.

Despite this recent growth of membership, the PAN still has an extremely reduced membership base. In a country of 100 million people, by the year 2001 the party had only 182,000 active members.[32]

The Struggle between Ideology and Pragmatism: The PAN's Candidate Selection Process

In the past, when the expectation of winning office was low, few people wanted to become candidates of the PAN. Running a campaign for elections that were regarded as virtually impossible to win required a great degree of sacrifice and commitment. As former Governor Ruffo said, throughout the 1950s, 1960s, and 1970s, "candidates perceived themselves as 'martyrs' whose mission was to 'resist' electoral fraud and turn the other cheek."[33] Rather than win elections, campaigns were regarded as opportunities to promote the party's ideology and educate the public. "Nepotism," as Castillo Peraza said, "was considered heroic then. One had to beg family members to help out with the campaigns. It was considered a symbol of solidarity. Had I won an election during the early 1980s, I would have had to form my government with members of my family."[34]

With an expanding electorate and growing office-holding opportunities, this situation has completely changed. Candidacies are now highly prized, and a large number of people are interested in joining the party, hoping either to become candidates for office or to work closely with a candidate and be rewarded with a government position if he or she wins the election.

The surge in the number of office seekers has created enormous tensions in the party's candidate selection process. Unlike the past, the party now has to reconcile the interests of its longtime members who feel they deserve the party's nomination—regardless of whether they are qualified—with those of newcomers who are motivated by political ambition and who often are not only more qualified but also can be more attractive to the electorate at large. More important, the party has to find mechanisms to preserve its ideological commitments without losing sight of its pragmatic objective, winning elections. But the existing rules for selecting candidates are designed to ensure the preservation of the party's ideological integrity, and they disproportionately benefit the traditional faction of the party.

The procedures for selecting candidates were formulated long before the party became competitive in the electoral arena, when party members did not actively seek candidacies. Moreover, these procedures were designed to assure that disaffected members of the PRI, or any other *caudillo* type of leader, could not use the party as a political platform to launch his or her own political career. As I argued in chapter 3, notwithstanding the recent modifications in the party statutes, candidate selection continues to be an internal party affair. Candidates for the lower chamber of Congress (at the federal and local levels) continue to be nominated by delegates at party conventions. These delegates are selected by the party's municipal and state committees, which have typically remained in the control of longtime party members. The criteria for selecting delegates to these conventions are rudimentary: any active member can sign up to be a party delegate. He or she still has to find the means to attend the party conventions; the party does not pay its delegates to attend.[35]

Until 2001, before the introduction of primary elections, candidates for the Senate and governorships needed only to collect forty signatures from active party members in support of their nomination.[36] Currently, these candidates need the approval of their state party organization before they can register to run in the party's primary elections. Similarly, presidential candidates also need the approval of the National Executive Committee to run in the party's primary election (Articles 37 and 38). Furthermore, in an effort to reduce and "filter" the growing number of office seekers, the party now obliges all prospective candidates to take a "candidate's exam" designed and administered by the party's National Executive Committee. This exam tests prospective candidates' analytic capacity and psychological profile and evaluates whether they are prepared for the job they seek. People who fail these exams do not obtain the party's approval to register as candidates.[37]

Since the nominating procedure is still very much an internal party affair, candidates need to appeal only to the core of their party to win their nomination; they have no incentive to organize their own campaigns and appeal to the general electorate. Therefore, while candidates may appear attractive to the panista core, they may not appeal to the electorate at large.[38]

Recognizing that this constitutes a serious problem for the party, many panistas began to talk about the need to design new procedures for selecting their candidates. Former Governor Ruffo, for example, argued in the mid-1990s that the party "needed to introduce some sort of 'filter' to determine who can and cannot become a candidate." "What we need," he said, "is something similar to an 'elders' council' to determine who deserves the nomination."[39] Other members of the PAN did not share this opinion and believed that the party needed to find mechanisms to convince old-time activists who do not meet the requirements for office to "give way to those who are better qualified and trained to become candidates."[40] Yet other panistas believed that the party needed to reform the party's statutes and include more stringent requirements for becoming a party candidate.[41]

In the midst of this discussion, in 1997 then-Governor Vicente Fox came up with yet another alternative for selecting the presidential candidate when he decided to seek his party nomination for the 2000 presidential election. Mobilizing well in advance of the elections, Fox decided to organize his campaign independently from his own party. He was convinced that if he let the nomination procedure run its traditional course, he did not have a chance of winning the party's nomination as presidential candidate. Traditional panistas did not trust Fox because he was perceived as a newcomer and a populist leader with little attachment to the PAN's ideological principles. As Fox said, "I know that I do not stand a chance of winning the party's nomination if I leave it to the party apparatus. My strength lies in my capacity to appeal to the public at large."[42]

Since no party regulation proscribes the organization of an electoral campaign before the party's convention, Fox decided to build his organization two years ahead of the party's national convention. The so-called Amigos de Fox (Friends of Fox) became the launching pad to finance his campaign organization. This organization was extremely successful in recruiting a wide variety of people who without any necessary ties to the PAN, wanted to support Fox's candidacy. Eventually, Amigos de Fox became a much bigger organization than the PAN itself, with a membership of about three million throughout the country. Fox's unparalleled success in the end discouraged any other active member from seeking the party's nomination. By the time the PAN was getting ready to organize its national convention, Fox was the only registered presidential candidate.

Given Fox's ability to appeal to a much wider electorate, the PAN's national leadership became convinced that its existing procedures to select the presidential candidate were anachronistic and that substantial reform was necessary. But arriving at any consensus inside the party was difficult. In its National Assembly in 1999, the party finally accepted a partial reform: the party's presidential candidate was to be selected through a closed primary election, in which active and adherent party members could vote. Although this reform eliminated the party convention, it still confined the nominating procedure to a small number of party activists and supporters. But it effectively increased the incentives for prospective candidates to appeal to the larger electorate.

In 1999 the nominating procedures did not make any difference, for Fox, the only candidate, would have won the nomination in any case. By 2001, however, the party rolled back its path to reform: it amended the 1999 statutes one more time, now restricting the privilege of voting in primary elections to the core of the party's *active* members and subjecting prospective candidates to a qualifying mandatory exam. Although this statutory reform also introduced a primary election as a method for selecting candidates for senators and governors, by limiting the voting rights to active members of the party, the reforms fell short of opening the nominating process to the larger electorate. Moreover, the resistance to expanding the base of active party militants grants the party apparatus some power over the candidate selection procedure, for they still control who votes in the party's primary elections.

The consequences of these nominating procedures are twofold. First, the party still lacks flexible mechanisms to select electorally more attractive candidates for office. This can seriously weaken the party's electoral competitiveness.

In the case of Chihuahua, for example, the candidate for the 1998 gubernatorial election was a traditional panista who strongly criticized the governor, even though the latter was extremely popular with the electorate.[43] In Baja California and Jalisco, the party also nominated traditional panistas as candidates for governor in subsequent elections. In Guanajuato, in contrast, the PAN nominated a newcomer but one who because of his conservative views received strong support from the traditional faction of the party.[44] Although in these states the PAN won the gubernatorial elections a second time, the victories were not due to the appealing qualities of its candidates but to the implosion of the PRI. I return to this point below.

Second, the party typically selects more traditional party members as candidates for Congress, at the federal and the state level. In the vast majority of cases, these candidates are well versed in the party's philosophical principles, but they are not well trained technically and lack the capacity to translate the party's ideological concerns into effective policies and feasible legislative proposals.[45] For example, in 1995 the PAN's federal legislators decided to reject President Zedillo's initiative to increase the value added tax from 10 to 15 percent. According to a high-level party official, the party's legislators decided to reject the president's initiative because the increase would not be popular, without really knowing or understanding the financial implications of their decision.[46]

Furthermore, given the different economic and political backgrounds that have characterized public officials in the executive and legislative branches of government, governors—particularly those who come from the business community—often are not supported by their own party in Congress. Governor Barrio in Chihuahua complained that the PAN in fact behaved like an opposition party, blocking his initiatives in Congress.[47] Similarly, Governor Fox once jokingly said that compared to other panista governors, he was lucky because he did not have to deal with a panista majority in Congress.[48] Now, as president, Fox has found it difficult to work closely with members of his own party in Congress. During the much debated and highly politicized discussions over fiscal reform, a reform deemed central by the administration, the PAN did not fully support the government's proposal to tax food and medicines, which are exempt from value added tax. Because of the PRI's unwillingness to support this reform, only a watered-down version was approved by Congress in 2002.[49]

As the midterm election of 2003 approaches, some leaders of the PAN who advocated for the introduction of more far-reaching reforms in 2001 are worried that the party's current statutes might not help the PAN to select more attractive candidates for office. As one member of the party's National Executive Committee who led the statutory reform committee in 2001 complained,

The statutory reform that was approved in 2001 fell short of our expectations. We could not convince the majority of the National Council and the National Assembly to approve a more comprehensive reform. In the meantime, we need to assure that we select more attractive candidates for the upcoming election. Unfortunately, our statutes do not help us in this matter. We will need to find "extra-statutory" means to nominate more attractive candidates. That is, we need to invite outsiders to run as candidates, and this is something we can do because the National Executive Committee needs to approve all the nominations. Although we cannot do this in every single district, we know full well that we cannot win the elections if we only nominate panistas as candidates.[50]

Clients versus Citizens: The PAN's Linkages to the Electorate

Before 1989, when the PAN did not win elections routinely, the party invested most of its resources in organizing attractive electoral campaigns. It exploited the existing discontent with the PRI and the government to mobilize wide sectors of the population and portrayed itself as the alternative against corruption, inefficiency, and authoritarianism. Without access to power, the PAN did not have enough incentives to design further strategies of political mobilization beyond the electoral period, other than preparing for the next electoral campaign. With growing access to government positions, however, the PAN has now been forced to overcome its traditional electoral bias and to define new strategies to support its governments and maintain its hold on power. But here also is where the party has confronted serious problems.

As a self-conceived "party of citizens" based on individual and voluntary affiliation, the PAN has rejected the notion of building a mass-based party organization. To do so would mean catering to the demands of its constituencies, including extending patronage and individual favors in exchange for political support.[51] The PAN associates these activities with the PRI and rejects them on the grounds that they are illegal and illegitimate.

According to Gibson (1996), governing parties in competitive party systems face two fundamental tasks: they need to win elections, and they need to introduce effective public policies. That is, parties need to demonstrate competence in office, and they need to design strategies to survive in the electoral arena. To achieve these ends, political parties must bring together a policy coalition and an electoral coalition. The former is important for allowing the party to define its priorities and implement its policies; the latter is critical for mobilizing and keeping its ties with the electorate.

Although these tasks are interrelated and reinforcing, once in office the PAN has tended to give higher priority to the policy arena than to keeping and broadening its ties with the electorate. In part, this stems from the entrepreneurial origin of many panista government officials and their conviction that the electorate will increasingly judge the party on its successful government's performance.[52] But as we shall see, good government performance is not necessarily rewarded at the polls. As the PAN has come to realize, people do not necessarily vote for the incumbent party even when they are satisfied with its performance in office.

The PAN's greater emphasis on the policy arena is also the result of its unwillingness to acknowledge the importance of servicing constituencies and engaging in community work as a means of maintaining and expanding its ties to the electorate. The PAN rejects clientelism and corporatism as forms of social organization and political participation. But they have not been able to define a viable alternative for linking organized social groups to the party on a more permanent basis.

As Shefter contends (1994), although a political party can win an election by mobilizing the electorate in opposition to the existing regime, it usually needs to rely on the construction of a mass-based political organization to remain in power.[53] In short, to ensure their political survival, parties need to find new ways of linking the electorate to the party on a more continuous basis and of rewarding its constituencies with material incentives, private benefits, and clear public benefits. But herein is where the PAN encounters serious conceptual difficulties.

Panistas generally reject the distribution of "material incentives" as a way of maintaining and increasing their constituencies. They distinguish themselves from the PRI in this respect precisely because they regard this practice as morally questionable and illegitimate. A former president of the party expressed the matter clearly: "The party is not *caritas*. It is a group of citizens that get together to discuss public issues."[54] Even more revealing is the opinion of two panista deputies in Chihuahua who considered that "the task of deputies is to become agents of laws rather than agents of services."[55]

The PAN's failure to find an alternative means of social organization and its refusal to engage in patronage activities as a way to cater to its constituencies has become increasingly costly. The party often fails to win consecutive elections. Equally significant, panista public officials often feel abandoned by their own party.

In his confrontation with the teachers' union in Chihuahua, one of the state's most powerful organizations linked to the PRI, Governor Barrio was left alone. His party did not help him to establish new ties with teachers who might have benefited from the government's efforts to fight against a corrupt and inefficient union leadership.[56] Of his experience in Baja California, former Governor Ruffo said,

> The PAN is floating above society. It lacks a social structure of support. When I was governor I was left alone fighting against a myriad of corporatist organizations linked to the PRI. The PAN did not try to organize disaffected members of these groups and link them to the party. For example, they could have created an organization of "panista taxi drivers." . . . The PAN also did not want to engage in community service activities [*gestión social*]. Had they done that, they would have made my job much easier.[57]

Organizing people by trade or other shared interests does not necessarily entail replicating PRI's corporatist strategies of political control and manipulation. Furthermore, it is important to recognize that not all forms of clientelism or pork barrel politics are necessarily illegal and illegitimate. A local deputy of the PAN in Chihuahua who was critical of his party's lack of social involvement said, "The party needs to engage in casework activity; without doing anything illegal, it is important to recognize that people often need a little bit of circus and a little bit of theater."[58]

Political parties in democratic countries engage in clientelist practices as a matter of course. Casework, patronage, and community organizing are part and parcel of their activities (Fiorina, Cain, and Ferejohn, 1987; Coleman, 1996). As Jonathan Fox (1994, 153) argues, these activities become illegal and illegitimate when the right to associational autonomy is violated, that is, when coercion is employed to affect people's political choices. Material benefits might be distributed to different social groups in a democratic way when these benefits are not conditioned on the surrendering of social organizations' right to express their interests autonomously.

By leaving government officials alone and by failing to find alternatives to the PRI's clientelistic and corporatist strategies, the PAN tends to wear out as a result of its own electoral successes. This not only affects the party in subsequent elections; it also endangers the very institutions of political representation in a democratic government. Without solid political parties deeply entrenched in society, people have fewer mechanisms to hold their governments accountable and to reward or punish them for their actions. Perhaps more important, the fewer the number of electors who feel attached to political parties, the more vulnerable the political system becomes to demagogic, populist, and "delegatory" leaders (Budge and Farlie, 1976; O'Donnell, 1994).

Different Responses to the Same Constraints:
Chihuahua, Baja California, and Guanajuato

After the midterm elections of 1992 in Baja California, Governor Ruffo realized that the party needed to develop stronger electoral coalitions to remain in power. Although the PAN was able to retain control of the municipal governments it had won in 1989, it won by a small margin. Furthermore, the PAN lost one seat in the local congress (Lujambio, 2000).[59] In Ruffo's more pragmatic view, the PAN's ideology was ill suited to the realities of the country: "The PAN believes we are all citizens. The reality is that society still lacks political consciousness and organization. I agree that it is better to teach people to fish, but I became convinced that while they learn, it is also necessary to give them fish."[60]

Ruffo implemented a social program called Manos a la Obra (Hands On), which engaged party operators in public works projects throughout the state. In a fashion not too different from the PRI, Ruffo appointed panista activists in different communities to help people organize for public works projects.[61] He accepted that these activities were typically associated with the PRI, but, he said, "I realized I had to think as a priísta and become involved in their own logic. I basically decided I needed to go into the communities, encourage people to organize for community projects, and reap the political benefits of these efforts."[62] In the end, Ruffo's strategy proved efficient. The PAN was able to break into traditional priísta constituencies, further debilitating the PRI, which since its electoral defeat in 1989 had been besieged by factional strife.[63] Even though the PAN nominated a traditional panista, and one without any charismatic appeal, it won the gubernatorial elections in 1995.[64]

In Guanajuato, the PAN implemented a similar strategy, particularly after the midterm elections of 1994, in which the PAN lost almost all the municipal governments it had won in 1991. As the leader of the PAN in the state said,

> After the 1994 elections, we organized a strategy designed to establish a greater political presence at the neighborhood level. We sent political activists to different communities to work in social assistance projects. We realized that we had to work closer to the people and become involved with their concerns, particularly in the poor and rural neighborhoods where people only knew the PRI. At first, many panistas did not understand this strategy; they believed that an election could be won by organizing two months before the elections. The PAN is used to thinking about organizing the next elections, rather than devising a strategy for maintaining itself in power.[65]

Like the PRI's territorial organization, the PAN in Guanajuato created a territorial structure below the municipal committee, which is traditionally the PAN's lowest level of organization. According to the president of the PAN in the state, the PAN organized the so-called submunicipal committees throughout the forty-six municipalities in the state. By December 1996 they had established 850 submunicipal committees, and by 1998 they had 1,000. Their goal was to organize 2,000 submunicipal committees by the year 2000.[66]

This panista political machine is actively engaged in social assistance projects: it provides services such as legal advice and medical attention for the poor; it helps people find jobs, get scholarships for their children, and gain access to government officials. It also helps people organize at the neighborhood level to gain access to the government's programs and benefits. In addition, it distributes party literature and advertises the government's achievements throughout the community. The heads of the submunicipal committees meet regularly with the head of the municipal committee, as well as with local deputies and mayors (when they are panistas). As the leader of the municipal committee in León, Guanajuato, put it, "The key to anticipated success is the formation and training of party cadres."[67]

Many journalists, academics, and even some panista leaders have criticized the PAN in Guanajuato for creating a political machine like that of the PRI. Indeed, the PAN in Guanajuato not only built a similar machine; it also incorporated into its ranks the leaders and members of some of the former priísta peasant and urban-poor organized groups. The Liga Agraria (Agrarian League) and the Movimiento Popular Ciudadano (Popular Citizens' Movement) became two new institutional mechanisms for integrating these groups into the PAN in Guanajuato.[68]

In contrast to these more exceptional experiences in Baja California and Guanajuato, the PAN in Chihuahua and Jalisco collapsed after winning office in 1992 and 1995 respectively. As I argued above, in these states, the PAN not only failed to expand its organization; it also behaved as an opposition party, blocking many of the governors' initiatives in Congress. As a former high-level government official in Chihuahua said, "PAN has not developed strategies to defend their own governments. The PAN has been a party used to resisting, not supporting. If they only know how to push, when one asks them to pull, they don't know how to do that."[69]

After the 1995 midterm elections in Chihuahua, when the PAN lost its majority in Congress and in most of the cities it had won in 1992, the governor openly admitted that something in his administration had gone wrong; that he needed to establish closer ties to society as a whole (Aziz Nassif, 1996, 49).

The government introduced a new public works program modeled after the Manos a la Obra program in Baja California, designed to enhance its visibility at the community level. The governor's Jalemos Parejo (Working Together) program, however, did not have a political infrastructure. Lacking political PAN agents at the neighborhood level, the program fell into the hands of the PRI's well-structured territorial organizations.[70]

The PAN's electoral defeat in the 1998 elections was only a confirmation of a longer electoral trend. Since its victory in 1992, the PAN had lost all elections in the state. Its leaders at the state level recognized that they had failed to extend their organization beyond the municipal level. As the party's director of organization in the state admitted,

> We failed to seize the opportunity to expand our organization when we controlled the state government. . . . We now realize how important it is to be able to reach out to the neighborhood level, to service the constituencies, and increase the presence of the party between elections. Now we are doing it, but of course, without controlling the government, things are much more difficult now.[71]

In Jalisco, the PAN also performed poorly in the midterm elections. In 1998 the PAN lost 47 percent of the municipalities it had won in the previous election. In Congress, the PAN also lost the majority it had won in 1995.[72] As a scholar in Jalisco argued, "The problem in this state is that people perceive that their vote counts, but they do not know what democracy is for. The main problem is that parties do not engage in casework or social activities, and as a result, people perceive political parties as social clubs."[73] In other states controlled by the PAN, such as Querétaro, Morelos, and Nuevo León, the party has also failed to expand its organization and entrench itself in society.[74]

A consequence of political parties' failure to establish strong roots in society is that people do not develop long-term ties to them. That is, they do not develop strong partisan identities. This leaves parties extremely vulnerable in the electoral arena. As many authors now recognize, while candidates and issues are important electoral determinants, partisan identity is still the single most important determinant of electoral preference (Campbell et al., 1960; Fiorina, 1981).

According to Mainwaring (1995, 385), weak party roots are apparent not only in higher levels of electoral volatility but also in lower levels of partisan identification. The former is measured through electoral data; the latter is measured through survey questions.

Using survey data, the next chapter explores partisan identification and the extent of the PAN's entrenchment in society in three states—two where it controlled the government and one where it was in the opposition. While this is important for explaining the PAN's electoral performance in these states, it also contributes to understanding the relevance of other factors, such as candidate and government performance, for influencing people's voting choices.

The Voters' Perspective

Explaining the PAN's Electoral Performance

In democracies elected officials are motivated to respond to people's needs and demands to remain in office. In authoritarian regimes, on the contrary, elected officials can be less responsive to the public because their political careers do not necessarily depend on the electorate's judgment about their performance in office. In a country that is experiencing a transition to democracy, such as Mexico, one might expect elected officials to become increasingly interested in their performance in office. Even where reelection is not permitted, electoral competitiveness motivates elected officials to worry about their reputations, for their political careers greatly depend on the performance of their party in subsequent elections.[1]

If competition leads government officials to demonstrate their competence in the task of governing, to what extent does the logic of competition also affect voters' electoral choices? How much do people really care about government performance when they cast their votes? Do people use their votes to "punish" or "reward" political parties for their performance in office?

In the case of Mexico these questions become extremely relevant, because opposition parties, in particular the PAN,[2] have faced enormous problems maintaining their electoral coalitions in subsequent elections. This is the case even when they introduce innovative reforms designed to increase the government's efficiency. Indeed, the PAN has endeavored to distinguish itself from the PRI by combating corruption, inefficiency, and authoritarianism, which traditionally have been associated with this party. Typically, when the PAN loses an election, the winner is not the left of center opposition party (the PRD) but the PRI.[3]

The central purpose of this chapter is to analyze people's evaluations of government performance and to explore the relationship between these evaluations and voting preference. I compare and contrast public opinion in three states that have experienced growing competition but different electoral trajectories: Chihuahua, Guanajuato, and Puebla.[4] The PAN controlled the former two states at the time of the survey; the PRI has controlled the latter uninterrupted since 1929. However, in Chihuahua, the PAN lost the elections in 1998; in Guanajuato, the PAN has become the dominant political force in the state.

By comparing two states controlled by the PAN with a state controlled by the PRI, I also attempt to shed light on the determinants of electoral behavior in an emerging democratic setting. More concretely, I explore whether the electorate behaves differently in states that have already experienced a change in power than in states where the PRI has never lost the governorship.[5]

As I elaborate below, the relationship between evaluations of government performance and voting preference has been widely analyzed in the literature on electoral behavior. According to the theory of party realignment, satisfaction with government performance greatly affects the propensity to vote for the incumbent party. Thus, as Flanigan and Zingale (1998, 57) argue, after a party has been rejected by the electorate, the new party in office faces greater incentives to introduce innovative policies, often in sharp departure from the past. If people perceive these policies as successful, then significant numbers of voters will become partisans of the new administration's party and will continue to vote for this party in subsequent elections. If, on the other hand, voters are not satisfied with the administration's policies, then they will reject the party in the next election, and its victory would be regarded, in retrospect, as exceptional.

Many panistas believe that the difficulties the PAN has encountered in consecutive elections stem precisely from people's propensity to become disappointed with their new government. Citizens, like consumers, tend to judge their sense of satisfaction in relation to their expectations of the future rather than in relation to their experience in the past. In their view, the PAN's most important weakness is its failure to adequately advertise the government's achievements. People do not necessarily know what their governments have accomplished. The corollary is that better communication could close the gap between people's expectations and actual delivery of results.[6]

In my view this interpretation is too simplistic. I argue that evaluations of government performance, while important, were not so decisive in shaping electoral behavior in the three states studied. First, there is no evidence that voters in Chihuahua were disappointed with the policies introduced by the panista administration. Second and more important, the relationship between evaluations of performance and voting preference is not direct. It is mediated by people's attitudes toward political parties and, more particularly, their degree of partisan identification. The latter, as I have discussed in this book, crucially depends on what parties (not only governments) do between elections.

People do not necessarily reward good performance with a vote in favor of the incumbent party if it fails to maintain strong links with the electorate between elections and if it does not select attractive candidates for subsequent elections. Parties gain a reputation not only for what their governments accomplish but also for the extent to which they cater to their constituencies, respond to their needs, represent them, and become involved in the life of the communities beyond the electoral period. The latter includes a wide range of activities: providing affordable legal advice, organizing free clinics and shelters for battered women, funding scholarships, pressing the relevant authorities to meet the demands of the community, making elected officials accountable, training leaders to organize for collective action, assisting mutual aid societies, and promoting cultural and other recreational events. In sum, parties are rewarded when they become relevant actors in the day-to-day affairs of the community.

Using the terminology developed in this book, I argue that catch-all parties are better prepared to maintain their constituencies in highly competitive electoral settings. These parties are greatly entrenched in society, and they also enjoy higher degrees of flexibility to respond to the needs of a diverse and increasingly demanding electorate.

Although evaluations of government performance exert a stronger influence on voting behavior in states that have experienced alternation in power (Chihuahua and Guanajuato) than in states where the PRI has never lost an election (Puebla), these evaluations are not sufficiently strong to determine voting preference. Partisan identity is still the single most important predictor of electoral preference in all three states. The main challenge therefore is to investigate the factors that shape people's attitudes toward political parties.

After a brief overview of the major theoretical approaches on electoral behavior, I present the results of the surveys and examine the determinants of electoral preference in Mexico.

Theories of Electoral Behavior in Democratic Elections

Political parties' electoral performance depends to a large extent on the voters' motivations and decisions. Analyzing the determinants of electoral preference thus becomes central to understanding parties' electoral performance. Given a range of choices, what makes people vote for one party and not another? Why do some people vote more consistently than others? What can parties do to expand their electorates? To analyze these questions, we turn to the theoretical approaches developed in the United States, where substantial research on electoral behavior has been conducted.[7] Traditionally, this research has been dominated by two main theoretical approaches. On the one hand, the sociopsychological approach introduced by the Michigan School (Campbell et al., 1960) emphasizes the importance of voters' *attitudes* as critical determinants of electoral preference. On the other hand, the rational choice approach introduced by Anthony Downs (1957) stresses that electoral preference is the product of the voters' rational *evaluation* of a particular economic or political situation (Fiorina, 1981; Niemi and Weisberg, 1992, 9). The first theoretical approach poses that electoral behavior is heavily determined by the voters' partisan identity and by the attractiveness of the candidates competing for office. Voters do not necessarily have to make judgments about the issues or evaluate the consistency of the proposals. They vote for a particular party either because they identify with that party or because they are simply attracted by its candidates. Electoral behavior reflects an attitude, not an evaluation. On the contrary, the second theoretical approach gives greater weight to the voters' rational evaluations of the issues being discussed; the vote reflects a retrospective evaluation of the party (or candidate) in office or a judgment on the consistency of the proposals.

At the center of the voting behavior debate is the relative weight of candidates, party identity, and issues as determinants of voting preference. Specifically, the controversy revolves around how rational the electorate is after all. Recent studies have attempted to demonstrate how attitudes and rationality are not necessarily mutually exclusive. It is not irrational to vote against a charismatic and attractive candidate that is judged incompetent to solve a particularly pressing problem. Similarly, it is not irrational to support an incumbent party that is negatively evaluated for its performance in office if the alternative is considered worse (Fiorina, 1981, 56; Niemi and Weisberg, 1993, 143). As Fiorina argues, electoral preference is multidetermined, and it might be self-defeating to try to segment electoral behavior into its constituent parts.

> We tend to think of voting behavior as a neatly divisible act: so many parts to issues, so many parts to candidates, so many parts to retrospective evaluations, the rest to party affiliations. Logically then, when we expect someone to rely more on retrospective evaluations, we expect that person to rely less on other things. But maybe what we think of as separable parts are actually intertwined, with the current issues and experiences becoming part of the stuff of retrospective evaluations that cumulate into a kind of long-term party judgment that in turn affects the interpretation of current issues and experiences. (1981, 56)

Candidates, party affiliations, and retrospective evaluations are all interrelated, yet most analytic perspectives on electoral behavior tend to stress one of these factors above the others. Accordingly, the "personal vote" theory stresses that the personal qualities and attributes of the candidates exert a strong influence on electoral preference. In the age of mass media and advertising, the personalities and records of the candidates, independent of their parties, are what becomes most attractive to the electorate.

Candidates build their campaigns around their personal qualities as leaders; they rely heavily on the mass media to promote their image and convince the electorate and are sometimes ready to depart from the traditional lines espoused by their parties in order to broaden their appeal. In countries where public officials can be reelected, candidates also build their personal reputations based on their past records in office (Fiorina, 1987).

While the impact of candidates is undeniable, in reality it is difficult to separate the candidates from their parties. As Aldrich (1995, 48) points out, even if today's elections seem "candidate centered," few candidates have any serious chance of winning an election on their own: "Candidates with any serious hopes are always invariably partisan." Moreover, although it is conceivable that candidates may depart from certain positions espoused by their parties to attract electoral support, it is unlikely that they will go too far. Parties are still crucial for providing candidates with a point of reference and thus reducing the cost of information about their policies and issues. Affiliation with a political party brings the candidate a "natural reputation" (Aldrich, 1995, 49).

Recognizing the difficulty of isolating the candidates from their parties, Fiorina and others have sought to analyze the weight of the candidate's personal attributes on electoral preference. Their conclusions are that while party identification has primacy in influencing voters' choice, the personal characteristics of candidates is a close second (Fiorina, 1987, 167).

Given that Mexican elected officials cannot be reelected, the candidates' previous record in office seems unlikely to exert a strong influence on voting preference.[8] Without the possibility of reelection, the candidates' personal reputations are linked to their parties' collective reputations. Still, personal characteristics such as communication skills and even appearance can be quite important in attracting electoral support. And, as we shall see below, the majority of the Mexican electorate believes that the candidate is more important than the party in deciding whom to vote for.

Although on closer examination it becomes clear that party identity filters people's opinion about their candidates, we can still hypothesize that candidates and policies exert a more important influence on electoral preference for people who lack partisan identification, the so-called independents (or neutrals).

Candidates can also become critical factors in those cases in which the election is defined in terms of a PRI–anti-PRI cleavage. That is, in states that have not experienced alternation in power, elections are often mechanisms to express the extent of the support for or opposition to the PRI and the regime (Moreno, 1999b). People vote for the opposition because their candidates seem able to defeat the PRI and not because they like their policies or identify with their parties. To the extent that opposition voters are primarily interested in defeating the PRI and not in advancing their particular ideological positions, they can give their support to whatever opposition candidate seems more likely to win (Magaloni, 1996).[9] But in those states where the PRI has already been defeated once, non-PRI candidates can no longer mobilize the voters on the basis of opposition to the PRI regime. In addition to their attributes or qualities as leaders, they become attractive to the electorate if they successfully define the issues they stand for and are able to articulate a convincing political program. To do that effectively, they are often forced to rely on their parties and to appeal to their parties' collective reputation.

The party's collective reputation leads us to the second major theoretical approach on electoral preference. The "theory of retrospective voting" (Fiorina, 1981) posits that parties gain a reputation not only for their ideological positions but also for what they do once they are in office. That is, people make subjective evaluations of government performance and use their votes to express their degree of satisfaction or dissatisfaction with the government. If satisfied, they vote for the incumbent party (or candidate); if not, they vote for the opposition. The vote is thus used as a tool to punish or reward the government for its performance in office. According to this theory, people do not need to be sophisticated to form an opinion about government performance. They can recognize good government when they experience it. As Fiorina argues,

> They need not know the precise economic or foreign policies of the incumbent administration in order to see or feel the *results* of those policies. . . . If jobs have been lost in a recession, something is wrong. . . . If thugs make neighborhoods unsafe, something is wrong. . . . And to the extent that citizens vote on the basis of such judgments, elections do not signal the direction in which society should move so much as they convey an evaluation of where society has been. Rather than a prospective decision, the voting decision can be more of a retrospective decision." (1981, 5)

The question of course becomes whether citizens in fact vote on the basis of such judgments. Although rationally it may seem quite logical to punish or reward the government with one's vote, the relationship between government performance evaluations and electoral preference is far more complicated. The first problem is that parties do not always get credit for what their governments accomplish. If elected officials distance themselves from their parties and are considered responsible for their own actions, then the judgment about their performance might not be transferred to their parties. This is especially the case if officials cannot be reelected. Second, party identity may bias one's opinion about government's performance. Democrats tend to evaluate Democratic governments better than Republicans, and vice versa (Weisberg, 1984, 456). Third, not all aspects of government performance have the same importance for voters. While the state of the economy is usually recognized as critical in influencing electoral behavior (MacKuen, Erikson, and Stimson, 1992; Markus, 1993), other issues such as unemployment and public safety might be more relevant for voters (Fiorina, 1981). A negative evaluation regarding a particular policy might be electorally damaging even if on all other realms the government is positively evaluated. Fourth, in the case of Mexico, where opposition parties have only recently begun to gain access to government, their record is still too meager to gain a reputation for their performance in office. While people can tell a good government from a bad one, they do not necessarily associate the government's performance with their party if the latter fails to work closely with the government, advertise the government's achievements, represent its constituencies, and become present and relevant in the life of the community. Furthermore, we can hypothesize that while a poor performance is more readily punished at the polls, a good performance is not always rewarded if people fail to develop stronger and long-term ties with the incumbent party.

The development of long-term ties to a party relates to the question of party identity, the third major analytic approach on electoral behavior. As many authors recognize, party identification is the single most important predictor of voting behavior (Campbell et al., 1960; Fiorina, 1981). People vote for a particular party because they identify with this party's ideological positions and policy stands. Moreover, particularly in the United States, partisan identity is considered more stable than the actual voting choice (Le Duc, 1981). The question is, what are the bases of partisan identity? In part, partisan identity is undoubtedly based on emotional, not rational, grounds. It might derive from long-rooted family traditions or from deep ideological convictions that sometimes go beyond a rational argumentation. But partisan identity is also based on rational evaluations of the party's performance in office. These evaluations include judgments about the government's capacity to deal with major policy issues (Flanigan and Zingale, 1998) as well as concrete experiences with the party's engagement in people's daily life. The latter ranges from casework and constituency service activities to patronage and clientelism (Lawson, Pomper, and Moakley, 1986; Coleman, 1996).

In Mexico, in particular, where for decades opposition parties played a marginal role in the electoral arena, the number of people strongly identified with them on ideological or traditional grounds is still too limited to be electorally significant. In those places where the opposition was able to win an election, it managed to attract a large percentage of voters who were discontented with the status quo and who did not have a strong partisan identity. Once in power, however, the main challenge for these parties is to build a large base of loyalists who remain active between elections and safeguard their grip on power.

As I have argued elsewhere (Mizrahi, 1999), winning against the PRI the first time is no guarantee of future victories, because the first victory might have more to do with an effective mobilization in opposition to the PRI than with a positive identification with the party in question. To that end, opposition parties need to become more proactive and programmatic and to maintain a close check on elected officials' behavior.

Here is precisely where the different approaches to electoral behavior interrelate. In contrast to the PRI, which can largely build on tradition, habit, and an extended patronage network, opposition parties have to build their mass of loyalists using their record in office, the nomination of attractive candidates, and an alternative network of patronage as an incentive. The latter, in particular, requires disassociating patronage activities from the corrupt and authoritarian clientelist practices traditionally associated with the PRI.[10] The aim in the long run is to forge partisan identities, for this is still considered the stablest basis of electoral support.

Partisan Identity, Retrospective Evaluations, and Candidate Attractiveness:
Electoral Preference in Chihuahua, Puebla, and Guanajuato

The results of the 1998 elections in the states of Chihuahua and Puebla are
intriguing and seem paradoxical. The government in Chihuahua was generally positively evaluated for its performance in office, and yet the PAN lost the
elections in the state. In Puebla, in contrast, despite a less favorable evaluation
of government performance, people overwhelmingly continued to support
the incumbent party, the PRI.

Furthermore, if we look at the parties' electoral trajectories, it becomes
even more puzzling that throughout the *sexenio* (six-year term) of Governor
Francisco Barrio, the PAN failed to maintain its leading position in Chihuahua, a state considered one of the most important electoral strongholds of
this party. As Chart 6.1 shows, after 1992, the PAN lost in virtually all subsequent elections. Moreover, abstention increased substantially, from 37 percent
in 1992 to 43 percent in 1998.[11] The results of the 1998 elections only confirmed
a longer electoral trend. As the first state to be "reconquered" by the PRI in a
clean election, these outcomes pose important questions about the strength
of the PAN, particularly when one considers the PRI's eroding prestige at the
national level.

Chart 6.1   Electoral Results in Chihuahua, 1992–1998

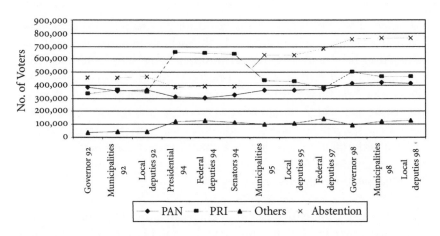

In Puebla, in contrast to Chihuahua, the PRI was able to maintain its dominant position throughout the sexenio of Governor Manuel Bartlett. As
Chart 6.2 shows, the PRI won most of the subsequent elections at the local,

state, and federal levels. Although the PAN won a number of important cities in 1995,[12] it by no means challenged the dominance of the PRI in the state. By 1998 the PRI managed to regain control in most of these cities. Moreover, in the federal elections of 1997, the PAN's share of the vote fell even behind the left-of-center PRD. Puebla can be regarded as a typical case of PRI dominance in the context of growing electoral competitiveness.[13]

Chart 6.2   Electoral Results in Puebla, 1992–1998

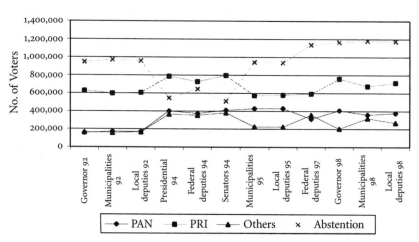

Compared with these two states, the electoral trend in Guanajuato shows that unlike Chihuahua but like Puebla, the incumbent party (the PAN) has managed to maintain its dominant position in the state. After Governor Vicente Fox was elected in 1995 (see Chart 6.3), the PAN won in subsequent state and local elections. Furthermore, in the 2000 gubernatorial race, the PAN won the election with a margin of 22.6 percentage points.[14]

How can we explain these electoral outcomes? How important are government performance evaluations in influencing electoral behavior after all?

Evaluations of Government Performance

In increasingly competitive electoral environments, public officials have greater incentives to become more responsive and responsible to the electorate, for they have to account to this electorate at the polls. Even if elected public officials cannot be reelected, their political careers greatly depend on their party's electoral performance. A vote against the incumbent party can

Chart 6.3   Electoral Results in Guanajuato, 1991–2000

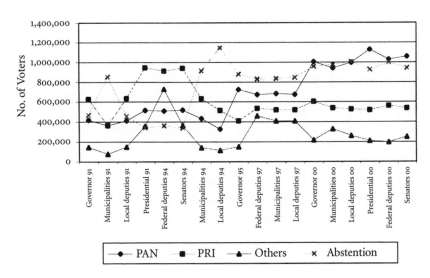

be interpreted as public repudiation for their performance in office, a situation that profoundly damages their reputation for subsequent elections.[15] Electoral competitiveness enhances the incentives for good government performance to the extent that people base their electoral preference on their judgments about government performance.

If we compare the evaluations of government performance in Chihuahua, Puebla, and Guanajuato, it is not clear that these evaluations exert a direct influence on electoral behavior. But in the two states that have experienced alternation of power, these evaluations play a more significant role in shaping electoral preference.

The main goal of analyzing evaluations of government performance is to provide some measures of people's degrees of satisfaction with their government's administration and its capacity to solve important problems in their state. To be fair, however, it is important that we take into account the policy areas for which the state government, rather than the federal or local governments, is mainly responsible. In a heavily centralized country like Mexico, this is particularly important, for many policy areas still remain in the hands of the federal government.

Thus, in designing the surveys, we considered people's evaluations in the areas of education, public works, public safety, employment, and the government's capacity to solve the most important problem in the state. The questionnaire did not include health or housing, for these areas began to be decentralized only in 1998.

The evaluation of government performance in each of these policy areas was given a value on a scale of 0 to 10, where 0 means an extremely poor evaluation and 10 an excellent evaluation of government performance.[16] We then created an Index of Government Performance (IGP) that averages people's evaluations in these five policy areas. The index also uses a scale of 0 to 10.[17]

According to this index, in Chihuahua, government's performance was rated at 5.75, and as can be seen in Table 6.1, 62 percent of the population surveyed rated government performance above 5.[18]

In Puebla, the electorate overall rated the government's performance at only 3.8, and as this table shows, 52.5 percent of the population surveyed rated government performance below 5.[19] In Guanajuato, government performance was rated at 5.4, and 57 percent of those interviewed rated government performance above 5.[20]

Table 6.1   Evaluations of Government Performance in Chihuahua, Puebla, and Guanajuato

IGP (scale 0–10)

	Very bad (0–2.5)	Bad (2.5–5)	Good (5–7.5)	Excellent (7.5–10)
Chihuahua	7%	31%	43%	19%
Puebla	2.5%	50%	22%	3%
Guanajuato	6%	36.1%	49.1%	8.7%

We see a similar pattern in the evaluations of the governor. The governor was more favorably evaluated in Chihuahua (64%) and Guanajuato (60%) than in Puebla (42%).

We asked people to evaluate whether their economic situation as well as that of their state in general improved or worsened during the course of the year. In the case of Chihuahua, 45 percent of the surveyed population believed the state's economic situation had worsened and only 36 percent believed their personal economic situation had deteriorated. Thirty-two percent believed that their personal and the state's economic situation had improved.

In contrast, in Puebla, 72 percent of the people surveyed believed the economic situation in the state had worsened and 61 percent believed their personal economic situation had deteriorated. Only 14 percent believed that their personal as well as the state's economic conditions had improved. In

Guanajuato, only 19 percent of those surveyed believed the state's economic situation had worsened and 22 percent believed their personal economic situation had deteriorated. Thirty percent believed their personal economic situation had improved, and 40 percent believed the state's economic situation had improved.

Finally, we asked people to tell us what they considered more important for the next governor, that there be continuity or change? As we see in Charts 6.4 and 6.5, more than half of the surveyed population in Chihuahua (64%) said they wanted continuity, while in Puebla, more than half of the population (62%) said they wanted change. The survey did not include this question in Guanajuato.

The surveys demonstrate that the governments of Chihuahua and Guanajuato were evaluated more positively than the government in Puebla. Yet the

Chart 6.4   Electoral Preference According to Desire for Change or Continuity

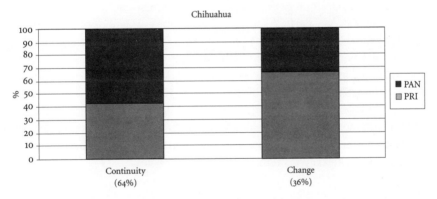

Chart 6.5   Electoral Preference According to Desire for Change or Continuity

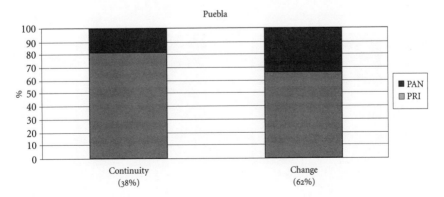

negative evaluations of performance in Puebla did not seem to affect the PRI in the electoral arena, particularly when the great majority of the people said they wanted change rather than continuity. In Puebla, 60 percent of the people surveyed said they would vote for the PRI in the next election, and only 22 percent said they would vote for the PAN. The opposite was the case in Chihuahua. Positive performance evaluations did not reflect the voters' electoral preference: a majority (49%) of the people surveyed said they would vote for the PRI in the next election, and 41 percent said they would vote for the PAN.

This is a puzzling outcome. First, in Puebla, notwithstanding the negative evaluations of government performance, the PRI enjoyed a comfortable cushion of support. In contrast, in Chihuahua, the PAN was "punished" by the electorate even when the vast majority of the electorate was relatively satisfied with the government's performance. And finally, in Guanajuato, similar to the PRI in Puebla, the PAN continued to be supported by the majority of the electorate.

To examine more closely the relationship between government performance evaluations and electoral preference, we combined these two variables in Charts 6.6, 6.7, and 6.8. As Chart 6.6 shows, in Puebla, the evaluations of government performance seem to bear a weak relationship to electoral preference. The PRI was the net winner among those who evaluated government performance poorly as well as among those who evaluated government performance positively. Although the PAN had its highest percentage of the vote among those who evaluated the government negatively, the PRI still managed to become the net winner with more than 60 percent of the vote. This cushion of support evidently stems from other sources: a strong partisan identity and/or the lack of a viable and attractive alternative. I return to these points below.

Chart 6.6   Electoral Preference According to Evaluations of Government Performance

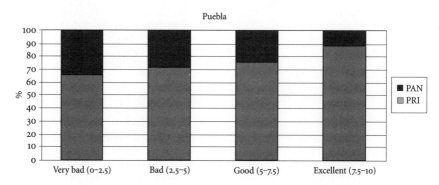

In contrast, in Guanajuato and Chihuahua, a clearer relationship seems to exist between government performance evaluations and electoral preference. Indeed, in both states, the majority of those who evaluated government performance negatively said they would vote for the PRI, and those who judged the government's performance positively said they would vote for the PAN. But, as Chart 6.7 shows in Guanajuato, the PAN had a greater cushion of support than the PAN in Chihuahua, for the majority of those who gave bad evaluations of the government (between 2.5 and 5), still said they would support the PAN. In Chihuahua, as Chart 6.8 shows, those who evaluated the government poorly were readier to punish the PAN with their votes.[21]

Chart 6.7   Electoral Preference According to Evaluations of Government Performance

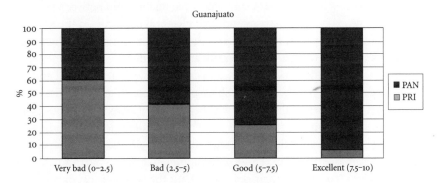

Chart 6.8   Electoral Preference According to Evaluations of Government Performance

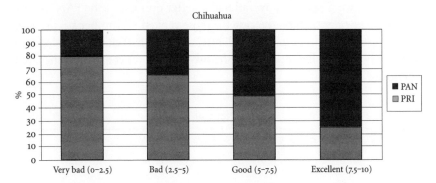

We might conclude that retrospective evaluations of government performance are more important in states that have experienced alternation in power. People might be readier to use their votes as a tool to express their degree of satisfaction with the government only when they have tried out an alternative to the PRI. Given their propensity to become disappointed with the government's results, voters tend to punish a bad performance while not necessarily rewarding a positive one. Yet if these evaluations are such important determinants of electoral preference, the PAN should have won the elections in Chihuahua, not the PRI, for the majority of the people evaluated the government satisfactorily, with a rate above 5. Evidently there are other factors influencing electoral behavior.

Partisan Identity

Given that performance evaluations do not seem to exert such a definitive impact on voting behavior, we explore now the relationship between people's attitudes toward political parties and their electoral behavior. At the end of a six-year term of government, what was the spectrum of partisan alignment in these states? On what is party identification based?[22]

To analyze attitudes toward the two main political parties, the PRI and the PAN, in each of these states, we classified people according to their degree of identification. We first asked people whether they considered themselves priístas or panistas or whether they lacked any political identification. Those who said they identified with the PRI or with the PAN were asked the intensity of their partisan identification. Those who claimed to have no partisan identity were ranked according to their opinions about the two political parties. Accordingly, those who said they were strong panistas, were ranked 1 on the scale and those who said they were strong priístas were ranked 9. Moderate panistas were ranked 2, and soft panistas 3. Moderate priístas were ranked 8, and soft priístas 7. Those without a partisan identity were ranked 4, 5, and 6. But the people who were ranked 4 overall had a better opinion of the PAN than of the PRI. The opposite was the case for those ranked 6. Number 5 represents those voters who had no partisan identity and who had either no opinion or an equally good or bad opinion of the two parties. We considered the latter "neutrals."[23]

Panista	Neutral	Priísta
1	5	9

As we can see in Chart 6.9, in Chihuahua at the end of the panista administration, there was a larger proportion of hard-line priístas than of hard-line panistas (21% vs. 15%). Although the total percentage of priístas and panistas in the state was similar (39%), their distribution on the scale of partisan identity (intensity level) was quite different. The so-called neutrals accounted for 21 percent of the population, a significant percentage, but not enough to have made a difference in terms of the final electoral outcome.

Chart 6.9   Partisan Identity

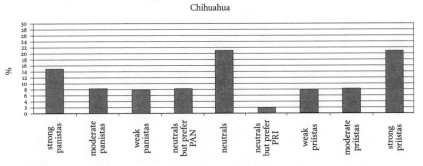

If we now analyze the scale of partisan identity in Puebla, we can see in Chart 6.10 that the proportion of priístas is enormous when compared to the panistas. Twenty-three percent of the total population were identified with the PAN, whereas 58 percent identified with the PRI. Furthermore, if we compare the proportion of hard-core panistas and priístas (1 and 9 on the spectrum), the disparity becomes even more obvious, for only 4 percent were identified as strong supporters of the PAN, while 27 percent were identified as strong priísta supporters. Given that the government was so badly evaluated for its performance, these results lead us to conclude that in the case of Puebla, the identification with the PRI was not related to a judgment about the quality of the government.

Chart 6.10   Partisan Identity

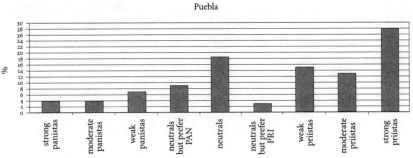

Finally, as Chart 6.11 shows, in the case of Guanajuato, the percentage of panista loyalists is far greater than that of the priísta loyalists (49% vs. 26%). Evidently, a major partisan realignment occurred in this state, since the PAN became a major political force only after 1991. The similarities between the scales of partisan identity in Puebla and Guanajuato (strong identification with the incumbent party), despite the obvious differences in the evaluation of government performance in these two states, lead us to conclude that partisan identity relies on something beyond the evaluation of government performance, namely, the party's activities between elections.

Chart 6.11   Partisan Identity

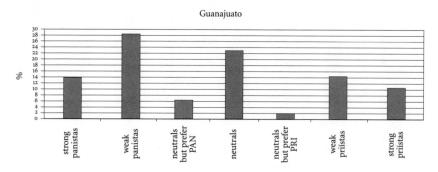

As is the case in many states controlled by the PRI, in Guanajuato the PAN was able to organize a widespread machine that allowed it to penetrate deep into the communities. Although the PAN did not change its candidate selection rules,[24] in terms of its territorial organization, it began to resemble a catch-all party more than a sectarian or electoral party at the state level. By contrast, in the case of Chihuahua, the PAN remained sectarian. After its victory in 1992, the governing PAN shrunk and became virtually paralyzed between elections. Many panista leaders in the state believed that the PAN would consolidate its presence throughout the state on the merits of the successful performance of its government. As one local deputy who became the leader of the PAN in the state said, "There is no doubt that we are better than the PRI. It is a matter of time before the results can be appreciated by people who have great expectations for the government."[25] The result was that even when people judged the government's performance satisfactory overall, the PAN failed to maintain its electoral coalitions in the state.

The corollary is that the presence and visibility of the political party on the ground is critical for building partisan identities. Political parties need to cater to their constituencies continuously, not only during electoral periods. Parties, not only their governments, need to build their reputations based on their own records of caring for their constituencies. While a large part of this activity can be based on patronage, it is important to recognize that not all forms of patronage are necessarily corrupt or morally questionable. Parties can service their constituencies by distributing goods and services without undermining people's freedom to express themselves, associate in political organizations, and freely decide who to vote for. Positive evaluations of government performance are not necessarily rewarded at the polls if the party fails to work closely with the community.

One of the methods to gauge people's perceptions about the relevance of political parties in their daily lives is to ask whether or not parties get involved in solving problems in their neighborhoods. Unfortunately, we do not have this question in the Guanajuato survey, but we can compare the cases of Puebla and Chihuahua.

Although in both Chihuahua and Puebla only a minority of people responded affirmatively to this question, in Chihuahua a mere 9.6 percent of the surveyed population believed political parties were relevant actors in their community, whereas in Puebla, 28.3 percent said political parties were engaged in their community's problems. Moreover, as could be expected, the majority of people named the PAN in Chihuahua (59%) and the PRI in Puebla (80%).

What these results suggest is that through their activities, political parties *can* promote a growing mass of supporters that become bound to parties on practical and not necessarily on ideological or programmatic terms. People may feel attached to a particular political party not because they are convinced of its ideology or policy proposals but because the party *does things* for them and helps them solve their problems. This form of identification with a political party is based on *rational* rather than *affective* grounds. And as Biorcio and Mannheimer (1998, 208) suggest, citizens can establish a "pragmatic" link with their parties when they "regard a political party as having the capacity to act effectively on what they consider to be important issues."

Moreover, as Fiorina, Cain, and Ferejohn (1987) argue for the United States and Great Britain, constituency service and casework activities have an important influence on voting behavior. In a country like Mexico where there is no reelection, it is the party, rather than the public official, that has the greatest incentive to become involved in these types of activities. More important, given the scarcities and unfulfilled needs that exist in Mexico, this type of community servicing seems even more rational as a method of promoting stronger links between citizens and political parties and of attracting greater electoral support.

To examine the strength of the relationship between partisan identity and voting behavior, we combined the scales of partisan identity with electoral preference in our three states. As Charts 6.12, 6.13, and 6.14 suggest, those people who identify with a political party voted overwhelmingly in support of that party. This is the case even for those who did not identify with the party but who had positive opinions of the party in question (numbers 4 and 6 for Chihuahua and Puebla, and 3 and 5 for Guanajuato, according to the scale of partisan identity).

In all three states, the party loyalists determined the electoral outcome; the neutrals were not decisive in any of our three cases. However, it is still interesting to analyze how the neutrals tended to vote. One might expect that for them, evaluations of the candidates and the government's performance are the most important factors in their voting decisions.

Chart 6.12   Electoral Preference According to the Scale of Partisan Identity

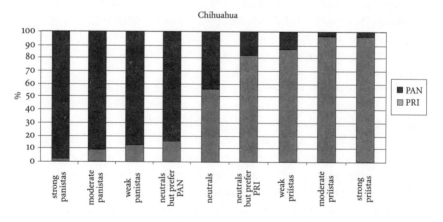

In the case of Chihuahua, the majority of the neutrals (58%) decided to support the opposition party, the PRI. The neutrals, accounting for 21 percent of the electorate, could have altered the electoral outcome only if they had voted overwhelmingly (by more than 70%) in support of the PAN. This could have happened only if these voters had evaluated the PAN's candidate much higher than the PRI's candidate or if they had evaluated government performance exceptionally well. Neither of these conditions was true. The neutrals evaluated government performance more like the priístas.[26] And, as we shall see below, these voters gave better evaluations to the PRI's candidate.

Chart 6.13   Electoral Preference According to the Scale of Partisan Identity

In the cases of Puebla and Guanajuato (Charts 6.13 and 6.14), the neutrals gave their support to the incumbent party by comfortable margins. However, these voters evaluated the government's performance more like the opposition (the panistas in Puebla, and the priístas in Guanajuato).[27] For these voters it seems that performance evaluations were not critical in deciding electoral preference. We might conclude that neutrals in these two states decided to support the incumbent party simply because they did not perceive a better alternative. This is clearer in the case of Puebla, where the panista candidate was barely known by the majority of the electorate.

Chart 6.14   Electoral Preference According to the Scale of Partisan Identity

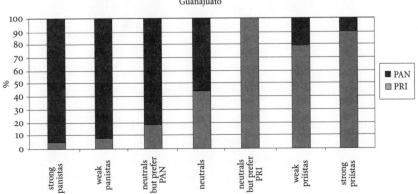

Candidates

In Chihuahua and Puebla, the surveys were conducted a month and a half before the elections.[28] The candidates for governor in these two states were actively engaged in their campaigns. In the case of Chihuahua, both candidates were widely known by the great majority (67%) of the electorate.[29]

In the case of Puebla, only the PRI candidate was widely known. More than 65 percent said they recognized the PRI's candidate, whereas only 39 percent recognized the PAN's candidate. Recognition, however, did not seem to affect the electoral outcome; among those voters who knew both candidates, the PRI candidate was still the overwhelming winner (62% vs. 38%).

To examine the importance of candidates for electoral behavior, we asked people what was more important in their voting decision, the party or the candidate. We then analyzed the voting preference among those who responded that the candidate was more important. As we see in Charts 6.15 and 6.16, in Chihuahua, the PRI wins by a slight margin of 52 percent against the PAN. In the case of Puebla, the PRI wins overwhelmingly with 69 percent of the vote.

Chart 6.15   Electoral Preference According to the Relative Importance of the Party or the Candidate

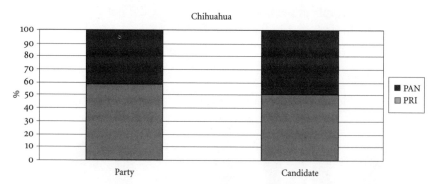

What these results reveal is that in highly competitive electoral contexts, as in Chihuahua, candidates could have made a difference in the final outcome. In the case of Puebla, on the other hand, it seems unlikely that a better or more widely known opposition candidate would have made much of a difference. In a state with this partisan profile, only an extremely charismatic candidate helped by an impending political or economic crisis could have made a difference in the final electoral outcome.

Chart 6.16   Electoral Preference According to the Relative Importance of
the Party or the Candidate

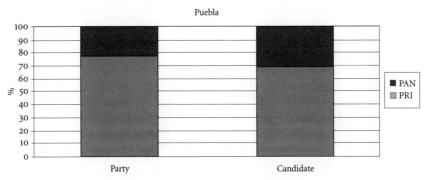

To measure people's evaluations of their candidates, we created an Index
of Candidate Evaluations that includes people's opinions regarding the candidates' attributes: honesty, capacity to rule, and proximity to the people. The
index goes from a scale of −3 to 3, where −3 means an extremely negative
evaluation and 3 an excellent evaluation. In the case of Chihuahua, the PAN's
candidate paradoxically obtained a higher evaluation than his PRI counter-
part. We might conclude that something more than the opinion about attributes, such as the image or the message, was at work. In the case of Puebla, the
PRI's candidate was better evaluated, but we know that the PAN's candidate
was virtually unknown.

As is the case with government performance evaluations, candidate evaluations are heavily influenced by voters' partisan identification. If we analyze
how voters across the spectrum evaluated the two main candidates, we see
in Charts 6.17 and 6.18 that party identification filters people's perception of
the candidates: panistas evaluate their candidate better than the priístas and
vice versa.[30]

The neutrals in both states, on the other hand, gave similar evaluations to
both candidates. In Chihuahua, where the margin of victory of the PRI was
8 percentage points, this outcome suggests that the neutrals could have voted
differently if the PAN had presented a more attractive candidate. But as we
have seen in previous chapters, the PAN nominated a traditional panista who
appealed mainly to the core of the panista constituency but could not reach
out to the larger electorate. Moreover, knowing that the majority of the electorate wanted continuity rather than change, the PRI's candidate, a businessman who resembled the types of candidates supported by the PAN in the past,

Chart 6.17   Evaluation of Candidates Across the Scale of Partisan Identity

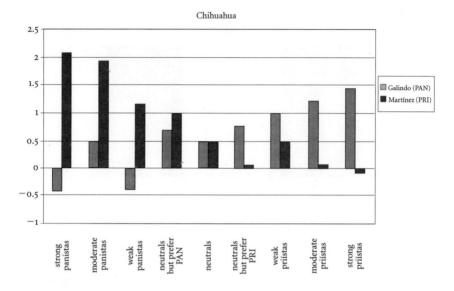

Chart 6.18   Evaluation of Candidates Across the Scale of Partisan Identity

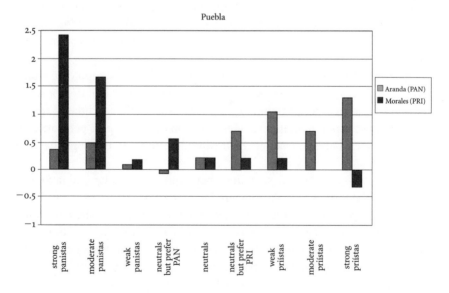

built his campaign around the topic of continuity. He promised to maintain the "continuity of change." The panista candidate, on the other hand, attacked the government for abandoning its commitment to the principles advocated by the PAN and promised to bring about change.

Given the lack of alternatives in the state of Puebla, the preference for change was circumscribed within the PRI. This was an issue that could have been relevant for the PRI's primary election but totally irrelevant for the general election. Given that the PRI's candidate was not the governor's favorite, it is plausible to suggest that people perceived that this candidate could bring about change.[31] The opposition was too marginal to make any difference.

We can conclude that in the case of Chihuahua, the PAN's candidate could have made a difference in altering the electoral outcome had he been more able to attract a significant percentage of neutrals. Although to a great extent the results of the election were defined by the people who were strongly identified with political parties, the neutrals could have altered the electoral results if they had been more convinced by the panista candidate. In the case of Puebla, on the other hand, candidates played a much smaller role. Given that the neutrals could not have altered the results of the elections, only an extremely charismatic leader helped by the sense of an impending crisis could have convinced people to change their voting preferences in this state. This did not occur.

Building "Cushions of Support" in Competitive Elections

In emerging competitive electoral settings, where political parties effectively compete for votes and where parties regularly win and lose elections, voters become increasingly sophisticated. They take into consideration a variety of factors that range from the attractiveness of the candidates and the consistency of their messages to the evaluation of the incumbent governments, identification with a particular political party, and an assessment of the existing alternatives, including abstaining from participating in the election. As Fiorina (1981) argues, the voting decision is not a neatly divisible act; it is rather a decision based on multiple and interrelated factors. And it becomes even more complex as the electoral environment becomes more competitive.

In Puebla, a state where the PRI has never lost power, the electorate votes primarily on the basis of its identification with the main political parties. In the absence of viable political alternatives, voters tend to be less sensitive to short-term factors such as government performance or the persuasiveness of the candidates' messages. People continued to identify with the PRI and to vote for this party despite their negative evaluation of government performance, the nomination of a priísta candidate who was strongly associated with the most conservative wing of the party, and a generalized opinion that change, rather than continuity, was preferable for the next government.

It is clear that in Puebla the PRI continues to enjoy a broad base of party loyalists, despite its reputation for corruption and authoritarianism and its eroding levels of support at the national level. As in many other states in the country, in Puebla the PRI operates as a mass bureaucratic party, a party with a widespread territorial organization that services its constituencies but that severely constrains office seekers' attempts to gain nomination. The PAN in Puebla, on the other hand, is too weak to make any electoral difference. With a fragile machine, a weak presence between elections, and a propensity to nominate sectarian candidates, the PAN is still unable to challenge the PRI. In states with this electoral and political profile, only an impending political or economic crisis coupled with the opposition's success in nominating a charismatic and electorally attractive candidate can bring about a change in electoral behavior.

In contrast, in Chihuahua and Guanajuato (which have both experienced an alternation of power), short-term factors became more and more relevant in people's voting decisions. While partisan identification still continues to be the single most important determinant of electoral preference, it is increasingly intertwined with the evaluations of government performance, the perceptions of competing candidates, and the activities of the party between elections. Together, these factors make up the political parties' reputation, a critical element in forging new partisan identities.

In Chihuahua, the PAN failed to build a cushion of support that could have protected it against the negative evaluations of government performance with regard to crime and the selection of a sectarian candidate. During the six years of panista government, the PRI managed to maintain (or expand) a larger base of hard-core supporters than the PAN. These voters were crucial for the final electoral outcome. Moreover, against its authoritarian tradition, the PRI introduced a primary election to select its candidate for governor. The candidate appealed to a broad electorate and promised to continue the panista government's achievements. Following our terminology, we can say that in Chihuahua, the PRI increasingly came to resemble a catch-all party. The PAN, on the other hand, remained essentially sectarian. In line with its traditional rules, the PAN nominated a candidate that appealed to the core of panista voters but that failed to attract the larger electorate. This candidate, moreover, distanced himself from the panista administration, arguing that it had failed to promote the traditional panista ideals and concerns, and he promised to bring about change.

In contrast to Chihuahua and Puebla, in Guanajuato, the PAN succeeded in building a machine that, like the PRI, worked closely with communities between elections. As a result, the PAN managed to create a larger base of hard-core supporters that outnumbers that of the PRI. Although in Guanajuato the PAN nominated a candidate associated with the most traditional and conservative wing of the party,[32] it has managed to become the dominant political party in the state. In the 2000 gubernatorial elections, the PAN won by a substantial margin.

In a country that is emerging from more than seventy years of one-party rule, partisan identity—other than priísta—is not well developed or entrenched. While many people have become discontented with the PRI, they are not ready to align themselves with a different political party. Electoral support for opposition parties does not necessarily reflect a longer-term commitment to these parties. If these parties do not work closely with their constituencies, their voters are easily lost.

The survey data collected in three Mexican states show that people are not fools; they can distinguish a good government from a bad one. Moreover, in competitive electoral contexts, good evaluations of government performance are critical in justifying and legitimating the party in power. But in isolation, good performance evaluations do not have a strong impact on electoral preference.

People do not reward a positive evaluation of performance with their votes if the governing party fails to work closely with them. The party is crucial for making the government's achievements relevant to the people. An administration that is left alone is too weak to persuade voters to continue to support the party. As Coleman (1996, 810) argues, strong parties are those that "live beyond election campaigns, have a sense of permanence and ongoing involvement in the community and in politics, and are engaged in matters such as party building that have effects beyond the next election."

To the extent that parties succeed in maintaining a mass of party loyalists, they build a cushion of support that protects them when they face short-term difficult economic or political situations or when the party fails to nominate an appealing candidate. People may continue to support a party that enjoys a good collective reputation even if they do not agree with the way some of its administrations are run or if they dislike some of its candidates. More important, strong parties exert a powerful counterweight to elected officials who once in office might be tempted to act arbitrarily. Parties are not only electoral machines; they are important actors in the daily life of democratic systems. Parties that have strong roots in society are more effective in preventing charismatic leaders such as Fujimori in Peru or Chávez in Venezuela from destroying the very institutions that make democracy work (Coppedge, 2000; Conaghan, 2000).

While electoral outcomes cannot be predetermined, for this is the very nature of competition, political parties can work to increase their chances of getting elected in competitive elections. Without building and maintaining a core of supporters, parties remain too fragile and volatile to play the democratic game. And without strongly rooted parties, the very nature of democracy is at stake.

Conclusion

Vicente Fox and the PAN: A Happy Marriage?

On December 1, 2000, Vicente Fox came into office, ending seventy-one years of PRI hegemony. In his inauguration speech, Fox promised to fight against corruption, promote stable and sustainable development, reduce the gap between rich and poor, improve the quality of public services, guarantee the rule of law, solve the conflict in the southern state of Chiapas, encourage greater political participation, and end once and for all the unchecked power of the president.

The victory of the PAN at the presidential level is a watershed in Mexico's political history. On one level, it marks the conclusion of a prolonged transition to democracy. The election of Vicente Fox is in effect the last brick in the centripetal path to democracy, one that started at the local level and gradually moved toward the center. By accepting its defeat, the PRI acknowledged that fair elections are now the only legitimate means of gaining access to power. Although this seems obvious and simple, it is quite a substantial accomplishment if one considers that only a few years ago there was not a general and accepted consensus in the country on this matter. Today, electoral democracy and the institutions that support it are fully consolidated.

On another level, the victory of the PAN has inaugurated a new political era in Mexico, one characterized by plurality in government, effective separation of powers, a freer and more assertive media, and an entirely different profile in the composition of the executive cabinet. In contrast to the past, when members of the cabinet were also members of the "official party" and were appointed on the basis of their proximity and loyalty to the president, Vicente Fox vowed to use merit and competence as selection criteria and appointed to his cabinet many people who were neither members of the PAN nor part of his inner circle of friends and collaborators. On the other hand, as members of the cabinet were being appointed, prominent leaders of the PAN announced that unlike the past, the governing party would not give its unconditional support to the administration.

While these are without doubt giant steps in the path toward democratization, two years after President Fox's victorious election, Mexico still faces enormous problems in building and consolidating more democratic governing practices. In today's more plural political environment, where the president does not have a majority in Congress, Fox has had an extremely difficult relationship with Congress, which has blocked the executive's most important pieces of legislation.[1] The PAN's unenthusiastic support for the administration and its overt criticism of many of the executive's speeches and actions has further complicated the administration's quest for substantive reforms.

As the Congress awakens from its lethargic past, the main political actors in the country (members of the cabinet, members of Congress, mayors and governors, and leaders of the main political parties) have failed to find the means for building consensus through compromise and negotiation. The once too powerful president has given way to one who has serious problems getting things done. This becomes all the more significant given the difficult challenges the new administration confronts.

Notwithstanding the progress on the electoral front, many of the country's old and grave social problems so far remain unaffected. Crime is rampant, more than 40 million people still live in extreme poverty, the rule of law is weak, there are no effective mechanisms to make government officials accountable for their actions, human rights continue to be violated, the conflict between the federal government and the Zapatista rebels in Chiapas has not been resolved, and corruption is still perceived by the majority of the population as a serious problem.[2]

After more than seventy years of priísta rule, it is of course extremely hard for a new president to reverse the course of history and show clear and evident signs of change. Yet President Fox raised enormous expectations of change and faces unparalleled pressure to produce results in a short period. These expectations have already given way to disappointment, as the president's approval rating declined from an all-time high of 70 percent in 2000 to 47 percent in 2002.[3]

Increasingly frustrated by the seeming obstruction of Congress and declining levels of support, President Fox has sought to increase his popularity by appealing directly to the public, bypassing Congress, and blaming political parties for the administration's ineffectiveness.[4] However, in a country that has little experience with democracy, this erosion of support for its practices and institutions casts disquieting shadows on the viability of democratic governance.

The consolidation of democracy depends to a large extent on whether democratic institutions produce results. Moral support for democracy is not enough; democracy also has to be effective. This is perhaps the greatest challenge confronting the Fox administration and the PAN, for so far democracy has not made a significant difference for the average citizen. In fact, democracy has been proven to make change all the more difficult.

As I have argued, political parties play a critical role in making democracy work. Although President Fox has made serious mistakes in the way he has handled his relationship with Congress,[5] it is political parties who bear the greatest responsibility for the slow pace of change in the country, for they have been unable to go beyond their short-term goals, respond to the demands of their constituencies, and find grounds for cooperation, negotiation, and compromise.

Mexican political parties are generally highly disciplined political organizations. Given the ban on reelection, parties exert enormous influence on how their legislators vote in Congress, for lack of discipline seriously affects the future of a politician's career. While this discipline might be good for the cohesiveness and unity of a party, it becomes problematic for an administration that needs the collaboration and coordination of different parties to govern.[6] Highly disciplined parties are not always flexible enough to reach political compromises with other political forces. More important, without the possibility of being reelected, elected officials and their parties have fewer incentives to respond and become more accountable to their constituencies. The latter requires a more pragmatic approach, going beyond the party's narrow and self-defined interests and becoming more receptive to the varied and changing demands of the electorate. In short, it requires that parties adopt strategies to strengthen their ties to their constituencies while at the same time maintaining flexibility. These strategies are more suitable to catch-all types of parties.[7]

In the case of the PAN, the party's weak electoral entrenchment and lack of flexibility to attend to the demands of the larger electorate have deeper roots than Mexico's electoral legislation and particularly the ban on reelection. Weak electoral entrenchment stems primarily from the party's own rules and organizational structure. As I have argued in this book, the PAN has remained above the electorate by design; it is still a sectarian type of party despite its electoral progress during the past two decades. Thus, even if Mexico's electoral legislation were further reformed to allow for the reelection of legislators,[8] the party's internal rules would still require substantial revision to meet the new challenges it confronts.

While the PAN's internal rules allowed it to survive in a hostile and uncompetitive political environment, they are a hindrance to a governing party. The PAN's refusal to expand its base of activists, its tendency to choose candidates that appeal to the core of the PAN but not to the larger electorate, its refusal to engage in community work and become more accountable to its constituencies, and its propensity to become active only during electoral periods seriously affect the party's electoral performance. Moreover, a party that fears the consequences of political ambition and that gives priority to the preservation of its doctrine and the purity of its members becomes too aloof from the day-to-day concerns of the electorate and is ill equipped to find the flexibility and pragmatism necessary for governing in a more democratic environment.

The Legacies of Martyrdom

When the PAN was created in 1939, its founding members knew that they were committing themselves to a "struggle for eternity" (Gómez Morin, 1946), for they confronted an environment that made competing and defeating the PRI in the electoral arena virtually impossible. The creation of an opposition party was at once a denunciation of what was then becoming an authoritarian regime dominated by an official party and a commitment to democracy and to principles of justice and the common good deeply inspired by the Social Christian Doctrine.

The limited electoral opportunities available to opposition parties in Mexico shaped their internal structure and their relationship with the environment. Since winning elections was not a realistic possibility, the PAN became an inward-looking party, focusing on the consistency of its doctrine and ideological principles. Panistas defined their mission as an educational one: they had to win over people's consciences, teach Mexicans the art of citizenship by disseminating their ideals, and expose the authoritarian features of the Mexican political regime. Panistas conceived of themselves as "martyrs" of an unfair and authoritarian system and justified their activism in mystical terms. They were moved by higher moral and ethical principles; power and ambition were neither in their scope nor recognized as legitimate goals of political action.

Panistas knew that they would see the rewards of their actions in the long run. Theirs was a life of "sacrifice," and they had to be prepared.

The doctrinal and moralistic profile the PAN adopted at its creation was crystallized in its internal rules. To survive in a hostile electoral and political environment, panistas devised an organizational structure that guaranteed their doctrinal integrity and protected them against political opportunists. The rules for affiliating with the party and selecting candidates and their administrative and organizational structure ensured that only those committed to the party's ideological principles could participate in the party's internal affairs.

The PAN was an extremely small political party. It had meager resources, operated with volunteers, and was concentrated in just a few states. It was a sectarian party that operated like a club of friends. Although electorally ineffective, its internal rules and fragile political organization allowed this party—like no other opposition party in Mexico— to survive in an adverse environment.

By the mid-1970s the government introduced an electoral reform that significantly increased the electoral opportunities for opposition parties. The PAN faced a dilemma: continue with its educating mission or adopt a more aggressive and explicitly vote-seeking strategy. Both paths entailed enormous risks. The first strategy ensured the party's ideological integrity but condemned the party to political isolation in a more open electoral environment. The second strategy was electorally more promising but threatened the party's ideological integrity and exposed its members to the "polluting" influences of power and ambition.

The PAN's leaders opted for the latter strategy, although they encountered strong internal opposition. In 1976 the PAN confronted its most serious internal crisis, but by 1979 this crisis was overcome. Since then the PAN has adopted an open-door policy, accepting all those who wanted to vote and work for the party but without formally changing its membership rules. Until the 1980s, however, the electoral gains of the party were so meager that few people found it attractive.

The situation started to change after 1982, when President López Portillo decided to nationalize the Mexican banks. A significant number of entrepreneurs, particularly owners of small and medium-size businesses in the north, were profoundly angered by the president's decision, which was perceived as unilateral and arbitrary. They decided to organize in opposition to the PRI and gave their support to the PAN. The PAN welcomed these entrepreneurs into its ranks.

The participation of entrepreneurs considerably strengthened the PAN in the electoral arena. They infused the party with much-needed financial resources, new campaign techniques, and organizational strategies drawn from their own businesses. More important, entrepreneurs also became the party's candidates. In most cases it was these candidates who won elections for the PAN.

At first the influx of entrepreneurs did not create problems inside the party ranks. But once the party started to win elections, an internal struggle for nominations began. Longtime members of the party felt that given their sacrifices, they deserved to be nominated. The newcomers, on the other hand, believed they were more qualified. More important, many longtime members of the PAN felt that the entrepreneurs threatened to erode the party's doctrinal and ideological principles.

Although traditional panistas could not compete against newcomers in terms of their resources or professional profiles, they had one important advantage in party affairs: the party's rules. Indeed, these rules, which have not been substantially modified since 1939, benefit the most traditional members of the party. The rules can be used to filter and select party activists, to control the candidate selection process, and to decide the party's activities and legislative agenda.

In most of the places where the PAN was able to win an election against the PRI with an entrepreneurial candidate, the party selected a traditional panista for the next consecutive election. And in most cases, the PAN either lost these elections or won by narrow margins and with high levels of abstention. One of the most difficult challenges the PAN confronts as it becomes a governing party is precisely to maintain its unity and ideological profile and at the same time preserve its constituencies in consecutive elections.

During the 1990s, the PAN expanded significantly, winning important elections at the local and state levels. The party's internal rules, however, remained intact. Today the PAN's sectarian rules are becoming increasingly out of sync with the broader concerns of the electorate. And its leaders are much more conservative and ideologically cohesive than the electorate at large. This disparity can seriously undermine the party's electoral and political prospects. If the party fails to respond to and represent its constituencies and to address the issues that affect society today, it will face serious difficulties remaining a viable political option in the years to come. The PAN's preoccupation with Social Christian Doctrine might not reflect the more practical needs and interests of its constituencies. Similarly, the party's preoccupation with the "moral integrity and honesty" of its members might not allow it to expand and to choose the best and more attractive candidates for office.

The party's anachronism became evident in the process that led up to Vicente Fox's nomination as PAN's presidential candidate. As a typical newcomer, Vicente Fox was distrusted by a significant number of panistas. They were intimidated by his assertive and charismatic personal style; they were also skeptical of his adherence to panista ideology. As governor of Guanajuato, Fox surrounded himself with people who were not identified with the PAN. Moreover, he knew that to defeat the PRI he needed a broad coalition and was therefore ready to make alliances with anyone, regardless of ideological orientation.

As no other panista seemed capable of defeating the PRI at the national level, panistas faced a difficult dilemma. If they supported Fox and became actively involved in the campaign, they could win the elections. But winning with such a candidate entailed the risk of losing the party's ideological profile.

Perhaps no one understood this dilemma better than Fox himself. He knew that to win the party's nomination, he needed to take innovative steps. Left to the regular nominating procedures, he could not assure his nomination. Fox decided to challenge his own party by organizing his candidacy three years before the elections. Similar to what prospective candidates in the United States do, he created his own organization, Friends of Fox, independent of his party. By the time the PAN had to nominate its presidential candidate, Fox had acquired such strength and political visibility that no other candidate wanted to register for the party's nomination.

Fox won the party's nomination, but many party leaders did not campaign actively on his behalf. As was feared—or expected—by many panistas, Fox appealed to the electorate at large and was able to attract voters whose only commonality was a desire to defeat the PRI. His campaign organization included a heterogeneous team, many of whom not only lacked a relationship with the PAN, but also came from the opposite end of the ideological spectrum.[9] Recognizing the need to go beyond the PAN's core electorate, a member of the campaign team even said that to win the elections, they "needed to save the PAN from the panistas."[10]

In the end, and despite—or perhaps because of—the differences with his own party, Fox was able to win the presidential elections by a substantial margin. In many ways the July 2 victory was a personal one. With the PAN's candidate now in office, however, the distance between the PAN and the president not only threatens to undermine the executive's governing capacity, it can also weaken the party's prospects in future elections.

Given that Mexican electoral laws prohibit Fox's reelection, the PAN needs to find ways to maintain its constituencies if it wants to stay in power. In great part, the government's performance will be critical to maintaining the party's constituencies. But as has been the case in other regions where the PAN has been in government, good evaluations of government performance are not enough to preserve the voters' loyalty to the party. To hold on to its constituencies in future elections, the PAN will have to work hard and continuously, not only during elections. This is perhaps the greatest test ahead for this party—surviving as a party in government. The PAN will have to overcome its propensity to mobilize mainly during electoral periods and to devise ways to service its constituencies. If the PAN cannot convince broader sectors of the electorate of its central ideological principles, at least it will have to show its effectiveness in responding to and representing citizens' demands and needs. The PAN's success in these activities can help it forge stronger and more permanent links with its constituencies. Furthermore, the party will have to elaborate substantive and practical proposals, to support its own administration, and to expand its organization to be able to penetrate into the life of the community.

As a party in government, the PAN will have to gain credit for the government's performance, and at the same time, it will have to infuse the government's actions with panista ideology. Furthermore, in contrast to the past, when the PAN could afford to attract voters by criticizing the PRI and the government without defining a specific agenda, today the PAN will have to draft a more programmatic, responsible, and realistic government agenda, one that goes beyond the mere wishful thinking of the past. At the same time, the PAN will have to bridge the gap between the party elite and its voters.

All of the above implies that the PAN needs to cease to operate as a sectarian party. This requires a substantial transformation of its internal rules and organizational structure. This was already recognized by one of the PAN's most celebrated members, Juan Manuel Gómez Morin, son of the PAN's founder, Manuel Gómez Morin, during the celebration of the party's sixty-first anniversary. In his speech, Gómez Morin said that "PAN needs to adapt to the new realities, and it needs to revise its ideological principles and modify its internal rules." [11] A high-level party official expressed the same idea more metaphorically when he said that the problem with the PAN today is that it "looks like an adult dressed in a sailor suit." In other words, the PAN grew beyond its organization and internal statutes, and now a new "organizational outfit" is required. [12]

To the extent that political parties are successful in defining their agendas, maintaining their cohesion, and aggregating and articulating the demands of their constituencies, they will succeed in fostering greater partisan identity among broader sectors of the population. While this is crucial for strengthening political parties in a more democratic setting, it is not a small task.

Now that defeating (or protecting) the regime is no longer the main issue that defines and divides Mexican political parties, they are facing a major identity crisis. As the PRI–anti-PRI cleavage disappears, it is not yet clear what are the new issues on which political parties position and distinguish themselves from one another.

The PRI and the PAN share fundamental views on the economy; the PRI and the PRD share views on social policy issues; the PAN and the PRD share views on democracy, particularly in states still controlled by the PRI. Moreover, despite the absence of clear ideological cleavages that could increase the opportunities for cooperation, the three major parties have resisted abandoning the all-or-nothing style of the past, a political attitude that seriously undermines their ability to negotiate and reach agreements. Finally, reforming political parties' rules and organization alters the balance of power inside the parties, creating new sets of winners and losers. While successful reforms entail overcoming internal resistance to change, the shape and breath of these reforms critically depends on the internal compromises parties forge among their own base of activists.

The Foxista Style of Government: Finding a Third Way

Just as Vicente Fox found it necessary to distance himself from his own party to win the elections, as president he believed he needed to find a way to reconcile the PAN's ideas of subsidiarity, the common good, and the importance of the market and private initiative with the left's traditional commitment to social justice, equality, and improving the lot of the poor. This effort to devise a third way between neoliberalism and socialism, between the PAN and the PRD, and between the PAN and the PRI is evident in the make-up of his cabinet.

At first sight, the so-called economic cabinet seems ideologically and politically distant from the PAN. Indeed, it is dominated by people who come from the business sector and have little or no relationship with the PAN. As the "Cinderella" cartoon that appeared in a Mexican newspaper eloquently illustrates,[13] in the distribution of cabinet positions, panistas lost against members of the private sector.

A closer look at the cabinet, however, shows that Fox in fact sought to get closer to the PAN and at the same time create an all-inclusive cabinet.[14] He appointed panistas to important positions such as in the Ministry of Social Development and the General Comptrollers Office, and he appointed a leftist to the Ministry of Foreign Affairs.

CENICIENTA

The inclusion of nonpanistas in the cabinet is not unusual. Most panista governments at the state level have drawn staff from among their closest advisers and collaborators, many of whom have come from the private sector. While this leads many panistas to feel ignored, partisanship is not always the best criterion for government appointments. One of the challenges ahead for the PAN is precisely to train its own cadres and prepare them for public office.

Vicente Fox's search for a third way was also evident in his inauguration speech. He committed himself to overcoming poverty and promised to maintain a healthy economy; he justified the need for introducing a substantial tax reform and promised to promote economic growth and an attractive business environment. He also talked about fighting corruption and moving beyond a paternalistic conception of the state, one that distributes goods and services to the poor without giving them the tools and incentives to become more productive. But at the same time, he stressed that he would make special efforts to bring education and health services to those who have been excluded from the privileges of economic development. While President Fox's speech was not typically panista, it included many keywords from panista ideology such as federalism, the common good, solidarity, and the notion of governing as servicing the community.

Fox's creativity and innovations will most likely mark his style of governing. He is unorthodox in every sense of the word. He challenged official inauguration protocol by visiting the Basílica de Guadalupe (Church of the Virgin of Guadalupe, one of the most sacred shrines in Mexico) and then going for breakfast with street children in one of Mexico City's poorer neighborhoods. He has already said that he will not spend time in his office; that his work will be outside, for one cannot be effective while sitting at his desk. Indeed, he will be a president who is in permanent campaign mode. When someone asked him whether the public could visit Los Pinos, the official residence, he said that anyone could come because he would not be there.

On the international front, President Fox also inaugurated a new and more assertive style, promoting a closer and more unambiguous relationship with the United States and adopting a more prominent role in international affairs. The participation of Mexico in the United Nations Security Council and Mexico's vote against Cuba at the UN's Human Rights Commission are all part of this redefinition of Mexico's foreign policy.

For the PAN, coexisting and supporting this unorthodox government represents a big challenge. But introducing substantial internal reforms to adapt to the new political reality represents an even bigger challenge for this party.

The Challenges of Governing

The "struggle for eternity" that panista founders envisioned in 1939 finally came true in less than a century. Sixty-one years after its founding, the PAN won the presidential elections. However, as the PAN relishes its victory, it needs to transform its anachronistic organization. A party that was built to survive electoral defeat needs to reinvent itself for success. This involves finding a balance between pragmatism and ideology, between ambition and political integrity, between electoral efficacy and idealism.

Political parties are fundamental to making democracy work. Democracy requires parties that survive after the elections, that become entrenched in the electorate, and that adopt identifiable positions with regard to certain issues. Furthermore, parties need to be flexible enough to collaborate and negotiate with other political forces in the country. Rigid political organizations lead to polarization and stalemate. This induces frustrated executives to bypass the institutions of democracy and appeal directly to the public.

The 2003 midterm elections will be important for defining the new configuration of power in Congress. If the PAN wins a majority of seats, and to the extent that it agrees to collaborate more closely with the administration, President Fox will have greater room to introduce substantial reforms. However, the president will still need the cooperation of the other two larger parties, for the Senate elections are not held at this time and the PRI still controls the majority of state governments and local congresses in the country.

In democratic Mexico, the three main political parties face important challenges as they adapt to the more pluralistic political environment. Although compared to the PRI and the PRD,[15] the PAN has been more successful in solving its internal divisions, it is a party that clings to the past and in many respects behaves as if it were still in the opposition. It holds firmly to its traditionally held positions and beliefs, proudly exposes its differences with the president as signs of its independence, and refuses to introduce substantial reforms to modernize and grow as a political organization. This would not be so important if it were merely an internal party affair without implications beyond the party's electoral performance. As I have argued in this book, however, the strength and vitality of parties is critical to the very viability of democracy, particularly in a country that is emerging from a long period of authoritarian rule. The fate of the PAN, the new governing party, is central to the fate of democracy in Mexico.

N O T E S

Introduction

1. In 1983 the PAN won seventeen municipal elections. This was an unprecedented victory, which is in great part explained by a temporary openness of the electoral arena at the municipal level. President Miguel de la Madrid (1982–88) came to power facing one of the worst economic crises the country had confronted. To gain legitimacy, the president promised a "moral renovation" of society, which included not only a fight against corruption, which was rampant during the previous administration of López Portillo, but also cleaner elections. Given the strengthening of the PAN at the local level, by the midterm elections of 1985, the government decided to return to its usual practice of election tampering. One of the most manifest and widely publicized cases of fraud were the elections in the state of Chihuahua in 1986, where the PAN had acquired unprecedented strength and electoral fraud was instrumental to ensuring the victory of the PRI. Francisco Barrio was the PAN's candidate for governor in 1986. The PAN organized a massive postelectoral mobilization to protest against fraud, but it was to no avail. For an elaboration of the 1986 elections in Chihuahua, see Molinar 1987 and Mizrahi 1994a.

2. In the 1994 presidential elections, the PAN received 27 percent of the total vote, a substantial increase but still too limited to become a dominant political force.

3. According to a survey conducted in Mexico in September 2000, only 20 percent of Mexicans have some level of confidence in political parties; 76 percent of Mexicans had no or little confidence. I thank Roderic A. Camp for sharing this information with me.

4. Using Elster's (1985) logic of *adaptive preference formation* following the fable of the fox and the sour grapes, we can say that panistas defined their preferences according to the nature of the constraints they faced. Knowing that

power was out of their reach, they defined as their main objective educating civil society rather than winning elections. They adjusted their preferences to their possibilities. They did not want power because they knew they could not attain it. Once power is within their reach, however, the entire logic of the party becomes questionable. New possibilities bring about the definition of new goals. But for many traditional panistas, the old logic is tied to their identity and thus they resist adapting to the new state of the world. Anchored in the past, they still believe that power is damaging to ideals, that it jeopardizes the ideological coherence of the party. They prefer to "win by losing elections."

5. The president was the virtual head of the party and therefore the "grand elector" in the country at large. Political careers depended heavily on the decisions of the head of the executive branch. I elaborate this point below.

6. According to the trimonthly survey conducted by the newspaper *Reforma,* Vicente Fox's popularity fell fourteen points, from 61 percent in December 2001 to 47 percent in March 2002. The decline in the president's popularity is even more striking when compared to his approval rating of 70 percent in February 2001. *Reforma,* March 1, 2002.

Chapter One.   The Paradoxes of Electoral Success

1. Although the 1968 student massacre in Tlatelolco revealed one of the first signs of the exhaustion of the political regime, most of the slow process of transition toward democracy occurred in stable and peaceful conditions. After the student repression, the government of Luis Echeverría (1970–76) was able to co-opt many student leaders and selectively repressed those who preferred to challenge the regime by organizing guerrilla wars. For a description of student leaders' political careers after 1968, see de Mauleón (1988). Until the violent upsurge of violence in the southern state of Chiapas in 1994, most democratic movements were channeled through the electoral system. The Chiapas rebellion, however, was another sign of the regime's exhaustion. Through the eloquent writings of the leader of this indigenous revolt, "Sub-Comandante Marcos," the world became aware of the extreme poverty and the exclusion of a significant group of indigenous groups from the benefits of economic development. Armed struggle became a symbol of the regime's inability to bring about social justice, an important theme that gave life to the PRI after the revolution.

2. The president was the most important determinant in the selection of candidates for governor, federal deputy, senator, and, of course, the presidency. Candidates for the office of local deputies and municipal presidents were usually left to the state governors to appoint. For an elaboration of this topic, see Langston (2000).

3. President Cárdenas introduced a substantial reform in the party's organization along sectoral and corporatist lines. In 1938 the PNR became the PRM (Partido de la Revolución Mexicana). In 1940, when the military sector of the party was eliminated, the PRM became the Partido Revolucionario Institucional (PRI) (Garrido, 1982, 304).

4. José Vasconcelos, for example, an intellectual and follower of Madero during the Mexican Revolution, was excluded. He ran against the PNR candidate in the 1929 presidential elections but lost in an electoral process characterized by widespread fraud (Garrido, 1982).

5. An amorphous sector that included middle-class professionals, state employees such as teachers and bureaucrats, women's groups, and even some small-scale entrepreneurs.

6. In addition to strong presidential control over the party and the electoral restrictions on the opposition, political discipline was maintained by a constitutional amendment introduced in 1933 that prohibited the consecutive reelection of governors, mayors, and members of Congress. Since elected officials could not be reelected, the future of their political careers depended to a large extent on maintaining political discipline within their party. Although this law contributed to strengthening political discipline, it also meant that elected officials were not accountable to their constituencies. One of the most important constitutional amendments the PAN has proposed is precisely to allow the consecutive reelection of members of Congress and mayors. See Nacif (1997).

7. When corruption and co-optation did not work, repression was also used, but this was restricted and focused

8. Throughout the years, the government and the PRI fostered so-called satellite parties, parties that were nominally in the opposition but that voted in Congress along with the PRI. The purpose of parties such as the Partido Auténtico de la Revolución Mexicana (PARM) and the Partido Popular Socialista (PPS), was twofold. First, they helped to legitimize the formally democratic facade of the Mexican political regime. Second, they allowed the regime to divide the opposition and prevent non-priísta voters from eventually organizing a unified front against the PRI.

9. For a historical analysis of the origins of the PAN, see Mabry (1973). For a detailed analysis of the party's experience in the political arena, see Loaeza (1999).

10. Cárdenas's main objective was to use public education to reduce the influence of the Catholic Church and to inculcate in students the values of communal work and the legitimacy of labor and peasants' rights. See Vaughn (1997).

11. Gómez Morin in his speech to the party's national convention, February 2, 1946.

12. According to Loaeza (1999), Gómez Morin was influenced intellectually by the Spanish secular right of the 1920s as well as by the thought of the French Catholic thinkers Charles Péguy, Charles Maurras, and Henri Bergson (Loaeza 1999, 115–17). However, as some historians argue, Gómez Morin can also be regarded as a chapter (and product) of the Mexican Revolution. See Meyer (1991).

13. José Vasconcelos was nominated by the Partido Nacional Anti-reeleccionista, the same party that emerged to propose the candidacy of Francisco I. Madero against Porfirio Díaz in 1910. Vasconcelos presented his candidacy as opposition to Calles, whom he regarded as a new revolutionary *caudillo*, or chief. The Partido Anti-reeleccionista

claimed the 1929 elections had been fraudulent. Vasconcelos proclaimed himself the winner but later left the country. See Garrido (1982).

14. It is important to mention that Cárdenas's policies did not harm the business sector, as it feared. The creation of state-owned industries provided industrialists with cheap subsidized products, such as electricity and oil. The incorporation of workers and peasants in the official party became an effective means of controlling their demands and peacefully resolving conflicts between workers and entrepreneurs. And the strengthening of workers' purchasing power expanded consumer demand, which greatly benefited domestic entrepreneurs (Reynolds, 1970, 77; Haber, 1989, 189; Yañez Maldonado, 1990).

15. The peasants who live in an ejido own what they produce but do not own the land itself. Thus *ejidatarios* could not legally sell or rent their land use rights. In 1991 a constitutional amendment to Article 27 redefined ejidatarios' property rights. To attract private capital to agricultural production, the reforms allow ejidatarios to sell or rent their lands. For more on this topic, see Grindle (1996); de Janvry, Gordillo, and Sadoulet (1997).

16. Besides González Luna, the Catholic activists were Miguel Estrada Iturbide, Rafael Preciado Hernandez, Luis Calderon Vega, Manual Ulloa Ortiz, and Jesús Toral Moreno (Mabry, 1973, 17–32).

17. Article 130 of the Mexican Constitution forbids the church from participating in politics and prohibits it from owning property. Clergymen were not allowed to vote, and the state had extensive powers to regulate their activities, for example, to determine the number of clergy allowed in a particular state.

18. Cárdenas launched the CTM and the CNC, organizations of workers and peasants respectively that were incorporated in the PRI. Workers and peasants were organized in separate organizations to check one against the other and to allow the government to control them. The CNC and the CTM became pillars of the official party, a mass-based party that did not seek to attract individual affiliations. Moreover, these organizations also became the means to subject popular organizations to state control. See Garrido (1982).

19. Avila Camacho also did not share Cárdenas's views on education. Article 3 of the Constitution was amended in 1946 to eliminate the "socialist" character of public education and to give more flexibility to private education. According to von Sauer (1974, 67), the PAN attributed the redrafting of the Constitution to its pressure.

20. The bloody conflict between church and state during the 1920s, the Cristero Rebellion, had convinced Gómez Morin that politics had to be separated from the religious sphere. Although the PAN founders shared many ideological principles with Christian Democratic parties, a confessional party was simply not viable. Furthermore, as Mabry (1973) argues, the Catholic activists who formed the PAN were politicized members of the reform wing of Mexican Catholicism. They were inspired by their religious beliefs but were convinced that they needed to act through secular-based organizations (Mabry, 1973, 158). The PAN was not formally a member of the International Organization of Christian Democratic Parties until 1998.

21. The subsidiarity principle establishes that "the greater and more perfect society should not do what the minor one can and should do, except if the latter is unable to do it, in which case the intervention of the former is justified, only to the extent that it promotes that the minor society shall reestablish the possibility of carrying out by itself its goals." PAN, *Principios de doctrina*.

22. The PAN is not opposed to public education, but it opposes the adoption of a single, mandatory textbook. It also opposes constitutional prohibitions against religious education, although in practice these prohibitions have been largely ignored.

23. The PAN's doctrine establishes that "the human being, by nature is a social being, thus he is responsible not only to his own destiny but also to that of his community. . . . Solidarity rests on the linkage between persons and society and implies a relationship of mutual respect. . . . Each person has the right and the duty to participate in the public affairs of the community of which he is part." PAN, *Principios de doctrina*.

24. On the ideological and doctrinal positions of the PAN, see González Luna (1940); Mabry (1973); González Morfín (1977); Loaeza (1999).

25. In the party's celebration of its sixty-first birthday, Juan Manuel Gómez Morin, son of the PAN's founder, Manuel Gómez Morin, expressed these ideas in his speech. He wanted to stress that panistas come from a long tradition of self-sacrifice and strong convictions. Now that the PAN has won the presidential elections, his words seemed like a reminder of where panistas originally came from. This reunion took place on November 30, 2000, a day before Vicente Fox was sworn in as president.

26. In 1958 the PAN won six seats in an election it regarded as fraudulent. In previous elections the PAN won only four or five seats. I elaborate on this in chapter 3. Of the six elected deputies, four refused to abandon their seats in Congress and were expelled from the party (Mabry, 1973, 59).

27. Until 1963 members of Congress were selected by majority rule, a system that made it extremely hard for opposition parties to gain access to Congress. They had to win the majority of votes in each district to obtain a seat. To increase the costs of withdrawing members of Congress, the 1963 electoral reform also penalized parties that refused to take their seats in Congress with the loss of their registration (Molinar, 1991, 65).

28. In 1993 the so-called governability clause, which guaranteed substantial overrepresentation to the majority party in Congress, was formally eliminated. In the 1994 elections the PAN won 119 seats in Congress, a substantial improvement over the past but still not enough to challenge the majority of the PRI in Congress.

29. The PAN argued that many of these amendments, such as the reform of the ejido system and the relations between church and state, originally had been introduced by their legislators. The government of Carlos Salinas de Gortari, in their view, "stole" their proposals. In retrospect, the Salinas de Gortari administration represented a crucial shift in Mexico's economic policy, moving away from a closed economic system in which the state played a major role in the economy to an open and liberal economic system with minimal direct state involvement. The PAN had been an advocate

of economic liberalism since its foundation, stressing the importance of private capital and free markets for economic prosperity. As I argue above, this was consistent with the PAN's principle of subsidiarity, which holds that the government should intervene in the economy only in matters that exceed the capacity of private capital.

30. In 1992 the PAN won the second gubernatorial election in the state of Chihuahua. Although in other states the electoral process was far from clean, the PRI and the government adopted a much more conciliatory position toward the PAN than toward the PRD. The PRD's radicalism stems in part from the lack of tolerance it confronted; it was "pushed" toward a more confrontational attitude. Cárdenas was regarded not like other opposition leaders but as a traitor.

31. The independence of electoral authorities started in 1994, when President Salinas de Gortari introduced his third electoral reform in a highly charged political environment after the assassination of his presidential candidate and the upheaval in Chiapas. Until 1996 the judicial system could not intervene in electoral matters.

32. Indeed, many panistas claimed that the Salinas de Gortari administration actually stole its economic program from the PAN. They argue that they collaborated with the PRI in Congress because they were voting in favor of the programs they had traditionally endorsed. Voting against the PRI would have been politically inconsistent. Interview with Luis H. Alvarez, October 1996.

33. Interview with Carlos Castillo Peraza, October 1996.

34. Perhaps one of the most evident and recent examples of the PAN's lack of a practical and realistic government program is the attitude of the new secretary of social development, Josefina Vázquez, a panista federal deputy appointed by President Fox. Pressed by his own party, the president was compelled to include some old-time panistas in his cabinet. In one of her speeches, Vázquez claimed that the poor need to be treated with dignity; that poverty can be fought by changing people's attitudes; that instead of combating poverty, we need to start talking about creating prosperity; and that she still did not know whether the social programs currently under way would continue (*Reforma*, 11 December 2000). Unlike the president's team of advisers (many of them recruited from the private sector), Vázquez did not have a blueprint for action and her approach was inspired by the panista ideology of solidarity and self-improvement. The secretary for social development had good intentions but no program. I elaborate on this point in the conclusion.

35. This is explained in part by the combination of an economic (market versus planned economy) and a political (democracy versus authoritarianism) dimension in the left-right scale. Thus many voters identify the PRI as more "right-wing" than the PAN because it is perceived as closer to the authoritarian dimension. This shows that as the democratic-authoritarian dimension becomes less salient, the electorate defines the left-right scale predominantly along the economic dimension.

36. According to Moreno (1999a, 57), in a postelection survey conducted in 1997, 70 percent of the population placed themselves on the center-right of the ideological spectrum.

37. From 1989 to 1998 the PAN won elections in a total of 542 municipalities. However, the party was able to win consecutive elections in only 123 cases. That is, the party won consecutive elections in only 22.6 percent of the total municipalities that were up for elections. These data were given to me by the party's Office of Electoral Affairs.

At the congressional level, it is more difficult to calculate the party's rate of repetition. This is due to the mixed system of representation and of the numerous electoral reforms introduced over the past twenty years that have changed the size of Congress as well as the districts and the formulas for allocating seats in Congress.

Chapter Two.   Political Parties as Organizations: A Typology of Parties

1. As I argue in chapter 1, from 1943 to 1963, when an electoral reform was introduced, the PAN had an extremely marginal presence in Congress. Because deputies were chosen on the basis of majority rule, it was difficult for the opposition to win a seat in Congress. In 1963 a "semiproportional" system of representation was introduced, entitling parties with 2.5 percent of the total vote five seats in Congress and an additional seat for each 0.5 percent of the vote up to a maximum of twenty seats. In 1964, with 11.5 percent of the total vote, the PAN obtained twenty seats in Congress, two on the basis of majority rule and eighteen on the basis of this new system of proportional representation. See the tables in chapter 3 for a historical account of the PAN's performance in the electoral arena. For an elaboration of the electoral reforms, see Medina Peña (1994) and Molinar (1991).

2. In the presidential elections of 1940, the PAN did not have a presidential candidate but supported the candidacy of Juan Andrew Almazán, a general who defected from the official party. In that same year, the PAN did not present candidates for Congress. It was not until 1943 that the PAN participated in legislative elections for the first time, fielding twenty-one candidates for the offices of federal deputy. The PAN won its first seats in Congress in 1946.

3. One of the most puzzling questions this literature has addressed is why opposition parties were willing to participate in elections they knew were unfair when by participating they contributed to the legitimation of the regime they so fiercely opposed. Crespo (1995) convincingly argues that the government was always concerned with giving the opposition enough incentives to prevent them from boycotting and thus delegitimating the regime. This explains why the government paradoxically introduced the broadest electoral reforms when the opposition seemed weakest and rolled back these reforms when the opposition was strongest.

4. The theoretical argument developed herein is influenced by Kitschelt's (1994) analysis of the transformation of social democratic parties in western Europe.

5. The party's internal organization constrains party leaders' decision-making capacity. However, confronted with changing environmental circumstances, leaders can decide to change the organizational structure by reforming the party's rules.

6. In 1999 a set of partial reforms in the method of selecting the presidential candidate were introduced. However, the old rules still hold for the selection of candidates for other positions.

7. These analytic tools are conceived in the context of presidential systems, in which elections for the executive and legislative branches are separate and based on the principle of majority rule. Political parties have to come up with candidates for these offices. In many Latin American countries, congressional elections are based on a method of proportional representation. In these cases, parties can gain political representation without necessarily having to create large electoral coalitions. That reduces some of the burden on parties since they have easier access to power. In the Mexican case, congressional elections are based on a mixed system of majority rule and proportional representation. Moreover, the nonreelection clause only increases the burden on parties, since they not only have to create large electoral coalitions but also have to select new candidates for each electoral cycle.

8. In the case of Mexico, for example, the opening of the electoral system created a series of opportunities and constraints for the opposition. While opposition parties could increase their presence in Congress, their chances of competing (and defeating) the PRI at the national level were very limited. The PRI and the government started to acknowledge that opposition parties had won some elections—at the municipal level. During the 1980s, the opportunities to compete effectively at the state level were also restricted. This changed in 1989, when the PAN obtained its first electoral victory in the state of Baja California. During the 1990s, however, and especially throughout the administration of Salinas de Gortari, the chances for the opposition were extremely selective and restricted. The president was ready to accept the PRI's defeat in Baja California but was reluctant to accept Vicente Fox's victory in Guanajuato in 1991. This electoral environment defined the arena in which parties had realistic chances to compete. Both the PAN and the PRD reacted differently to this electoral environment: the PAN adopted a more collaborative position toward the PRI at the national level while becoming more aggressive and combative at the state and local levels. The PRD, in contrast, adopted an unrelenting radical position, focusing its criticisms against the regime at the national level. I return to this below.

9. Going against a nonwritten tradition of secretly picking his successor, the president refused to interfere in the PRI's nomination process. For the first time in history, the PRI organized a national primary election to select its presidential candidate for the 2000 elections. The process was not smooth, and the main challenge facing the party today is maintaining its unity and discipline in the face of open competition. In several states open primaries were also introduced for the selection of the gubernatorial candidate.

10. For an interesting analysis of the PRI's internal transformation, see Langston (1999).

11. Some examples of leftist parties that, like the PAN, were excluded from power are the Partido Comunista Mexicano (PCM) and the Partido Revolucionario de los Trabajadores (PRT). During the 1980s, these parties decided to create a unified leftist

party, the PSUM. And in 1988, the PSUM merged to become the Frente Democrático Nacional (FDN), a coalition of leftist parties and organizations that supported the priísta dissident Cuauhtémoc Cárdenas as presidential candidate. Later these parties also participated in the founding of the PRD.

12. By "fortune" I mean here not only the ability to survive as a political organization but also the ability to maintain and expand the party's electoral coalitions. Of course, parties may still fail to win elections even if they manage to change their internal rules and organizational structure. Parties that manage to transform their internal organization, however, have greater opportunities to win elections than do those that fail to introduce reforms.

13. This includes the promotion of party identity among the electorate. In Mexico, where one party has for a long time controlled most of the country's political life, fostering party identity is crucial for enabling opposition parties to cultivate more permanent ties to the electorate. I return to this point in later chapters.

14. Felipe Calderón, former national chairman of the PAN, expressed this clearly when he said after taking office as party's chairman in 1996 that the challenge of the party was "to win elections without losing the party."

15. For an interesting analysis of voting behavior based on constituency service, see Fiorina, Cain, and Ferejohn (1987). I develop the importance of this point later in this book.

16. For an interesting analysis of the consequences of party reform, see Polsby (1983).

17. These parties usually select their candidates through primary elections. The latter can be open—for all registered voters—or closed—restricted to party members. In both cases, and due to the growing influence of the media in the electoral arena, candidates appeal to the public at large in their campaign for the nomination. These parties are consequently readier to reinterpret and adjust the party's ideological positions to accommodate to the pulse of the electorate.

18. The electoral system in which parties compete is crucial in shaping the party's strategies. In majority rule systems, parties have greater incentives to adopt vote-seeking strategies, for they need to win the majority of votes to gain access to office. In proportional representation systems, parties can afford to reduce their political appeal for they can gain access to power without necessarily winning the majority of votes. Thus a highly ideological party with a reduced electoral coalition has greater chances of gaining access to power in countries where parties are elected on a system of proportional representation. The religious parties in Israel are a good example.

19. This, I believe, is in great part what happened to the Labour Party in England. See Tsebelis (1990).

20. For an excellent study of casework and constituency service in the United States, see Mayhew (1974).

21. In some parties, the links between the party and the electorate has a strong ideological basis. These are traditionally small and highly ideological parties, such as communist parties in many countries, religious parties in Israel, and, as we shall see

later, the PAN. While these parties maintain close ties to that portion of the electorate that is convinced of the party's goals and ideas, they may lack the resources and the bureaucratic structure to expand their electoral coalitions.

22. For an interesting analysis of the Peronist Justicialista Party in Argentina, see Levitsky (1998).

23. These linkages can be forged with specific social sectors, for example, the working class. But what is important is the presence of the party on the ground, close to where people live and work. The linkages between parties and constituencies can be forged by members of Congress and not necessarily by the party apparatus itself. The relevant question here is whether the constituencies are permanently courted. In the United States, members of Congress and their staffs maintain an active and constant linkage with their constituencies. These links have a powerful influence on people's voting behavior. See Fiorina (1987).

24. What this also means is that strongly rooted parties are better able to maintain party identities among the electorate based on their record in office. Parties become identified by the policies they pursue while in office. In a country that is just emerging from an authoritarian past and where party identities are not fully shaped or are in the process of change, the success of political parties in forging more permanent party identities among their followers is critical. As I show below, in the case of Mexico this is becoming important for both opposition parties.

25. As we shall see later, we can distinguish the breadth and intensity of a party's ties to the electorate: sectarian parties have intense ties to an extremely reduced core of party followers. I owe this comment to Kurt Weyland.

26. Typically, these parties appeal only to their convinced followers and have fragile bureaucratic structures made up mostly of volunteers.

27. Voters may be attracted to this party not so much by what the party stands for but for purely pragmatic reasons. This is what happened to the PAN in Mexico's 2000 presidential election.

28. In some respects, the PRD also has sectarian elements. Examples of sectarian parties outside Mexico are the National Front in France, the Freedom Party in Austria, and the America First Party in the United States.

29. The Democratic Party in the United States also belonged to this category before the introduction of substantial reforms in its candidate selection process during the 1970s.

30. Electoral parties can be formed through the amalgamation of preexisting social movements. When parties form on this basis, they encounter serious problems after elections. In struggling to maintain their identities and serve the interests of their constituencies, social movements may push parties to become more sectarian. On the other hand, social movements may find it expedient to remain more independent from the party they supported after the elections. Often social movements are more effective in negotiating with the government than in opposing the government through a common electoral front. Moreover, many social movements are better orga-

nized and have more resources than the political parties to which they adhere. See the case of the PRD in Mexico (Bruhn, 1998) and the PT in Brazil (Keck, 1992).

31. This is the case whether the party wins or loses the elections. If they lose, party activists wait for the next election. If they win, the party's contraction affects the government because it cannot count on the party to build a cushion of support for the next election. Furthermore, typically there are serious fights between those who move into the government and those who stay in the party. Being in office, government officials feel they need to appeal to the electorate at large, while party officials believe the government should be responsive and representative to its own—narrower— constituency.

32. This, however, might constitute one of the most serious dilemmas for parties founded around a critical core constituency, such as the working class. This is the case with the PT in Brazil; it was an amalgamation of working-class social movements but had difficulty appealing to the wider electorate because that contradicted their foundational principles and identity. See Keck (1992).

33. This bureaucratic apparatus includes the congressional staff, who work in their districts on a permanent basis. This part of the apparatus is important for maintaining the party's presence in the community between elections. See Schlesinger, 1994; Katz and Kolodny, 1994. Some analysts, particularly those who think that the increasing influence of the mass media and the importance of candidates in elections reveal a weakening of political parties in the United States, might disagree with me. For them, the Democratic and Republican Parties in the United States seem to belong more to the electoral type than to the catch-all type. This is a debate that is beyond the scope of this analysis. However, if the categories defined above are useful in framing this debate, the typology has a heuristic value in itself, which is the central purpose of this chapter.

34. As is evident from the 1999 election results in Argentina, these parties can lose elections. Once in office, voters' perception of government performance is another important component of the party's electoral performance. However, as is evident in Argentina, the Peronista Party's defeat at the presidential level does not by any means suggest the total defeat of the party. It still controls numerous seats in Congress and the government in important cities, including the capital.

35. The party may benefit the urban more than the rural electorate, or it may give greater benefits to the business than to the worker sector.

36. The parties' organization also varies according to the nature of the electoral system. In countries where members of Congress are elected on a proportional representation basis, parties gain enormous power in the selection of their candidates for office. In the case of Mexico, deputies and senators are elected under a mixed system: some are elected through majority rule, and some are elected from party lists on a proportional representation basis.

37. In the first case, the electorate might be more willing to support opposition parties. In the second case, the electorate might become more interested in issues that

are less related to the economy and more to the quality of life. See Inglehart (1977). For an analysis of the emergence of new parties in Europe, see Kitschelt (1989).

38. This strategy makes sense in mixed electoral systems, where some seats in Congress are distributed on a proportional representation basis. The party might decide to try to increase its representation in Congress rather than attempt to win the presidency. Alternatively, in a federal system, the party may decide to try to win local and gubernatorial elections rather than to attempt to win national elections. As we shall see below, for many years, this was the PAN's strategy.

39. In electoral parties, however, the "party on the ground" is ephemeral; it organizes during electoral periods but tends to disintegrate afterward.

40. Thus these parties do not necessarily become the electoral opportunists imagined by Downs (1957), because they often include a core coalition of activists who defend the parties' original ideas and who prevent them from going beyond their central programmatic and ideological concerns in their search for votes (Panebianco, 1982, 72).

41. This conclusion is different from Mair's (1994). He argues that the party on the ground is the element that has weakened the most in political parties in the industrialized world. Both the party in central office and the party in government have taken the lead. I am not so sure of this conclusion, but in my typology and considering the types of regimes I am dealing with (presidential regimes in underdeveloped countries), I think that it is the party in central office that is losing power vis-à-vis the party in government and the party on the ground. As Aldrich (1995) argues, the parties now follow their candidates and perform an important service for them, both when they are working on the ground and when they are in office.

42. Interview with Arturo Garcia Portillo, a member of the party's National Executive Committee and of the Statutory Reform Committee. Mexico City, March 2002.

43. I elaborate this point in chapter 5.

Chapter Three.   The PAN as a Sectarian Party

1. After 1976, when the PAN failed to nominate a presidential candidate due to its internal divisions, the government decided to penalize political parties that did not present presidential candidates by withdrawing their official registration. Incentives for participating in elections, even if these were fraudulent, increased with this reform.

2. The reluctance of important sectors of the party to support the nomination of Vicente Fox as the PAN's presidential candidate in the 2000 elections stems in large part from their fear that Fox, a "newcomer" to the PAN, would not follow the party's traditional ideological principles. Indeed, a major obstacle Fox faced was convincing members of his own party to support him.

3. An important outcome of this law was limiting the number of parties and making it harder for political parties to compete against the PRI. Many regionally based parties could not gain official recognition after this reform. See Molinar (1991, 27–28).

4. The National Council is composed of three hundred active members selected by the National Assembly. These *consejeros* are drawn from the states and selected according to the electoral weight of the party in each state. In addition, the council includes the PAN's president and general secretary, the former presidents of the PAN, the presidents of the State Directive Committees, the leaders of the party in Congress, the governors, and the president of the republic (if in office). The National Executive Committee is composed of no less than twenty and no more than forty active members selected by the National Council and includes the president of the party, the former presidents of the national executive committees, and the leaders of the party in Congress, as well as the heads of the women's and youth organizations. The National Executive Committee is responsible for the day-to-day operation of the party (Articles 44–61).

5. Estatutos del Partido Acción Nacional, Serie de Documentos Básicos, 2. Articles 12, 13, 14, 40, 41, 42.

6. The party statutes recognize the right of party members to organize on the basis of age, professional interests, or any other activity. This, however, rarely occurred. With the exception of the youth organizations and the recently created women's promotion group, the PAN has failed to promote the organization of trade or professional groups (Reveles, 1996).

7. Being confined to the opposition and without access to state resources, the issue of patronage was purely ideological. The PAN did not even have the opportunity to distribute "selective" incentives to its followers. Once the party gained access to office, however, the distribution of selective incentives ceased to be a merely theoretical issue and became, as I discuss in a later chapter, a major political and practical concern.

8. Interview with Juan Antonio García Villa, General Secretary of the PAN in 1996, Mexico City, November 1996.

9. Interview with Castillo Peraza, longtime member of the PAN and former president of the PAN, Mexico City, October 1996. Castillo Peraza left the party after he lost the 1997 mayoral election in Mexico City.

10. As of 2000, the party has not been able to establish its presence in every municipality in the country. Mexico has 2,432 municipalities. The PAN has municipal committees in 1,671 municipalities. However, according to Wuhs (2002), the secretary of organization of the PAN lacks information on 801 of those municipal structures. That is, the PAN does not know if these are accredited municipal committees or not. Therefore, we can say that the PAN has 867 municipal committees in place. I thank Steven Wuhs for sharing this information with me.

11. Interview with Luis H. Alvarez, October 1996.

12. Interview with Jesus Mesta, Secretary of Finance, Chihuahua, June 1998.

13. Interview with Ernesto Ruffo, Tijuana, June 1996.

14. In 1997 the PAN relaxed the rules for accepting "adherents": anyone who wanted to register as an adherent could do so. However, the party did not accept adherents as full members until they complied with the established process for gaining full membership.

15. Interview with Carlos Castillo Peraza, Mexico City, October 1996.

16. Interview with Juan Antonio García Villa, Mexico City, November 1996.

17. Interview with Castillo Peraza, Mexico City, October 1996.

18. The *diputados plurinominales*, and *senadores de representación proporcional* are selected from a party list according to the total percentage of votes the party obtains in federal legislative elections. These candidates continue to be selected at the party's national conventions.

19. According to Article 37 of the new statutes, aspiring candidates still have to be approved by the party's National Executive Committee.

20. Only senatorial candidates elected by majority rule. The two additional senators—the proportional representation senators—are selected at the party's national convention.

21. Some leaders of the PAN, who favored the relaxation of the membership requirements and who advocated for more significant reforms of the party's candidate selection process, believe that the 2001 reforms constitute a regression in the party's adaptation to its new condition as a governing party. Interview with Arturo García Portillo, member of the Statutory Reform Committee, Mexico City, February 2002.

22. This is the case even if a candidate does not agree with some of the issues elaborated in the platform. Until recently, this was a purely hypothetical situation. I return to this point below.

23. According to some panista leaders, any active member can sign up to be a delegate to the party's conventions. In the past this was not a problem given the small number of people who actually attended the conventions. Interview with Juan Antonio García Villa, former secretary general of the PAN, August 2000.

24. Interview with Eliseo Martínez, former mayor of León, Guanajuato, July 1999. Martínez competed for the party's nomination for governor of the state of Guanajuato in 1999 but lost. He complained that the party apparatus in his state had controlled the convention.

25. As is the case at the federal level, the state conventions select the local deputies elected by proportional representation. Local deputies elected by majority rule are selected by a party convention at the district level.

26. Interview with Carlos Castillo Peraza, Mexico City, October 1996. Another longtime member of the PAN also said that the national conventions were so small that the theater where these were held was usually half empty. Not more than five hundred people attended. Interview with Juan Antonio García Villa, Mexico City, April 1999.

27. Interview with Felipe Calderón Hinojosa, president of the PAN (1996–99), Mexico City, August 1998.

28. The National Convention used to draft the party list for these positions. But given the size of the National Convention, in 1999 the party decided to have the states draft the lists. The National Convention then reviews the lists and draws up the final list of the party. Wuhs (2002).

29. Interview with Bernardo López, Fundación Rafael Preciado Hernández, April 1999.

30. Party activists were asked what was more important for the party, attracting new voters, even when this could risk losing traditional voters, or assuring that the party's traditional voters continue to vote for it. On a scale of 1 to 5, where 1 meant total agreement with the first position and 5 total agreement with the second, the mean was 2.8; that is, the majority of activists were more inclined to the second option. Interestingly, party leaders were slightly inclined to the first option. This could be explained by the presence of a greater number of newcomers in the party's Consejo Político Nacional (National Political Council). Survey of party militants and party leaders, conducted by Ken Greene in conjunction with the newspaper *Reforma*. Partial results published in *Reforma*, July 2, 1999.

31. Survey conducted at the XVII National Assembly in 1998 by the Fundación Rafael Preciado Hernández. I thank the Rafael Preciado Hernández Foundation for giving me access to these materials.

32. Manuel Gómez Morin, second address to the National Convention, 1940. Cited in Loeaza (1999, 179). This speech was delivered after the elections, which were condemned for being fraudulent and violent.

33. However, it did not present a presidential candidate but rather supported the candidacy of Almazán, a disaffected general who organized in opposition to the PNR.

34. Gómez Morin retired after he believed two basic goals of the party had been achieved: turning the Mexican government away from its antibusiness and anticlerical position (Mabry, 1973, 145–47).

35. The party lacked a registry of party activists, so the number of militants is unknown. But according to Reveles, by the late 1980s, when the PAN "modernized" its registry, it had 58,000 active members throughout the country (Reveles, 1996, 29).

36. Until 1972 all presidents of the PAN had been members of Catholic organizations and movements.

37. In presidential elections it won less than 15 percent of the total vote. See Tables 3.1 and 3.2.

38. The electoral environment in 1958 was tense. Luis H. Alvarez, the PAN's presidential candidate, received various death threats and was attacked during his campaign. The elections were plagued with irregularities: stuffing ballot boxes, allowing people to vote multiple times, opening ballots in places that were hard to find, closing ballots ahead of time, intimidating voters, and so on (Lujambio, 1994, 54).

39. This was the only amendment of the party's doctrinal principles since its foundation. These amendments referred to the social responsibility of the PAN and its distancing from economic liberalism; the party's tasks as an opposition party; the explicit dissociation from Christian Democracy; and the precautions militants should take given the risks of losing the party ideology and values when it won power (Rodriguez Prats, 1997, 149). No further amendments have been introduced in the party's doctrinal principles since.

40. By the intermediate elections of 1961, the PAN's share of the total vote decreased significantly (see Table 3.1). The weakening of opposition parties to the point of extinction was too dangerous for the PRI and the government. Without an effective opposition, the PRI could not claim legitimacy. The PAN conditioned its participation in further elections on the introduction of a substantive electoral reform.

41. During Echeverría's administration, government expenditures increased substantially. In 1971 federal expenditures accounted for 26.8 percent of GDP; by 1975, 40 percent; and in 1976, 39.6 percent. The number of public employees increased 62.8 percent between 1971 and 1976. See Tello (1979).

42. Other changes involved the method of selecting the party's president and the duration of his term, the composition of the internal bodies of the party, and the extent to which the party's National Executive Committee could intervene in state and local affairs (Reveles, 1996, 33). However, the central rules for maintaining the party as an organization—that is, the rules for affiliating members, for selecting candidates, and defining the structure of the party and its relations with civil society—remained untouched.

43. *La Nación* is the PAN's official newspaper.

Chapter Four.   The PAN as an Electoral Party

1. With the exception of the presidency of Lázaro Cárdenas, which gave rise to the PAN. For an excellent analysis of why Argentina's business elites resorted to the military to protect their interests, see Gibson (1996).

2. For an analysis of the transformation of the PNR into the PRM in 1938, see Garrido (1982).

3. This term was coined by Reynolds (1970).

4. The strongest conflict since Cárdenas was during the presidency of Luis Echeverría (1970–76). This conflict, however, did not spill over to the electoral arena. On closer analysis, Echeverría did not really attack business interests. In fact, his government promoted policies that favored the consolidation of holding companies in Mexico. For discussion of this topic, see Mizrahi (1994a).

5. For further discussion of the politics of entrepreneurs during the 1960s and throughout the 1980s, see Heredia (1992); Tirado, Luna, and Millán (1985); Labastida (1986); Mizrahi (1996).

6. According to the Chambers Law of 1941, business organizations were divided into two large confederations, the National Confederation of Chambers of Commerce (CONCANACO) and the National Confederation of Chambers of Industry (CONCAMIN). Entrepreneurs were obliged to affiliate with one of these two confederations. By formally dividing the business community into different confederations, the government attempted to limit the capacity of the private sector to form horizontal linkages and organize in opposition to the government (Purcell and Kaufman Purcell, 1977, 196). The other major business confederation, COPARMEX, created in 1929 by

Monterrey industrialists, is a multisectoral business union whose member firms affiliate on a voluntary basis. Since its creation, COPARMEX has maintained its independence from the government and has been the most radical and confrontational business organization in the country. However, COPARMEX's influence was limited by its small membership. Until 1970 it had only five thousand members (Bravo Mena, 1987; Saragoza, 1988; Buendia Laredo, 1989; Mizrahi, 1994a). In 1997 the Chambers Law was amended and affiliation with the business confederations became voluntary. In addition to these confederations, entrepreneurs also participated in a number of associations that were voluntary. See note 7.

7. Unlike the business confederations, these were voluntary associations. The ABM was created in 1928 and became the most prestigious business association in the country. Most of the ABM's members lived in the Federal District. The CMHN was established in 1962 by the thirty largest entrepreneurs in the country. It is an informal and multisectoral association without a permanent address or a president. Its members join only by invitation. This association had direct and permanent access to the president and the highest-level authorities. By the 1980s the CMHN had only thirty-two members. Interview with Juan Sánchez Navarro, prominent entrepreneur and a member of the CMHN. January 1990.

8. Interview with Emilio Goicochea Luna, a medium-size entrepreneur from Sinaloa who actively supported the PAN after 1982, San Francisco, California, July 1990.

9. The creation of the Banca Múltiple during the 1970s allowed various financial services (commercial and investment banks and nonbank financial firms such as fiduciary institutions, mortgage firms, insurance companies, and leasing firms) to become integrated into a single financial institution. The banking law of 1974 promoted mergers, particularly among the small and medium-size banks, as a way to foster competition in a financial market heavily dominated by two large banks, Bancomer and Banamex (Cardero and Quijano, 1982, 186).

10. For an excellent analysis of how the internationalization of financial markets disproportionately benefited large multisector conglomerates, see Maxfield (1990). In 1970 less than 1 percent of industrial establishments controlled 67 percent of industry's fixed assets and accounted for 63 percent of the total value of production. On the other hand, 92 percent of industrial establishments controlled 5.2 percent of fixed assets and accounted for only 6 percent of the total value of production. Fifty-five percent of the total production in the manufacturing sector was generated in the Federal District and the state of Mexico (Tello, 1979, 21). Almost all of the largest firms in the country were founded before the 1970s and were located primarily in the Federal District, the state of Mexico, Nuevo León, and Jalisco (Cordero, Santín, and Tirado, 1983, 92–95). By 1980, 1 percent of industrial establishments controlled 85 percent of industry's fixed assets and accounted for 69 percent of the total value of production (INEGI, Censos Industriales, 1976 and 1981).

11. They were overall more successful in the CONCANACO, the Commerce Confederation of Chambers, than in the CONCAMIN, because the former has a

decentralized organizational structure while the latter is heavily centralized. They also succeeded in gaining leadership positions in COPARMEX, which is also more decentralized and in general was more open to allowing the participation of entrepreneurs. See Mizrahi (1994a).

12. Between 1982 and 1986 three new associations were created, the Asociación Nacional de Micro, Pequeña Industria (AMIN), the Asociación Nacional de Industriales de la Transformación (ANIT), and the Consejo Coordinador de Asociaciones de Industriales (COCAI). "The AMIN and ANIT stated that they emerged as a response to the chambers' and confederations' indifference [to small and medium-size entrepreneurs because these organizations] were controlled by the biggest national and international firms. The COCAI, for its part, stressed that it was created to defend businessmen against government's attacks after the nationalization of the banks" (Hernández Rodríguez, 1991, 462).

13. The oil boom gave López Portillo's administration a false sense that all that was left to do was to "administer abundance." His administration was characterized by rampant corruption and government excesses. One entrepreneur from Ciudad Juárez summarized the feeling against López Portillo when he remarked, "López Portillo forgot he was president. He was frivolous and was consumed by corruption." Interview with Francisco Villarreal, an active supporter of the PAN in Ciudad Juárez who later was elected municipal president, Ciudad Juárez, July 1991.

14. COPARMEX was founded by Monterrey industrialists in 1929. Like the PAN, COPARMEX is heavily influenced by social Christian doctrine and endorses the principles of solidarity and subsidiarity. COPARMEX sponsors courses on social Christian doctrine and promotes among its members a sense of businessmen's "social responsibility," that is, the idea that in addition to making a profit, businessmen have to care for the well-being of their community and promote greater social justice. This requires acquiring political education and adopting an active role in politics, both of which are attitudes the business community did not consider important in the past. See Mizrahi (1994a).

15. Clouthier died tragically in a car accident in 1990. Other examples of former COPARMEX officials who played important roles in the PAN are Francisco Barrio, president of COPARMEX in Ciudad Juárez before he became mayor of Ciudad Juárez in 1983 and later governor in 1992; Ricardo Villa Escalera, president of COPARMEX in the city of Puebla and candidate for the governorship in 1992; Ernesto Ruffo, president of COPARMEX in Ensenada and governor of Baja California in 1989; Adalberto Rosas, president of COPARMEX in Hermosillo, Sonora, and gubernatorial candidate in 1985; Carlos Medina Plascencia, president of COPARMEX in León, Guanajuato, and governor of Guanajuato in 1991; and Vicente Fox, president of COPARMEX in León and the PAN's presidential candidate in 2000.

16. This doctrine is also fundamental to the PAN. These entrepreneurs saw support of the PAN as a logical extension of their training and socialization.

17. One of the attractive features of the PAN during the 1980s was that it was taken over by a new breed of leaders who were political outsiders but with enormous social

prestige. Unlike traditional politicians, these entrepreneurs did not seem to need politics to make a living. Quite to the contrary, they were perceived as people who were willing to risk their comfortable lives to fight for democracy. Hunger strikes and civil disobedience after allegedly fraudulent elections gave these entrepreneurs an ever greater aura of heroism, for entrepreneurs had never before been seen organizing events typically reserved for the most disadvantaged and marginal sectors of society. See Lau (1989) and Puga (1984).

18. Interview with Miguel Fernández, an entrepreneur from Ciudad Juárez, Chihuahua, June 1992.

19. Most of these entrepreneurs were later accepted as full members of the party after being actively involved in party affairs.

20. Interview with Carlos Abedrop, president of ABM at the time the banks were nationalized. Mexico City, August 1989.

21. For example, during the Echeverría administration, the largest entrepreneurs openly challenged the government and opposed the president's "populist" policies. For an analysis of the conflict between entrepreneurs and the government during the Echeverría administration, see Luna, 1984; Martínez Nava, 1984.

22. Interview with Federico Muggenburg, former director of the Centro de Estudios Económicos y Sociales del Sector Privado (CEESP), Mexico City, July 1991.

23. It is important to mention, however, that many of these entrepreneurs were in fact punished with audits orchestrated by the federal government.

24. Interview with Lic. Guillermo Pérez, president of the Chihuahua Chamber of Commerce in 1986, Chihuahua, July 1991.

25. Interview with Francisco Barrio, Ciudad Juárez, July 1991.

26. In many cases, entrepreneurs ran as external candidates, on the "invitation" of the PAN. Some examples are Francisco Barrio in Chihuahua and Manuel Clouthier in Sinaloa. They both started their campaigns without being members of the PAN and organized their campaigns without much interference from the party. The manner in which Francisco Barrio ran his candidacy in Ciudad Juárez in 1983 is a good example of the extent to which entrepreneurs were able to impose their agenda on the party. Barrio accepted the candidacy on two conditions: first, that the party would not interfere with the organization of his campaign, and second, that his candidacy would be launched first by a civic organization and only later by the PAN. The PAN accepted both conditions. Interview with Francisco Barrio, Ciudad Juárez, July 1991.

27. Interview with Eduardo Sojo, Chief of Economic Advisors, Government of Guanajuato, April 1999.

28. Interview with Alberto Mesta, February 1992.

29. Interview with Carlos Castillo Peraza, Mexico City, 1996.

30. By the end of the 1960s, the long period of sustained economic growth had come to an end. The country started to experience inflationary pressures and economic slowdowns. From 1970 to the present, the economy has not been able to maintain sustained growth.

31. Quoted in La Nación, November 15, 1974, 15.

32. As many party activists recognized, however, without a realistic chance of winning elections, few people had an interest in becoming members of the PAN. At best, the party could obtain the votes of discontent voters without necessarily increasing its membership.

33. This faction, strongly influenced by Catholic thought, also stressed the importance of social justice and the party's commitment to the poor. They were opposed to the influence of entrepreneurs within the party because they thought they were less interested in the social aspects of the PAN's doctrine. Entrepreneurs were concerned more about power and profits than about fairer distribution of income and the promotion of the "collective good." There are some facets of panista thought that make it more akin to socialism than to capitalism, a philosophy that has a long tradition in the Catholic Church.

34. While the PAN failed to nominate a candidate, the other "opposition" parties supported the candidacy of López Portillo. Most of these parties (the Partido Auténtico de la Revolución Democrática [PARM] and the Partido Popular Socialista, [PPS]) were in fact sponsored by the PRI and the government to divide the opposition and to maintain a democratic facade. This is why these parties were often called "satellite parties" (Molinar, 1991, 85). Only the Mexican Communist Party, which was not officially recognized at the time, ran a candidate for president, Valentín Campa. Lacking a registered opposition candidate, however, López Portillo ran against his own shadow in the 1976 presidential elections.

35. The reform also legalized left-wing parties and incorporated them in the electoral game. This was important in moderating their demands, giving them a stake in the electoral process, and decreasing their support for the guerrilla movement, a legacy of the student movement of 1968 (Crespo, 2000, 1).

36. Moreover, since then the party has increased its capacity to nominate candidates for all electoral districts in the country, as well as for all state governments. While from 1970 to 1976 the PAN nominated candidates for governor in only seven states, from 1976 to 1982 it nominated candidates in twenty-four states.

37. The electoral expansion of the PAN in the federal Congress can also be attributed principally to the new formula of proportional representation. The party still had a limited capacity to win majority rule districts. That did not change significantly until the 1980s.

38. From 1983 to 1986 the PAN won a total of twenty-three municipal elections. More than half of these victories (12) were in northern municipalities.

39. Some examples are Ernesto Ruffo in Baja Califonia, the first panista elected governor in 1989; Francisco Barrio in Chihuahua, elected governor in 1992; Vicente Fox in Guanajuato, elected governor in 1995 and the PAN's presidential candidate in the 2000 election; Manuel Clouthier in Sinaloa, the PAN's presidential candidate in 1988 and candidate for governor of Sinaloa in 1986; Fernando Canales Clariond from Nuevo León, elected governor in 1997; Alberto Cárdenas from Jalisco, elected governor in 1994; Ignacio Loyola in Querétaro; Felipe González in Aguascalientes; Rosendo

Villarreal from Coahuila, elected mayor of Saltillo in 1993; Adalberto Rosas in Sonora, candidate for the governorship of Sonora in 1985. Most of these entrepreneurs had never participated in politics before 1982. But they were actively involved in their business organizations, most notably in COPARMEX. I return to this point below.

40. For a full discussion of the case of Chihuahua, see Mizrahi (1994a, 1994b); Aziz Nassif (1987).

41. In 1988 the PRI encountered unexpectedly strong opposition from a loose left-wing coalition led by Cuauhtémoc Cárdenas. In that presidential election, the PAN fell to third place in terms of number of votes. Since then, the Salinas administration adopted a much more tolerant position toward the PAN than toward Cárdenas and his new party, the PRD. The PAN was heavily criticized by the PRD for allegedly adopting a more moderate role (for example, endorsing the results of the presidential elections and adopting a conciliatory stance toward the federal government and President Salinas de Gortari in particular). The PRD became the most radical and confrontational opposition to the PRI. Its radicalism, however, marginalized them in the electoral arena. Moreover, unlike the PAN, many PRD activists were persecuted and killed. According to Bruhn (1997, 17), more than 250 PRD activists were killed or disappeared between 1988 and 1994. For an analysis of the federal government's different attitude toward the PAN and the PRD during the Salinas government, see Crespo (1995).

42. In terms of the percentage of the population governed by the PAN, the expansion of the party has also been dramatic. Until 1983 the PAN controlled only 2 percent of the total population in the country and had not been able to overcome that limit. In 1998, by contrast, 38 percent of the population lived in municipalities controlled by the PAN (Lujambio, 2000, 84).

43. Interview with Raymundo Gómez, Chihuahua, June 1992.

44. Interview with Francisco Barrio, Ciudad Juárez, July 1991.

45. This support did not last beyond the elections, however. As I discuss in the next chapter, as a party in government, the PAN has not been able to maintain its electoral coalitions and work with organized social groups. In fact, many leaders of the PAN have expressed their distrust of and refusal to work with nongovernmental organizations (NGOs) and other social movements. They are particularly resentful of NGOs that in their view do not have the responsibility of governing and thus seem to maintain a more critical yet not committed attitude. Interview with Carlos Castillo Peraza, October 1996.

46. Most of these people came from the middle class and were educated and lived in urban areas. In many places the PAN also successfully mobilized large sectors of the nonunionized working class and some peasants. The latter, however, are not a typical panista constituency. See Magaloni and Moreno (2000) on the panista constituency.

47. In 1986 Francisco Barrio was the PAN's candidate for governor. He went on a hunger strike to protest election fraud and traveled to Washington, D.C., to present the Chihuahua case to the OAS. The election in Chihuahua caught the attention of the

international media and became a symbol of the PAN's electoral strength and its struggle against fraud. See Molinar (1987); Lau, Vicente, and Orozco (1986); Krauze (1986); Mizrahi (1994a).

48. Interview with Ernesto Ruffo, former governor of Baja California, June 1996.

49. As I argue above, when gaining access to power was not feasible, many traditional panistas adjusted their expectations by arguing that power was not really their ultimate concern but rather the promotion of certain ideological values and the education of civil society. However, once power is within reach, these panistas feel that they are the ones who deserve positions of power because they have endured in the party organization despite the lack of rewards. They believe that power is a means to "serve" the public and feel they are entitled to it for their years of activism. Following Elster's (1985) "sour grapes" logic, we can say that these panistas "adjusted" their expectations in light of the possibilities.

50. Interview with Luis H. Alvarez, president of the PAN from 1987 to 1993 and currently senator from Chihuahua, Mexico City, September 1996.

51. These are Fundación Rafael Preciado Hernández and Fundación Miguel Estrada Iturbide. The former serves the Chamber of Deputies and the latter the Senate. The Rafael Preciado Hernandez Foundation receives financial support from the Konrad Adenauer Foundation, an institution linked to the German Christian Democratic Party.

52. By 1996 the PAN had municipal committees in a total of 1,400 municipalities. There are 2,432 municipalities in the country. Most of the municipalities where the PAN does not have offices are in poor and rural regions of the country.

53. Confidential interview. I have heard numerous interpretations of Diego Fernández de Cevallos's behavior during the 1994 presidential campaign. Alvarez argued that Fernández de Cevallos had to be hospitalized and thus could not appear in public as frequently as he did before. Other panistas argued that Fernández de Cevallos actually did not withdraw from the public eye but that the media had limited his appearances. Finally, some panistas have told me that winning was not in his plans and that this became even more evident when he refused to run as the mayoral candidate in Mexico City in 1997, a contest he could have won against Cuauhtémoc Cárdenas from the PRD.

54. In 1987 dissident members from the so-called Corriente Renovadora del PRI left the PRI and decided to organize their own opposition movement. They were led by Cuauhtémoc Cárdenas, who they identified as a man who was deeply committed to improving the lot of the poor in the country. According to the members of this "corriente," the PRI had abandoned its revolutionary commitments by adopting neoliberal economic policies. These leaders had progressively lost positions of power within the PRI. During the infighting for the nomination of the presidential candidate, these priísta leaders decided to challenge the PRI from outside. See Bruhn (1997).

55. *La Jornada,* July 7, 1988; July 9, 1988; July 10, 1988; July 14, 1988; *Washington Post,* July 8, 1988.

56. The PRI won 52 percent of the total vote; the FDN, 31 percent; and the PAN, 17 percent (Loaeza, 1999, 468).

57. Being a defector from the PRI, Cárdenas was perceived by this party as a traitor. Moreover, Cárdenas's left-wing leanings and his opposition to the economic reforms introduced by the government of Miguel de la Madrid made him an unlikely candidate for cooperation with the new administration.

58. Clouthier continued to maintain the radical position he had assumed during the campaign. He called for the annulment of the elections on the grounds that no one could be sure who had won. The party increasingly distanced itself from this position as its leadership decided to recognize the official results and to work more closely with the new administration. Clouthier opposed the electoral reform, but after he was killed in a car accident, the reform was passed in Congress with the support of the PAN. Although most analysts accept the view that Clouthier's death was an accident, some panista members have raised suspicions that it might have been politically motivated, although the family did not make that claim, at least openly. In several interviews, I was told that the family believes Clouthier was assassinated but did not press the issue because of death threats.

59. The 1989 reform granted a greater margin of overrepresentation in Congress to the party that obtained the largest proportion of votes. For a thorough discussion of these reforms, see Lujambio (1995).

60. Interview with Luis H. Alvarez, Mexico City, November 1996.

61. These included strict sanctions against electoral delinquents, a provision that enhanced the authority of the electoral tribunal (Tribunal Electoral), the introduction of a photo electoral card, and a prohibition against party members becoming leaders of the *mesas directivas de casilla* (representatives at the electoral booths). According to Lujambio (1997, 39), the PRI also "promised" panista leaders that if they accepted the reform, the PRI and the government would be more willing to recognize panista victories.

62. One of the leaders of this group was Pablo Emilio Madero, who was supported by the pragmatists in 1976 as a presidential candidate.

63. In a way, however, the conflict in reality revealed an internal power struggle for control of the party. The Foristas had been displaced from many leadership positions they controlled during the mid-1970s and which they had won against the doctrinaire faction (Reynoso, 1993; Arriola, 1994).

64. Vicente Fox became actively involved in the PAN in 1988, at the invitation of Clouthier. Fox was elected to the lower chamber of Congress in 1988, when the PRI lost its two-thirds majority for the first time in history.

65. The most outspoken of these was Diego Fernández de Cevallos, the PAN's presidential candidate in 1994 and a moral authority inside the PAN. Fernández de Cevallos distrusts Fox for his failure to adhere to the PAN's traditional principles. In his view, and in that of many traditional panistas, Fox is perceived as an ambitious outsider who is ready to compromise his doctrinal and ideological positions to win

elections. For these panistas, it is better to "lose elections than to win at any price." Confidential interview, Mexico City, April 1999.

Chapter Five.   The PAN in Government: Obstacles to Building a Catch-All Party

1. In 1991 the PAN claimed it had won the gubernatorial election in Guanajuato. Although the PRI had already been declared the winner, faced with massive post-election demonstrations, President Salinas intervened and negotiated with the PAN and with the PRI to reschedule extraordinary elections and to appoint an interim governor in the meantime. Carlos Medina Plascencia, panista mayor of the city of León, was appointed interim governor. However, a priísta was appointed secretary of government, the second most important position after that of the governor. New elections were not held until 1995, when Vicente Fox won in the state.

2. In 1998, however, the PAN lost the elections in Chihuahua. I elaborate on this specific case in the next chapter.

3. With the exception of Mexico City, the PAN controlled most of the important cities in the country: Guadalajara, Ciudad Juárez, Tijuana, Mérida, Puebla, Veracruz, León, Monterrey, Mexicali, Tuxtla Gutiérrez, Oaxaca, Culiacán, Morelia, and Aguascalientes.

4. In 2000 the PAN controlled the state governments in Morelos, Aguascalientes, Jalisco, Guanajuato, Nuevo León, Querétaro, and Baja California. In the states of Nayarit and Chiapas, the PAN also won the elections in a coalition with the PRD and other opposition parties.

5. In 1992 the PAN won the governorship, the most important cities in the state, with the exception of Chihuahua, the capital, and a majority in the local congress. In the presidential election of 1994, the PRI won the election by a wide margin. In the midterm elections of 1995, the PAN lost its majority in congress, and with the exception of Ciudad Juárez, it also lost most of the cities it had won in 1992.

6. In the case of Jalisco, however, the PAN won the gubernatorial election by a very small margin of 2 percent and with an abstention rate of 70 percent. In 1995 the PAN won by a margin of 15 percent. The governor in 1995 was elected with more votes than the governor in 2001. The rest of the states controlled by the PAN, Nuevo León, Aguascalientes, and Querétaro, do not have elections until 2003.

7. For an analysis of the PRI as an organization at the state level, see Langston (2000).

8. As expected, this statement created a widespread reaction, and the mayor finally declared that it "was a personal comment and by no means reflected the municipality's official policy." Government's Bulletin, 25 August 2000.

9. The PAN had an absolute majority in Congress and thus passed the initiative without the support of the PRI or the PRD. The PAN's National Executive Committee condemned this legislation. As it was a highly divisive issue, the PAN's leadership did not want to foster a greater political controversy at a time when it had just won

the presidential elections. Moreover, although the PAN openly condemns abortion, this issue is not considered a national priority. The National Executive Committee of the PAN declared that "penalizing all types of abortion was ill-timed." *La Jornada,* 8 August 2000.

10. The governor claimed that he vetoed this legislation as a result of an opinion poll conducted in Guanajuato. According to this poll, 63 percent of the people in the state were opposed, and 83 percent considered that abortion should be permitted under certain circumstances. *La Jornada,* 8 August 2000. These results are interesting because Guanajuato is considered a very religious state.

11. According to Francisco Barrio, former governor of Chihuahua, during his administration, many of the innovations introduced, such as combating corruption and simplifying the procedures for obtaining a driver's license, a birth certificate, or a property title, were insignificant in terms of gaining greater political support for the PAN. This was so much the case that the current priísta administration has rolled back the majority of these administrative reforms. Interview with Francisco Barrio, Mexico City, August 2000.

12. In the case of Chihuahua, for example, the government decided to invest significant moneys in the restoration of the sewage system, which had not been repaired in decades. According to panista officials in the state, since the sewage is underground and no one sees it, the PRI refused to invest in this project. But it was imperative to restore it, for it had numerous leaks. Interview with Jesus Mesta, Finance Secretary, Chihuahua, 1996.

13. Interview with Felipe Calderón, former PAN national president. November 1999. This has been repeated to me in numerous interviews.

14. In large part, the problem is that elected officials cannot be reelected. Without this incentive, public officials tend to concentrate more on the administrative than the political aspects of government.

15. Interview with Jesus Mesta, Finance Secretary, Government of Chihuahua, Chihuahua, May 1996.

16. Interview with Ernesto Ruffo, Mexico City, June 1996.

17. As Mainwaring (2000) and Mainwaring and Scully (1995) argue, weak political parties are not conducive to democratic forms of government. Political parties are crucial institutions in democracies; without strong political parties, governments are tempted to develop their own ties to society and appeal to the "people" without any mediating institutions that can hold them accountable for their actions. Where government officials can be reelected, these "populist" strategies might allow them to maintain their hold on office. In countries like Mexico where government officials cannot be reelected, parties face greater incentives to build these networks of political support. The PRI's success and political longevity cannot be explained without exploring these ties. The refusal to build stronger and long-lasting ties to society is a recipe for electoral disaster. I return to this point below.

18. Interview with Carlos Castillo Peraza, former president of the PAN's National Executive Committee, Mexico City, October 1996.

19. There is also a difference in social class between longtime panista activists and the new generation of panista activists, who are generally wealthier. These differences have also led to resentment inside the party, for it is the so-called *perfumados* (those who use perfume) who have reaped all the benefits from access to office.

20. For example, Medina Plascencia had a secretary general from the PRI; Fox included a finance secretary who was a member of the PRI; and Barrio appointed as his secretary general a former priísta, Eduardo Romero Ramos. Ramos said in an interview, "I am the 'ambassador' to the PRI. The governor considered he needed a friendly mediator between the government and the interest groups linked to the PRI." Interview with Eduardo Romero Ramos, Chihuahua, August 1994.

21. These lists depend entirely on the party's endorsement. The composition of the PAN's legislators has other consequences in the formulation and promotion of public policies. I return to this point below.

22. This was one of his campaign mottoes when he was competing for the presidency of his party in 1996.

23. Personal conversations with various panistas who worked closely with President Fox during his campaign.

24. Interview with Felipe Calderón, Boston, Mass., November 1999.

25. Pablo Alvarez Padilla, former federal deputy and the PAN's president in Guanajuato, March 1990. Cited in Luis Miguel Rionda (1996, 30).

26. After the reforms introduced in 2001, this recruitment mechanism does not have such a direct impact on the nomination of senatorial and gubernatorial candidates, as these are now selected through closed primary elections rather than party conventions. However, conventions are still the party's most important decision-making and deliberative bodies. Moreover, since only active members are allowed to vote in primary elections, the recruitment of party members still affects the selection of candidates, albeit in a more indirect way.

27. Interview with Héctor Chávez Barrón, government official, Chihuahua, February 1998.

28. Interview with Eliseo Martínez, former municipal president of León, Guanajuato, and a candidate for the party's nomination at the 1999 party convention.

29. In the survey of party activists and leaders conducted by Greene and published by *Reforma*, the PAN's activists and leaders are clearly conservative with respect to their positions on these issues. Seventy-four percent of the PAN's leaders and 56 percent of the PAN's activists said that abortion should never be permitted. *Reforma*, July 2, 1999.

30. This is exactly what these activists perceive happens in the PRD, a party whose loose affiliation criteria are considered responsible for the lack of a coherent and unified ideological position.

31. Interview with Felipe Calderón, Mexico City, November 1999.

32. The other major "opposition" party, the left-of-center PRD, has 356,545 members who are only in the Federal District. The PRI does not have a registry of its members, but they are estimated in the millions.

33. Interview with Ernesto Ruffo, Mexico City, November 1996.

34. Interview with Carlos Castillo Peraza, Mexico City, November 1996.

35. However, a candidate can decide to pay for the transportation of delegates. Although delegates are not committed to any single candidate, paying their transportation becomes an informal means of influencing their vote. Moreover, some delegates are already committed to a particular candidate, although no statute exists to control how these delegates actually vote.

36. Municipal presidency candidates need only ten signatures. Party Reglamentos, Chapter VI. The party can also ask nonmilitants to run as candidates (Chapter VI, Art. 48). In the past, when party members had few incentives to seek the party's nomination, this became a means to recruit candidates. This was the procedure the party followed when entrepreneurs ran as party candidates during the 1980s. Given the expansion of its electorate, the party no longer resorts to this mechanism.

37. This further increases the party's control over the candidate selection process. According to the president of the PAN, Luis Felipe Bravo Mena, this exam guarantees a minimum standard of competence for all the PAN's candidates. In his view, this makes the PAN a "better party than the others, for both the PRI and the PRD do not really control the quality of the people they nominate for office." Interview with author, May 2002.

38. The party's National Executive Committee can veto a candidate for the Senate or a state government whenever an internal conflict threatens to divide the party. According to Wuhs (2001), during the presidency of Felipe Calderón, the National Executive Committee vetoed several candidacies. This, however, is intended as a mechanism of last resort and is not designed to select candidates with a particular ideological profile.

39. Interview with Ernesto Ruffo, June 1996. The candidate's exam referred to above is an outcome of this discussion.

40. Interview with Luis H. Alvarez, September 1996.

41. Interview with Raul Ramirez, the PAN's Director of Organization, November 1996.

42. Interview with Governor Vicente Fox, Mexico City, November 1997.

43. Indeed, during his campaign he criticized the governor for being too pragmatic and promised to become a real "opposition governor." Interview with Manuel Carrasco, General Director of the PAN's campaign in 1998, Ciudad Juárez, September 1998.

44. The case of Guanajuato is slightly different than those of Baja California, Jalisco, and Chihuahua, because the party did nominate a newcomer and one strongly supported by then-Governor Fox. The candidate, Juan Carlos Romero Hicks, was rector of the University of Guanajuato. Although he was not a member of the PAN, he won the support of the most traditional and conservative panistas in the state. His opponent, Eliseo Martínez, was an entrepreneur who was mayor of León in 1991. Because of local party disputes, Martínez lost the support of Fox's group, which seriously harmed his nomination. For an interesting analysis of the internal party disputes, see Shirk (1999).

45. I am not at all convinced that an exam is the best means for selecting more competent candidates for office. Rather it seems to strengthen the party's control over its nominating process and to stress those qualities that are more important for the party, such as the person's integrity and "honest way of living," as explicitly stipulated in the party's membership requirements.

46. Confidential interview.

47. Interview with Francisco Barrio, Mexico City, May 1999.

48. Conversation with Sergio Sarmiento, a Mexican journalist, Washington, D.C., 1999. The differences between the party and the administration also exist at the municipal level. The party usually appoints traditional panistas to run as candidates for the city council, even when they do not have a good relationship with the mayor. As one former mayor of a wealthy city in Nuevo León complained, "The members of the city council are longtime party activists who feel they have the authority to act on their own. Far from helping me, they frankly disturb me." Interview with Aldalberto Nuñez, mayor of San Nicolás de los Garza (Nuevo León), November 1996. This opinion was expressed in many interviews with both party and public officials.

49. The fiscal reform that was finally approved by Congress passed with the votes of the PAN and the PRD. Although the PAN considered that it worked hard to approve "the only fiscal reform that was feasible," the president's criticisms of what was finally approved by Congress profoundly angered the PAN's legislators. Confidential interview with a high-level party official, Mexico City, February and April 2002.

50. Interview with Arturo García Portillo, Adjunct Secretary, National Executive Committee, Mexico City, March 2002.

51. For an interesting analysis of the origins of mass-based political parties, see Shefter (1994).

52. Carlos Castillo Peraza, *Voz y Voto*, no. 34 (March 1996): 18.

53. In Shefter's (1994, 17) view, political parties are constructed not only to transmit to political leaders the concerns of the electorate; they are also institutions constructed by political leaders to mobilize (or retain) a popular following.

54. Interview with Carlos Castillo Peraza, October 1996.

55. Armendáriz (1996). It is important to note that in 1995 the PAN lost its majority in the local congress and most of the municipalities it had won in 1992.

56. Interview with Héctor Chávez Barrón, a government official in the Secretariat of Education, Chihuahua, February 1994.

57. Interview, Tijuana, Baja California, April 1997.

58. Interview with Leandro Luján, an entrepreneur and the PAN's state deputy from 1992 to 1995, Chihuahua, August 1994. What he meant by "circus and theater" is precisely that people need to perceive that politicians do great things for them, even if these are not so spectacular in the end.

59. In 1989 the PAN had 9 seats in Congress; the PRI, 6; and the PRD, 1. Smaller parties, the PC, PARM, and PPS, obtained 1 seat each. In 1992 the PAN obtained 8 seats in Congress; the PRI 7; and the PRD, 4 (Lujambio, 2000, 132).

60. Interview with Ernesto Ruffo, June 1996.

61. This program was run similarly to the Salinas PRONASOL program but with panista agents. People called Manos a la Obra PRONASUL, referring to the blue emblem of the PAN.

62. Interview with Ernesto Ruffo, Tijuana, April 1997.

63. For an excellent study of the PRI's factional strife in states where they lost control of the government, see Langston (2002).

64. Of course, electoral results are the product of a greater number of factors. The PRI in the state was not able to recuperate from its defeat in 1989. It was torn and plagued with internal conflicts. However, Ruffo's strategy enhanced the political position of the PAN. For an elaboration of the PRI's internal splits in Baja California, see Langston, 2000.

65. Interview with Juan Manuel Oliva, President of the Comité Estatal del PAN, Guanajuato, León Guanajuato, April 1999.

66. Interview with Juan Manuel Oliva, president of the PAN in Guanajuato, May 1998.

67. Interview with Luis Ernesto Ayala, president of the Comité Municipal de León, León Guanajuato, April 1999. It is interesting to mention here that the impetus to organize at the local level derived in part from the religious experience with community base organizations in which many panistas in the state had participated. These community base organizations also were instrumental in dismantling the territorial organization of the PRI in the state. Interview with Carlos Gadsden, member of the first panista government in Guanajuato, in charge of the government's project to decentralize resources to the municipalities in the state. He is currently the director of the Instituto Nacional del Federalismo. Mexico City, October 2000.

68. Interview with Luis Miguel Rionda, Professor, Universidad de Guanjuato, Guanajuato, 1999.

69. Interview with Eduardo Romero, Secretary General, Government of Chihuahua, April 1996.

70. The program stipulated that the neighbors could organize to decide which project they wanted to sponsor in their community. They needed to elect a political representative to take responsibility for each project. Most of these projects, launched in municipalities controlled by the PRI, were designed to bypass the municipal authorities and work directly with the people at the neighborhood level. However, the PAN failed to extend its political machine to the neighborhood level, and the elected representatives for these projects turned out to be recognized social leaders traditionally linked to the PRI.

71. Interview with Fernando Alvarez, Secretario de Organización, PAN Chihuahua, April 1999.

72. In Puerto Vallarta, Jalisco, the PAN introduced a "community action" program, designed to consolidate the party structure throughout the municipality and to foster more political participation. However, the program was not implemented. According to Garnica and Gasca (1999), while the PAN succeeded in breaking up corporatist organizations tied to the PRI, it failed to create new ones. This was because of a lack

of coordination between the party leadership and the party base. According to the authors, political participation in Puerto Vallarta was minimal. The high rates of abstention in the state are to a large extent a product of the failure of the PAN to entrench itself more firmly in society.

73. Interview with Maria Marván, professor, Centro Universitario de Ciencias Sociales y Humanidades, Universidad de Guadalajara, Guadalajara, Jalisco, November 2002.

74. In states such as Puebla, Veracruz, Durango, Morelia, Zacatecas, San Luis Potosí, Tamaulipas, Yucatán, and Sinaloa, where the PAN controls important municipal governments, the party has also faced many difficulties in winning consecutive elections. A few examples illustrate this point. In Puebla in 1989, the PAN won 6 municipalities. Three years later, in 1992, it lost 5 of these municipalities. In 1995 the PAN won 23 municipalities, but it lost all of the municipalities it had won in the previous election. Finally, in 1998 the PAN won only 14 municipalities and lost 16 of the 23 municipalities it had won in the previous election. In Veracurz in 2000, the PAN lost most of the municipalities it controlled in 1997, notwithstanding that these elections took place after July 2, the presidential elections won by the PAN. This path is similar in the other states. Even in the "more successful" states, such as Jalisco and Guanajuato, the PAN did not enjoy much success at the municipal level. In Guanajuato in 1994, the PAN lost 11 of the 13 municipalities it had won in 1991. In 1997 the party won 21 municipal elections, but it lost almost all the municipalities it controlled in 1994. In the case of Jalisco, the difficulties of the PAN have become more explicit at the municipal level. In 1995 the PAN won 49 municipalities in the state. In the following elections of 1997, the party lost 23 of these municipalities. This information has been compiled from data provided by de Remes (2000).

Chapter Six.   The Voters' Perspective: Explaining the PAN's Electoral Performance

1. Although elected officials in Mexico cannot be reelected, the future of their political careers greatly depends on the performance of their party in the electoral arena. Governor Francisco Barrio's plans to become a presidential candidate were thwarted after his party lost the gubernatorial election in 1988. We can make the same argument for second-term elections in the United States.

2. After July 2, 2000, the PAN can no longer be considered an opposition party, for it won the presidential elections. However, at the time this study was conducted, the PAN was still an opposition party at the national level.

3. As the popular saying in Mexico goes, people prefer what they know even if it is bad, rather than a better but unknown option ("Más vale malo por conocido que bueno por conocer").

4. Thanks to a grant from the Ford Foundation, I was able to design and conduct the surveys in Chihuahua and Puebla. These surveys were conducted by CONSULTA a month before the elections at the state level. One thousand people were interviewed

at their homes. The newspaper *Reforma* gave me the survey conducted in Guanajuato. Although I did not design this survey, it contains many questions similar to my own, which makes them comparable. People were asked which party they would vote for if the elections were held on that day, but as there were no elections in Guanajuato at the time the survey was conducted, we cannot analyze the impact of candidates there. The elections for governor in Guanajuato were on July 6, 2000, and as anticipated by the survey, the PAN won the elections. Although there are important social and economic differences among three states, the comparison is particularly interesting because, contrary to what could be expected, in Chihuahua, a northern state that is the most economically developed, with lower levels of poverty and illiteracy, the PRI won the elections in 1998. Puebla and Guanajuato, two central states with pockets of deep poverty, have a very different political profile. In the former, the PRI enjoys comfortable margins of support, while in the latter the PRI has been severely weakened after its defeat by the PAN in 1991. According to official information, Chihuahua ranks twenty-sixth in terms of the number of people living below the poverty line; Guanajuato ranks thirteenth, and Puebla sixth. Compared to Chihuahua, both Puebla and Guanajuato have higher rates of illiteracy (5.4% in Chihuahua, 14% in Guanajuato, and 16% in Puebla according to official data from the secretary of education). In terms of employment, Chihuahua grew faster than Guanajuato and Puebla, although Guanajuato grew faster than Puebla.

5. I use the case of Puebla as a prototype of PRI dominance. It is a state where the PRI still manages to win elections by large margins despite declining rates of support for the party at the national level.

6. Interview with Felipe Calderón Hinojosa, former president of the PAN in Mexico, Mexico City, August 1998. This opinion was repeated by many PAN leaders, both at the state and at the national level.

7. Research on electoral behavior is recent, for elections began to matter only a few years ago. While Mexico has a dramatically different electoral tradition, it shares with the United States the presidential structure of government. Mexico forbids reelection of all elected officials. Taking this critical difference into account, most of the theoretical approaches on electoral behavior developed in the United States can be used to explain electoral behavior in Mexico.

8. In the case of Vicente Fox, however, his record as governor helped him build his reputation as a respectable and capable statesman. But Fox had to resort to a more far-reaching advertising campaign to convey the message that he was the best candidate to defeat the PRI at the national level. This was the main issue at stake in the 2000 election. Although Fox was successful in persuading the majority of the electorate, his campaign could not have gained credibility without the support of the PAN. Fox needed the PAN as much as the PAN needed him to win the elections. The latter was later explicitly recognized by Fox himself, when he addressed his party after winning the presidential elections. *Reforma*, November 19, 2000.

9. Electoral parties, for example, usually rely on strong candidates for electoral mobilization. The case of Barrio in Chihuahua, Ruffo in Baja California, and Cardenas

in the Federal District are examples of this. Vicente Fox, the PAN's presidential candidate, is another relevant example. His candidacy was based on his personal record in the state of Guanajuato and on his consistent opposition to the PRI and the regime for which it stands.

10. For an interesting analysis of how authoritarian clientelism can give way to a more democratic system of patronage, see Fox (1994).

11. This increase can be interpreted as the failure of the PAN not only to maintain its constituencies but also to convince new voters to vote for this party. As we shall see below, the opposite was the case in Puebla and Guanajuato, where the abstention rate decreased from one gubernatorial election to the other.

12. The PAN won in 23 out of the 217 municipalities in the state, including the most important cities, Puebla, Tehuacan, Atlixco, and Cholula.

13. The opposition still claims that electoral processes in the state are not completely unbiased in favor of the PRI. However, during the 1998 gubernatorial elections, there were virtually no complaints of fraud. Political parties in the state widely approved the more independent electoral authorities.

14. The state of Guanajuato is peculiar because of its turbulent electoral past. In 1991, after a highly controversial election in which the PRI allegedly won the governor's race, the governor had to resign amid a growing popular mobilization against electoral fraud. Fox was then the PAN's gubernatorial candidate. An interim panista governor (Carlos Medina Plascencia) was appointed, but he was forced to appoint a priísta as interior secretary (Secretaria de Gobierno), the most important position after the governor. Extraordinary elections for governor were held in 1995. Vicente Fox ran again as the PAN's candidate. These elections were won by the PAN by a comfortable margin. Elections for governor were scheduled for the year 2000, to coincide with the presidential elections.

15. For example, this was the case with the priísta Governor Fernando Baeza in Chihuahua in 1992 and with the panista Governor Francisco Barrio in 1998.

16. The questions were the following: How would you evaluate the state government's actions in improving the quality of education in schools? How would you evaluate the state government's actions in solving the problem of unemployment? How would you evaluate the state government's actions in solving the problem of crime? How would you evaluate the state government's actions in building more roads and highways? How would you evaluate the state government's actions in solving the most important problem in the state? The values given to each answer were classified as very bad (0–2.5); bad (2.5–5); good (5–7.5); excellent (7.5–10).

17. The Index of Government Performance was constructed by adding and averaging the values given to these questions. The responses to these questions were reclassified and assigned a value from 0 to 2, where 0 meant the "government has been unsuccessful," 0.666 meant "the government has been somewhat successful," 1.333 meant "the government has been successful," and 2 meant "the government has been very successful." Thus, if the government was perceived to be very successful in all five policy areas, the Index of Government Performance would acquire a value of 10.

Because of the way this index was constructed, an evaluation higher than 5 is considered a positive one. It is extremely difficult for any government to be highly evaluated in all policy areas at the same time.

18. The government was rated 7.9 in public works, 6.7 in employment creation, 6 in education, 3.8 in public safety, and 3.9 in the state capacity to solve the most important problem. The latter was considered to be the problem of crime.

19. The government in Puebla was rated 5.1 in education and 5.2 in public works. In employment promotion, public safety, and the state's capacity to solve the most important problem in the state, it was rated well below 5 (3.5, 2.5, and 2.7). The most important problem in the state was considered unemployment.

20. The government was rated 5.6 in public works, 5 in public safety, 4.7 in employment creation, 6.3 in education, and 5.2 in the government's capacity to solve the most important problem. The latter was considered unemployment.

21. Interestingly, among those who evaluated the government between 5 and 7.5, the PRI still got a large percentage of the vote.

22. In the case of Guanajuato, I am exploring people's attitudes toward parties after four years in office.

23. In the case of Guanajuato, we had only two intensity levels in the survey, so the spectrum ranges from 1 to 7.

24. This would have required a national-level reform of the party's statutes. Although many panista leaders in the state believe there is a need to introduce reform in the candidate selection process, it was beyond their reach.

25. Interview, Chihuahua, 1994. The interview was conducted after the presidential elections of 1994, when the PRI obtained one of its highest percentages of the vote in Chihuahua. Indeed, after Zacatecas, Chihuahua became the second state with the highest vote in support of the PRI. Many panistas at the time believed that the electoral outcome was in large part the result of the failure of the government to advertise its accomplishments. The idea was that people do not see what the government is really doing and thus become disappointed and vote for the PRI. While there is some truth to this argument, I suggest here that the declining electoral support for the PAN stems from the party's own organizational weakness.

26. According to our Index of Government Performance, the panistas rated government performance 6.5, while the neutrals rated government performance 5.3 and the priístas 5.1. With respect to the most important problem in the state, the neutrals and the panistas pointed to crime, while the priístas said it was the state of the economy. We can hypothesize that the neutrals could have changed their electoral preference if the government had done a better job with regard to combating crime. The rising levels of crime in the state negatively affected the PAN, and it is not surprising that the PRI built its campaign around this problem.

27. In Puebla, panistas rated government performance 3.4, while neutrals rated government performance 3.5. Priístas, on the other hand, rated government performance 4.1. In Guanajuato, panistas rated government performance 6, neutrals 4.6, and priístas 4.8.

28. The survey accurately predicted the electoral results in these states.

29. In Guanajuato the survey was conducted during a nonelectoral period, so we do not have information about candidates.

30. It is also possible that people identify with a particular party because they like its candidate. This basis of partisan identity, however, is more ephemeral and thus more volatile.

31. The PRI's candidate was selected through a primary election. Flores was Governor Manuel Bartlett's candidate, but he lost the primary elections. Morales was perceived as someone who came from outside the domain of the governor, a change even if it was confined to the PRI.

32. The nomination of the PAN's gubernatorial candidate generated enormous divisions inside the PAN. The entrepreneurial wing complained that the more traditional wing controlled the party's convention and the selection process. In the end, Juan José Romero Hicks became the party's candidate, and in July 2000 he won the election by a substantial margin. As I have argued, this may have been due to the party's reputation rather than to the personal attributes of the candidate.

Conclusion.   Vicente Fox and the PAN: A Happy Marriage?

1. During his inaugural speech, President Fox said that in Mexico's new political reality, "the president proposes, and Congress decides." While at the time this recognition of the separation of powers was praised as a clear sign of the administration's commitment to democracy, Congress's obstruction of the executive's reforms has led to growing frustration. The most important piece of legislation blocked by Congress was fiscal reform, deemed by the government as crucial for meeting the country's urgent social needs. Congress eventually passed a fiscal reform, but it was a significantly amended version. The most important part of this reform, an increase in the value added tax, was rejected by Congress. Given the falling prices of oil in the world and the extremely low rates of tax collection in Mexico, President Fox stated that the tax increase was necessary to obtain the resources to fulfill his campaign promises. Congress has also blocked the president's initiatives to allow private investment in energy production, another crucial element in the president's reform agenda. In April Congress finally approved the Freedom of Information Act, granting public access to government information. Given the impasse between Congress and the administration, the passage of this act was a significant achievement. However, many other highly controversial reform initiatives—in the labor code, the energy sector, education, and allowing the reelection of members of Congress and mayors—do not have much chance of being approved.

2. In a survey conducted by *Reforma* on September 30, 2001, 45 percent of the people surveyed believed corruption had increased during the past year. Only 32 percent believed it had decreased, and 23 percent believed it had remained the same as the previous year. Moreover, 38 percent identified the federal government as the most

corrupt level of government. This is not encouraging for a new government that made the fight against corruption one of its most important promises during the campaign.

3. According to the surveys conducted by *Reforma*, March 1, 2002.

4. In March, Congress refused to grant permission to the president to travel to the United States and Canada on the grounds that he was traveling too much and seeking closer relations with the United States while departing from Mexico's traditional alliances with Cuba. The president blamed political parties for obstructing his administration, in particular, the PRI. *Reforma*, April 10, 2002. This was the first time the president openly criticized the PRI, for until then his administration was hopeful that the party would cooperate with the administration in passing fiscal reform.

5. The president has been criticized by all parties for not working more closely with members of Congress and appealing instead to the public in an effort to find support for his reform agenda. Moreover, the president has enraged members of his own party for not supporting the party's decisions at critical moments; for example, he first endorsed the indigenous reform bill and later criticized it when it was rejected by the Zapatista rebels. Finally, members of the cabinet have not been well coordinated and have aired their differences in public, while the president seemed to step aside and refrained from taking a clear position on issues. His passivity further contributed to a view of his administration as disorganized, incoherent, and ultimately ineffective.

6. The PRI and the PRD have great incentives to block the administration, for they believe they stand to gain from the president's failures in future elections. While this same logic should drive the PAN to collaborate more closely with the government, the party's commitment to its traditional ideology has precluded many of its leaders from demonstrating unequivocal support for the administration. This distance between the PAN and the government further contributes to eroding the support for the PAN among vast segments of the electorate.

7. The PRI's hegemony allowed it to use public resources to build an extensive and far-reaching electoral base, typical of bureaucratic parties, according to the typology developed in this book. Today the challenge for parties is to expand and maintain their electorates through more democratic means, that is, by representing their constituencies effectively.

8. The reelection of legislators has been widely discussed in academic and political forums. A broad consensus exists that the ban on reelection is anachronistic. The PAN has introduced a bill in Congress to reform the electoral legislation to allow reelection of mayors and legislators at the federal and local levels. This reform initiative, however, has not been seriously discussed in congressional committees, and it is not clear whether, given the current deadlock in Congress, it would pass. One of the most contentious aspects of this reform is whether current legislators would be allowed to seek reelection or whether reelection would be allowed only for legislators elected in 2003.

9. The most notable examples are Jorge G. Castañeda and Adolfo Aguilar Zinser, who are ideologically more identified with the left. They both supported Cuauhtémoc Cárdenas in the 1988 elections, when he competed against Carlos Salinas de Gortari

(PRI) and Manuel Clouthier (PAN). After their disappointment with the PRD and with Cárdenas, in particular, they decided to give their support to Fox. President Fox appointed Castañeda foreign relations minister and Zinser as Mexico's representative to the United Nations.

10. Confidential interview.

11. Speech delivered by Juan Manuel Gómez Morin at the PAN's sixty-first anniversary. Mexico City, November 30, 2000.

12. Interview with Arturo García, Secretario de Fortalecimiento Interno, PAN, June 2001.

13. I thank Mr. Calderón for allowing me to reproduce this cartoon. *Reforma,* November 18, 2000.

14. Vicente Fox offered some appointments to members of the PRD, but they declined to participate in the cabinet.

15. The PRI and the PRD faced enormous divisions when they had to elect new party leaders. In the PRI, Roberto Madrazo, the former governor of the state of Tabasco and a representative of the party's more conservative forces, won the internal election against Beatriz Paredes, representative of the more moderate wing of the party and strongly supported by the former presidential candidate, Francisco Labastida. Although Madrazo won, the election was marked by accusations of fraud and serious threats of rupture. In the case of the PRD, factional dispute has been even more conspicuous. The PRD's presidential election was won by Rosario Robles, former mayor of Mexico City and a candidate strongly supported by Cuauhtemoc Cárdenas, founder of the party and highly influential in its affairs. Although the PAN also had elections, they did not create divisions inside the party. The PAN reelected its president, Luis Felipe Bravo Mena, for a second term following its established and well-institutionalized procedures.

BIBLIOGRAPHY

Aguilar Villanueva, L. F. 1994. "El presidencialismo y el sistema político mexicano: Del presidencialismo a la presidencia democratica." In A. Hernández, ed., *Presidencialismo y sistema político: México y los Estados Unidos.* México: El Colegio de México/Fondo de Cultura Económica.

Aldrich, J. 1995. *Why Parties? The Origins and Transformation of Political Parties in America.* Chicago: University of Chicago Press.

Alvarado Mendoza, A., ed. 1987. *Electoral Patterns and Perspectives in Mexico.* Monograph Series, No. 22. La Jolla: Center for U.S.-Mexican Studies, University of California, San Diego.

Anzaldua Montoya, R., and S. Maxfield, eds. 1987. *Government and Private Sector in Contemporary Mexico.* Monograph Series, No. 20. La Jolla: Center for U.S.-Mexican Studies, University of California, San Diego.

Armendáriz, E. F. 1996. *Primer congreso local de oposición en México.* Chihuahua: Comité Directivo Estatal del Partido Acción Nacional de Chihuahua.

Arriola, C. 1977. "La crisis del Partido Acción Nacional, 1975–1976." *Foro Internacional* 17, no. 4. México: El Colegio de México.

———. 1988. *Los empresarios y el estado, 1970–1982.* México: UNAM/Miguel Ángel Porrúa.

———. 1994. *Ensayos sobre el PAN.* México: Miguel Ángel Porrúa.

Aziz Nassif, A. 1987. *Prácticas electorales y democracia en Chihuahua.* Cuadernos de la Casa Chata no. 151. México: Centro de Investigación y Estudios Superiores de Antropología Social.

———. 1996. *Territorios de alternancia: El primer gobierno de oposición en Chihuahua.* México: CIESAS, Triana.

Barraza, L., and I. Bizberg. 1991. "El Partido Acción Nacional y el régimen político mexicano." *Foro Internacional* 21, no. 2. México: El Colegio de México.

Bernal Gutiérrez, M. A. 1999. *Chiapas: Crónica de una negociación.* México: Editorial Rayuela.

Biorcio, R., and R. Mannheimer. 1998. "Relationships between Citizens and Political Parties." In H. Klingemann and D. Fuchs, eds., *Citizens and the State.* Oxford: Oxford University Press.

Brandenburg, F. 1964. *The Making of Modern Mexico.* Englewood, N.J.: Prentice Hall.

Bravo Mena, L. F. 1987. "Coparmex and Mexican Politics." In S. Maxfield and R. Anzaldúa Montoya, eds., *Government and Private Sector in Contemporary Mexico.* Monograph Series, No. 20. La Jolla: Center for U.S.-Mexican Studies, University of California, San Diego.

Bruhn, K. 1997. *Taking on Goliath: The Emergence of a New Left and the Struggle for Democracy in Mexico.* University Park: Pennsylvania State University Press.

———. 1998a. "The Partido de la Revolución Democrática: Diverging Approaches to Competition." In M. Serrano, ed., *Governing Mexico.* London: ILAS.

———. 1998b. "Cuauhtémoc Rey. The PRD in Power: Implications for Democratization." Paper presented at the XXI Conference of the Latin American Assocation, September 24–26.

Budge, C., and D. Farlie. 1976. *Voting and Party Competition: A Theoretical Critique and Synthesis Applied to Surveys from Ten Democracies.* New York: John Wiley.

Buendia Laredo, J. 1989. "Autoritarismo y participación empresarial: La Confederación Patronal de la República Mexicana, 1970–1988." B.A. thesis, El Colegio de México.

Camp, Roderic A. 1989. *Entrepreneurs in Twentieth-Century Mexico.* New York: Oxford University Press.

Campbell, A., P. Converse, W. Miller, and D. Stokes. 1960. *The American Voter.* New York: John Wiley.

Cardero, M. E., and J. M. Quijano. 1982. "Expansión y estrangulamiento financiero 1978–1981." *Economía Mexicana,* no. 4. Mexico: CIDE.

Chand, V. 2001. *Mexico's Political Awakening.* Notre Dame: University of Notre Dame Press.

Coleman, J. 1996. "Party Organizational Strength and Public Support for Parties." *American Journal of Political Science* 40, no. 3.

Collier, R. B., and D. Collier. 1991. *Shaping the Political Arena.* Princeton: Princeton University Press.

Conaghan, C. M. 2000. "The Irrelevant Right: Alberto Fujimori and the New Politics of Pragmatic Peru." In K. J. Middlebrook, ed., *Conservative Parties, the Right, and Democracy in Latin America.* Baltimore: Johns Hopkins University Press.

Conchello, J. A. 1974. *La Nación,* November 15, p. 15.

Coppedge, M. 1994. *Strong Parties and Lame Ducks: Presidential Partyarchy and Factionalism in Venezuela.* Stanford: Stanford University Press.

———. 2000. "Venezuelan Parties and the Representation of Elite Interests." In K. J. Middlebrook, ed., *Conservative Parties, the Right, and Democracy in Latin America.* Baltimore: Johns Hopkins University Press.

Cordera, R., R. Trejo, and J. E. Vega, eds. 1988. *México: El reclamo democrático.* México: Siglo XXI.

Cordero, S., R. Santín, and R. Tirado. 1983. *El poder empresarial en México*. Mexico: Terra Nova.

Cordova, A. 1988. "La Constitución y la democracia." In R. Cordera, R. Trejo, and J. E. Vega, eds., *México: El reclamo democrático*. México: Siglo XXI.

Cornelius, W., T. Eisenstadt, and J. Hindley. 1999. *Subnational Politics and Democratization in México*. San Diego, Calif.: Center for U.S.-Mexican Studies.

Cornelius, W., J. Gentleman, and P. H. Smith, eds. 1989. *Mexico's Alternative Political Features*. Monograph Series, No. 30. La Jolla: Center for U.S.-Mexican Studies, University of California, San Diego.

Crespo, J. A. 1995. *Urnas de pandora: Partidos y elecciones en el gobierno de Salinas*. México: Espasa Calpe/CIDE.

———. 2000. *Raising the Bar: The Next Generation of Electoral Reforms in Mexico*. Washington, D.C.: Center for Strategic and International Studies.

Crewe, I., and D. Denver. 1985. *Electoral Change in Western Democracies*. London: Croom Helm.

Crotty, W. 1984. *American Parties in Decline*. Boston: Little, Brown.

Crotty, W., ed. 1968. *Approaches to the Study of Party Organization*. Boston: Allyn and Bacon.

Dalton, R. J., S. C. Flanagan, and P. A. Beck, eds. 1984. *Electoral Change in Advanced Industrial Democracies*. Princeton: Princeton University Press.

De Janury, A., G. Gordillo, and E. Sadoulet. 1997. *The Second Agrarian Reform in Mexico*. La Jolla: Center for U.S.-Mexican Studies, University of California, San Diego.

De Mauleón, Héctor. 1998. "¿Dónde están y dónde estaban? Líderes y actores políticos." *Nexos*, no. 249.

De Remes, A. 2000. *Banco de datos electorales a nivel municipal: 1980–1999*. México: CIDE, División de Estudios Políticos.

Delhumeau, A. 1970. *México: Una realidad política de sus partidos. Una investigación psicosocial acerca de los partidos políticos mexicanos*. México: Instituto Mexicano de Estudios Políticos.

Diamond, L., and R. Gunther, eds. 2001. *Political Parties and Democracy*. Baltimore: Johns Hopkins University Press.

Downs, A. 1957. *An Economic Theory of Democracy*. New York: Harper and Row.

Elizondo, C. 2000. "El reto interno: Balance en un contexto democrático." *Gaceta de Economía* 5, no. 9.

Elster, J. 1985. *Sour Grapes: Studies in the Subversion of Rationality*. Cambridge: Cambridge University Press.

Espinoza Valle, V. 1996. *El sindicalismo regional en los noventa*. Tijuana: El Colegio de la Frontera Norte.

———. 1998. *Alternancia política y gestión pública: El Partido Acción Nacional en el gobierno de Baja California*. Tijuana: El Colegio de la Frontera Norte.

Fernández, E. 1996. *Primer congreso local de oposición en México*. Chihuahua: Comité Directivo Estatal del Partido Acción Nacional de Chihuahua.

Fiorina, M. 1980. "The Decline of Collective Responsibility in American Politics." *Daedalus*, no. 109.

———. 1981. *Retrospective Voting in American National Elections*. New Haven: Yale University Press.

Fiorina, M., B. Cain, and J. Ferejohn. 1987. *The Personal Vote: Constituency Service and Electoral Independence*. Cambridge, Mass.: Harvard University Press.

Flanigan, W., and N. Zingale. 1998. *Political Behavior of the American Electorate*. Washington, D.C.: Congressional Quarterly Press.

Fox, J. 1994. "The Difficult Transition from Clientelism to Citizenship: Lessons from Mexico." *World Politics* 46.

Garnica, D., and J. G. Gasca. 1999. *Los problemas de la participación ciudadana a nivel municipal, el caso del Programa de Acción Comunitaria (PAC) en el municipio de Puerto Vallarta*. México: CIDE and Miguel Ángel Porrúa.

Garrido, L. J. 1982. *El Partido de la Revolución Institucionalizada*. México: Siglo XXI.

Gibson, E. 1996. *Class and Conservative Parties: Argentina in Comparative Perspective*. Baltimore: Johns Hopkins University Press.

———. 1997. "The Populist Road Market Reform: Policy and Electoral Coalitions in Argentina and Mexico." *World Politics* 49, no. 3.

Gómez Morin, M. *Discurso en la Convención Nacional del PAN del 2 de febrero de 1946*. México: Documentos del PAN.

Gómez Tagle, S. 1990. *Las estadísticas electorales de la reforma política*. Cuadernos del CES, No. 34. México: El Colegio de México.

González Aréchiga, B., and R. Barajas Escamilla. 1989. *Las maquiladoras: Ajuste estructural y desarrollo regional*. Tijuana: El Colegio de la Frontera Norte.

González Luna, E. 1940. *El hombre y el estado*. México: Documentos de Acción Nacional.

González Morfin, E. 1977. "La doctrina de Acción Nacional." In E. González Morfin, J. González Torres, and A. Christlieb Ibarrola, *Tres esquemas*. México: Ediciones de Acción Nacional.

Graham, C. 1992. *Parties, Politics and the Elusive Quest for Democracy*. Boulder, Colo.: Lynn Rienner.

Grindle, M. S. 1988. *Searching for Rural Development: Labor Migration and Employment in Mexico*. Ithaca: Cornell University Press.

———. 1996. "La reforma de la tenencia de la tierra en México: Los campesinos, el mercado y el estado." In R. Riordan, ed., *Desafío de la reforma institucional en México*. México: Siglo XXI.

Guadarrama, G. 1987. "Empresarios y política: Sonora y Nuevo León." *Estudios Sociológicos* 5, no. 13. México: El Colegio de México.

Guadarrama Sistos, R. 1983. "Estado, banca y política económica." *Estudios Políticos* 2, no. 1. México: Nueva Epoca.

Guerra, J. N. 1998. *Historia personal de la Cocopa: Cuando estuvimos a punto de firmar la paz en Chiapas*. México: Editorial Grijalvo.

Guillén López, T. 1993. *Baja California 1989–1992: Alternancia política y transición democrática*. México: El Colegio de la Frontera Norte/UNAM.

Haber, S. 1989. *Industry and Underdevelopment: The Industrialization of Mexico, 1890–1940*. Stanford: Stanford University Press.

Hamilton, N. 1982. *The Limits of State Autonomy: Post-Revolutionary Mexico*. Princeton: Princeton University Press.

Hansen, R. D. 1971. *La política del desarrollo mexicano*. México: Siglo XXI.

Heredia, B. 1992. "Profits, Politics, and Size: The Political Transformation of Mexican Business." In D. A. Chalmers, M. D. C. Campello De Souza, and A. Borón, eds., *The Right and Democracy in Latin America*. New York: Praeger.

Hernández, A., ed. 1994. *Presidencialismo y sistema político en México y los Estados Unidos*. México: El Colegio de México.

Hernández Chávez, A., ed. 1994. *Presidencialismo y sistema político, México y Estados Unidos*. México: El Colegio de México/Fondo de Cultura Económica.

Hernández Rodríguez, R. 1991. "Los problemas de representación en los organismos empresariales." *Foro Internacional* 31, no. 3. México: El Colegio de México.

Higley, J., and R. Gunther, eds. 1992. *Elites and Democratic Consolidation in Latin America and Southern Europe*. Cambridge: Cambridge University Press.

Hirschman, A. 1970. *Exit, Voice and Loyalty: Responses to Decline in Firms, Organization and State*. Cambridge, Mass.: Harvard University Press.

Ignazi, P. 1996. "The Crisis of Parties and the Rise of New Political Parties." *Governance* 2, no. 4.

Inglehart, R. 1977. *The Silent Revolution: Changing Values and Political Styles Among Western Publics*. Princeton: Princeton University Press.

Instituto Nacional de Geografía y Estadística (INEGI). 1976, 1981. *Censos Industriales*. México.

Jacobs, E. 1981. "La evolución reciente de los grupos de capital privado nacional." *Economía Mexicana*, no. 3. México: CIDE.

Jacobs, E., and W. Pérez Núñez. 1982. "Las grandes empresas y el crecimiento acelerado." *Economía Mexicana*, no. 4. México: CIDE.

Katz, R., and S. Kolodny. 1982. "Party Organization as an Empty Vessel: Parties in American Politics." In R. Katz and P. Mair, eds., *How Parties Organize: Change and Adaptation in Party Organizations in Western Democracies*. London: Sage.

Katz, R., and P. Mair, eds. 1994. *How Parties Organize: Change and Adaptation in Party Organizations in Western Democracies*. London: Sage.

Keck, M. E. 1992. *The Workers Party and Democratization in Brazil*. New Haven: Yale University Press.

Kitschelt, H. 1989. *The Logics of Party Formation: Ecological Politics in Belgium and West Germany*. Ithaca: Cornell University Press.

———. 1993. "Social Movements, Political Parties and Democratic Theory." *Annals of the American Academy for the Political and Social Sciences*, no. 528.

———. 1994. *The Transformation of European Social Democracy*. Cambridge: Cambridge University Press.

Klingemann, H. D., and D. Fuchs, eds. 1998. *Citizens and the State*. Oxford: Oxford University Press.

Knight, A. 1992. "Mexico's Elite Settlement: Conjuncture and Consequences." In J. Higley and R. Gunther, eds., *Elites and Democratic Consolidation in Latin America and Southern Europe.* Cambridge: Cambridge University Press.

Krauze, E. 1986. *Por una democracia sin adjetivos.* México: Joaquin Mortiz Planeta.

———. 1997. *La presidencia imperial: Ascenso y caída del sistema político mexicano (1940–1996).* México: Tusquets Editores.

Labastida, J., ed. 1986. *Grupos Económicos y organizaciones empresanales en México.* México: Alianza Editorial/Universidad Nacional Autónoma de México.

Langston, J. 2000. *No More Local Leviathan: Rebuilding the PRI's State Party Organizations.* Working Paper, División de Estudios Políticos, No. 111. México: CIDE.

———. 2001a. *Changing to Compete or Learning to Lose? Mexico's PRI in the Era of Electoral Competition.*

———. 2001b. "Why Rules Matter: Changes in Candidate Selection in Mexico's PRI, 1988–2000." *Journal of Latin American Studies,* no. 33.

———. 2002. "Lessons from the States: Collective Action Problems in Mexico's PRI." Paper presented at the East-West Center Conference on One Party Dominant Systems, March, Honolulu, Hawaii.

Lau, R. 1989. "Las elecciones en Chihuahua (1983–1988)." *Cuadernos del Norte* 1, special issue.

Lau, R., J. Vicente, and V. O. Orozco. 1986. *Sistema político y democracia en Chihuahua.* México: Instituto de Investigaciones Sociales-UNAM/Universidad Autónoma de Ciudad Juárez.

Lawson, K., G. Pomper, and M. Moakley. 1986. "Local Party Activists and Electoral Linkage." *American Politics Quarterly* 14.

Le Duc, L. 1981. "The Dynamic Properties of Party Identification: A Four Nation Comparison." *European Journal of Political Research* 9.

Levitsky, S. 1998. "Crisis, Party Adaptation and Regime Stability in Argentina." *Party Politics* 4, no. 4.

Linz, J., and A. Valenzuela, eds. 1994. *The Failure of Presidential Democracy.* Baltimore: Johns Hopkins University Press.

Loaeza, S. 1999. *El Partido Acción Nacional: La larga marcha, 1939–1994.* México: Fondo de Cultura Económica.

Loaeza, S., and R. Segovia, eds. 1987. *La vida política mexicana en la crisis.* México: El Colegio de México.

López, B. 1999. *Gómez Morin, Precursor de la economía con justicia social.* Fundación Rafael Preciado Hernández. Unpublished ms.

———. 2000. *Historia del PAN.* México: Fundación Rafael Preciado Hernández.

Lujambio, A. 1994. "El dilema de Christlieb Ibarrola: Cuatro cartas a Gustavo Díaz Ordaz." *Estudios* 11, no. 38.

———. 1995a. *Federalismo y congreso en el cambio político de México.* México: UNAM.

———. 1995b. "De la hegemonía a las alternativas: Diseños institucionales y el futuro de los partidos políticos en México." *Política y Gobierno* 1.

————. 2000. *El poder compartido: Un ensayo sobre la democratización mexicana.* México: Océano.

————. Forthcoming. "Democratización via federalismo? El Partido Acción Nacional, 1939–1995. La historia de una estrategia difícil." In K. J. Middlebrook, ed., *Mexico's Partido Acción Nacional in Comparative Perspective.* San Diego: Center for U.S.-Mexican Studies.

Luna, L. M. 1984. "Los empresarios y el régimen político mexicano: Las estrategias tripartitas de los años setenta." *Estudios Políticos* 3, no. 1. México: Nueva Epoca.

Luna, M. 1992. *Los empresarios y el cambio político: México, 1970–1987.* México: Instituto de Investigaciones Sociales, Universidad Nacional Autónoma de México/ Ediciones Era.

Luna, M., R. Tirado, and F. Valdés. 1990. "Perspectivas teóricas en el estudio de los empresarios en México." *Revista Mexicana de Sociología* 52, no. 2.

Mabry, D. J. 1973. *Mexico's Acción Nacional: A Catholic Alternative to Revolution.* Syracuse: Syracuse University Press.

MacKuen, M., R. Erikson, and J. Stimson. 1992. "Peasants or Bankers? The American Electorate in the U.S. Economy." *American Political Science Review* 86 (September).

Magaloni, B. 1996. "Dominio de partido y dilemas duvergerianos en las elecciones presidenciales de 1994 en México." *Política y Gobierno* 3, no. 2.

Magaloni, B., and A. Moreno. 2000. *Catching All Souls: Religion and Ideology in the PAN.* Working Paper, Departamento de Ciencia Política. México: ITAM.

Mainwaring, S., and T. Scully. 1995. *Building Democratic Institutions: Party Systems in Latin America.* Stanford: Stanford University Press.

Mainwaring, S., and M. Shugart. 1997. *Presidentialism and Democracy in Latin America.* Cambridge: Cambridge University Press.

Mair, P. 1994. "Party Organizations: From Civil Society to the State." In R. Katz and P. Mair, eds., *How Parties Organize: Change and Adaptation in Party Organization in Western Democracies.* London: Sage.

Markus, G. 1993. *Controversies in Voting Behavior.* Washington, D.C.: Congressional Quarterly Press.

Martínez Nava, J. M. 1984. *Conflicto estado-empresarios en los gobiernos de Cárdenas, López Mateos y Echeverría.* México: Nueva Imagen.

Maxfield, S. 1990. *Governing Capital: International Finance and Mexican Politics.* Ithaca: Cornell University Press.

Mayhew, D. R. 1974. *Congress: The Electoral Connection.* New Haven: Yale University Press.

McDonald, R. H., and J. M. Rhul. 1989. *Party Politics and Elections in Latin America.* San Francisco: Westview Press.

Medina Peña, L. 1994. *Hacia el nuevo estado mexicano, 1920–1993.* México: Fondo de Cultura Económica.

Meyer, J. 1991. *La Revolución mexicana, 1910–1940.* México: Editorial Jus.

Middlebrook, K. J., ed. 2000. *Conservative Parties, the Right, and Democracy in Latin America.* Baltimore: Johns Hopkins University Press.

————. Forthcoming. *Mexico's Partido Acción Nacional in Comparative Perspective.* San Diego: Center for U.S.-Mexican Studies.

Mizrahi, Y. 1994a. "A New Conservative Opposition in Mexico: The Politics of Entrepreneurs in Chihuahua." Ph.D. dissertation, University of California, Berkeley.

————. 1994b. "Rebels without a Cause? The Politics of Entrepreneurs in Chihuahua." *Journal of Latin American Studies* 26.

————. 1996. "¿Administrar o Gobernar? El reto del gobierno panista en Chihuahua." *Frontera Norte* 8, no. 16.

————. 1999. *Voto retrospectivo y desempeño gubernamental: Las elecciones en el estado de Chihuahua.* Working Paper, División de Estudios Políticos, No. 100. México: CIDE.

Molinar Horcasitas, J. 1987. "El regreso a Chihuahua." *Nexos,* no. 111.

————. 1991. *El tiempo de la legitimidad: Elecciones, autoritarismo y democracia en México.* México: Cal y Arena.

Moreno, A., 1999a. "Ideología y voto: Dimensiones de competencia política en México en los 90." *Política y Gobierno* 6, no. 1.

————. 1999b. *Political Cleavages.* Boulder, Colo.: Westview Press.

Nacif, B. 1996. *Electoral Institutitons and Single Party Politics in the Mexican Chamber of Deputies.* Working Paper, División de Estudios Políticos, No. 48. México: CIDE.

————. 1997. "La no reelección legislativa, disciplina de partido y subordinación al Ejecutivo en la Cámara de Diputados en México." *Diálogo y Debate* 1, no. 2.

Niemi, R., and W. Weisberg. 1984. *Controversies in Voting Behavior.* Washington, D.C.: Congressional Quarterly Press.

————. 1992. *Classics in Voting Behavior.* Washington, D.C.: Congressional Quarterly Press.

North, D. C. 1990. *Insititutions, Institutional Change and Economic Performance.* Cambridge: Cambridge University Press.

O'Donnell, G. 1994. "Delegative Democracy." *Journal of Democracy* 5, no. 1.

Osborne, D., and T. Gaebler. 1992. *Reinventing Government: How the Entrepreneurial Spirit Is Transforming the Public Sector.* Reading, Mass.: Addison Wesley.

Panebianco, A. 1982. *Modelos de partido.* Madrid: Alianza Universidad.

Partido Acción Nacional. Comité Ejecutivo Nacional. 1986, 1992, 2001. Estatutos Generales. México: EPESSA.

————. 1989. *Principios de doctrina.* México: EPESSA.

Polsby, N. W. 1983. *Consequences of Party Reform.* Oxford: Oxford University Press.

Prud'Homme, J. F. 1996. "La negociación de las reglas del juego: Tres reformas electorales (1988–1994)." *Política y Gobierno* 3, no.1.

Przeworsky, A., and F. Limongi. 1997. "Modernization, Theories and Facts." *World Politics,* no. 49.

Puga, C. 1984. "Los empresarios mexicanos ante la catástrofe." *Estudios Políticos* 3, no. 1. México: Nueva Epoca.

————. 1992. *Empresarios medianos, pequeños y micro: Problemas de representación y organización.* Facultad de Ciencias Políticas y Sociales and Instituto de Investigaciones Sociales, Cuaderno no. 3. Universidad Nacional Autónoma de México.

Purcell, J. F., and S. Kaufman Purcell. 1977. "Mexican Business and Public Policy." In J. Malloy, ed., *Authoritarianism and Corporativism in Latin America*. Pittsburgh: University of Pittsburgh Press.

Reveles Vázquez, F. 1996. "El proceso de institucionalización organizativa del Partido Acción Nacional." Ph.D. dissertation, Universidad Nacional Autónoma de México.

Reyes del Campillo, M., ed. *Partidos, elecciones y cultura política en México: Los espacios de la democracia en la sociedad mexicana contemporánea*. México: UAEM/ UAM/COMESCO.

Reyna, J. L., and R. S. Wienert, eds. 1977. *Authoritarianism in Mexico*. Philadelphia: ISHI.

Reynolds, C. 1970. *The Mexican Economy: Twentieth-Century Structure and Growth*. New Haven: Yale University Press.

Reynoso, V. M. 1993. "El Partido Acción Nacional: ¿La oposición hará gobierno?" *Revista Mexicana de Sociología* 55, no. 2.

Rionda, L. M. 1996. "Guanajuato: El aprendizaje de la democracia y la difícil vivencia de un gobierno dividido." *Frontera Norte* 8, no. 16.

Roberts, K. 1994. *Renovation in the Revolution? Dictatorship, Democracy and Political Change in the Chilean Left*. Working Paper No. 203. Notre Dame: Kellogg Institute.

Rodriguez Prats, J. 1997. *La congruencia histórica del Partido Acción Nacional*. México: EPESSA.

Saragoza, A. M. 1988. *The Monterrey Elite and the Mexican State, 1880–1940*. Austin: University of Texas Press.

Sartori, G. 1976. *Parties and Party Systems: A Framework for Analysis*. New York: Cambridge University Press.

Schattschneider, E. E. 1942. *Party Government*. New York: Rinehart and Winston.

Schlesinger, J. A. 1994. *Political Parties and the Winning of Office*. Ann Arbor: University of Michigan Press.

Schmitt, H., and S. Holmberg. 1998. "Political Parties in Decline?" In H. D. Klingemann and D. Fuchs, eds., *Citizens and the State*. Oxford: Oxford University Press.

Secretaría de Hacienda y Crédito Público. 1998. *Situación de las finanzas públicas*. Documentos, México.

Serrano, M. 1998. *Governing Mexico*. London: ILAS.

Shadlen, K. C. 2000. "Neoliberalism, Corporatism, and Small Business Political Activism in Contemporary Mexico." *Latin American Research Review* 35, no. 2.

Shafer, R. J. 1973. *Mexican Business Organizations: History and Analysis*. New York: Syracuse University Press.

Shefter, M. 1994. *Political Parties and the State: The American Historical Experience*. Princeton: Princeton University Press.

Shirk, D. 1999. "Democratization and Local Party Building: The PAN in León Guanajuato." In W. A. Cornelius, T. A. Eisenstadt, and J. Hindley, eds., *Subnational Politics and Democratization in Mexico*. La Jolla: Center for U.S.-Mexican Studies, University of California, San Diego.

Stoddard, E. R. 1986. *Maquila Assembly Plants in Northern Mexico*. El Paso: Texas Western Press.

Stokes, S. 1998. "¿Son los partidos políticos el problema de la democracia en América Latina?" *Política y Gobierno* 5, no. 1.

Tamayo, J. 1985. "Frontera, política regional y políticas nacionales en México." Working Paper. México: CIDE.

Tamayo, J., and J. L. Fernández. 1983. *Zonas fronterizas (México–Estados Unidos)*. México: CIDE.

Tello, C. 1979. *La política económica en México, 1970–1976*. México: Siglo XXI.

Tirado, R. 1987. "Los empresarios y la política partidaria." *Estudios Sociológicos* 5, no. 15.

Tirado, R., M. Luna, and R. Millan. 1985. "Los empresarios en los inicios del gobierno de Miguel de la Madrid." *Revista Mexicana de Sociología* 47, no. 4.

Tsebelis, G. 1990. *Nested Games: Rational Choice in Comparative Politics*. Berkeley: University of California Press.

Ugalde, L. C. 2000. *Vigilando al ejecutivo: El papel del congreso en la supervisión del gasto público, 1970–1999*. México: Porrúa/Cámara de Diputados.

Valdés, L. 1994. "Partido de la Revolución Democrática: The Third Option in México." In N. Harvey and M. Serrano, eds., *Party Politics in an Uncommon Democracy*. London: Institute of Latin American Studies.

Valenzuela, A. 1978. *The Breakdown of Democratic Regimes: Chile*. Baltimore: Johns Hopkins University Press.

Vaughan, M. K. 1997. *Cultural Politics in Revolution: Teachers, Peasants, and Schools in Mexico, 1930–1940*. Tucson: University of Arizona Press.

Von Sauer, F. 1974. *The Alienated "Loyal" Opposition: Mexico's Partido Acción Nacional*. Albuquerque: University of New Mexico Press.

Ward, P., and V. Rodríguez. 1995. *Opposition Government in Mexico*. Albuquerque: University of New Mexico Press.

Ware, A. 1992. "Activist-Leader Relations and the Structure of Political Parties: 'Exchange' Models and Vote-Seeking Behavior in Parties." *British Journal of Political Science* 22.

Weldon, J. 1997. "The Political Sources of Presidentialism in Mexico." In S. Mainwaring and M. Shugart, eds., *Presidentialism and Democracy in Latin America*. Cambridge: Cambridge University Press.

Wilkie, J. W., and E. Wilkie. 1969. *México visto en el siglo XX*. México: Instituto Mexicano de Investigaciones Económicas.

Woldenberg, J., P. Salazar, and R. Becerra. 1997. *La reforma electoral de 1996: Una descripción general*. México: Fondo de Cultura Económica.

World Bank. 1997. *World Development Report 1977: The State in a Changing World*. Oxford: Oxford University Press.

Wuhs, S. 2002. "Opposing Oligarchy? Mexican Democratization and Political Party Transformation." Ph.D. dissertation, University of North Carolina, Chapel Hill.

Yañez Maldonado, M. 1990. "El Partido Acción Nacional: De la oposición 'leal' a la oposición real." Ph.D. dissertation, Universidad Nacional Autónoma de México.

INDEX

YEMILE MIZRAHI is an affiliate of the Woodrow Wilson Center for International Scholars as a public policy scholar and works as a consultant in Washington, D.C.